JEREMIAH

Text copyright © Rex Mason 2002

The author asserts the moral right to be
identified as the author of this work

Published by
The Bible Reading Fellowship
First Floor, Elsfield Hall
15–17 Elsfield Way, Oxford OX2 8FG
ISBN 1 84101 087 1

First edition
10 9 8 7 6 5 4 3 2 1 0

Acknowledgments
Unless otherwise stated, scripture quotations are taken from
The New Revised Standard Version of the Bible, copyright ©
1989 by the Division of Christian Education of the National
Council of the Churches of Christ in the USA.

The Revised Standard Version of the Bible, copyright © 1946,
1952, 1971 by the Division of Christian Education of the
National Council of the Churches of Christ in the United States
of America, used by permission. All rights reserved.

New English Bible copyright © 1961, 1970 by Oxford
University Press and Cambridge University Press.

Revised English Bible with the Apocrypha Copyright © 1989 by
Oxford University Press and Cambridge University Press.

The *Holy Bible, New International Version*, copyright © 1973,
1978, 1984 by International Bible Society. Used by permission
of Hodder & Stoughton Limited. All rights reserved. 'NIV' is a
registered trademark of International Bible Society. UK trademark
number 1448790.

Extracts from The Book of Common Prayer of 1662, the rights
of which are vested in the Crown in perpetuity within the
United Kingdom, are reproduced by permission of Cambridge
University, Her Majesty's Printers.

A catalogue record for this book is
available from the British Library

Printed and bound in Great Britain
by Omnia Books Ltd, Glasgow

JEREMIAH

THE PEOPLE'S
BIBLE COMMENTARY

REX
MASON

A BIBLE COMMENTARY FOR EVERY DAY

Introducing the
People's Bible Commentary
Series

Congratulations! You are embarking on a voyage of discovery—or rediscovery. You may feel you know the Bible very well; you may never have turned its pages before. You may be looking for a fresh way of approaching daily Bible study; you may be searching for useful insights to share in a study group or from a pulpit.

The People's Bible Commentary (PBC) series is designed for all those who want to study the scriptures in a way that will warm the heart as well as instructing the mind. To help you, the series distils the best of scholarly insights into the straightforward language and devotional emphasis of Bible reading notes. Explanation of background material, and discussion of the original Greek and Hebrew, will always aim to be brief.

- If you have never really studied the Bible before, the series offers a serious yet accessible way in.

- If you help to lead a church study group, or are otherwise involved in regular preaching and teaching, you can find invaluable 'snapshots' of a Bible passage through the PBC approach.

- If you are a church worker or minister, burned out on the Bible, this series could help you recover the wonder of scripture.

Using a People's Bible Commentary

The series is designed for use alongside any version of the Bible. You may have your own favourite translation, but you might like to consider trying a different one in order to gain fresh perspectives on familiar passages.

Many Bible translations come in a range of editions, including study and reference editions that have concordances, various kinds of special index, maps and marginal notes. These can all prove helpful in studying the relevant passage. The Notes section at the back of each PBC volume provides space for you to write personal reflections, points to follow up, questions and comments.

Each People's Bible Commentary can be used on a daily basis, instead of Bible reading notes. Alternatively, it can be read straight through, or used as a resource book for insight into particular verses of the biblical book.

If you have enjoyed using this commentary and would like to progress further in Bible study, you will find details of other volumes in the series listed at the back, together with information about a special offer from BRF.

While it is important to deepen understanding of a given passage, this series always aims to engage both heart and mind in the study of the Bible. The scriptures point to our Lord himself and our task is to use them to build our relationship with him. When we read, let us do so prayerfully, slowly, reverently, expecting him to speak to our hearts.

CONTENTS

PBC JEREMIAH: INTRODUCTION

The book of Jeremiah is one of the most moving of the prophetic books. It reveals a prophet who was commissioned by God when he was still quite young (1:6) and who seems to cut something of a lone figure, never quite at ease with a call which appeared to isolate him from society (15:17) and family (12:6) and to commit him to bringing a message of judgment which he would rather not have had to proclaim (17:16). While he was obedient to the call and faithful to his prophetic ministry, there appear to have been times when he wondered whether even God had deserted him (20:7). He felt the people's sin acutely but also felt anguish for the judgments that he saw were to come upon them for their persistent disobedience to God. Indeed, there are many times when this sense of solidarity with his nation makes it difficult to recognize when he is speaking as an individual about his own suffering and when he is speaking as the people's representative. While a few friends supported him—some in high places and some, like Baruch, who helped actively in the promulgation of his message—there is something tragic about his end when, after he had seen all he predicted come true in the destruction of Jerusalem and the exile of many of its inhabitants, he was subsequently taken to Egypt against his will where presumably he died in obscurity. He was not to live to see the salvation he had also predicted with a confidence based on his conviction in the ultimate triumph of God's love.

The early life and times of Jeremiah

Jeremiah was born of priestly line in Anathoth, a few miles north of Jerusalem. We are told that 'the word of the Lord came' to him in the thirteenth year of King Josiah (about 626BC), a king who is well spoken of by the editors of the books of Kings (2 Kings 22:2; 23:25). During his reign Judah managed to gain considerable independence from the, by now, waning power of Assyria, the empire which had swept away the northern kingdom of Israel and reduced it to vassalhood. This was probably the reason why Josiah was able to institute a sweeping programme of religious reform in which many measures were designed to purify the worship life of Judah, purging it of all foreign elements and centring the worship of Yahweh (the nearest we can get to the name for Israel's God) in the Jerusalem temple. The description of these reforms, following the discovery of the 'book of the law' (almost certainly some form of our book of Deuteronomy) is given in 2 Kings 22:8—23:24.

Jeremiah's early ministry must have been exercised throughout all this, although we know little detail about his life and ministry during this period. There are no oracles in the book explicitly dated in the reign of Josiah as there are in the reigns of those who succeeded him. Much of the preaching would fit the background of the conditions that prompted Josiah to his programme of reform, since they attack the religious apostasy and social evils that the reforms were designed to counter. However, while it is very difficult to date oracles by their contents alone, such attacks seem to have continued, for Jeremiah is clear that, right up to the time of the exile and beyond, the community continued its sorry story of unfaithfulness and apostasy. Perhaps Josiah's reform was not quite as successful or far-reaching as the books of Kings suggest, or else people lost faith in such new ideas when Josiah was killed in battle and national danger loomed again.

Nowhere does Jeremiah make unambiguously clear his attitude to the reform, but it is difficult to think that he who knew that human hearts were always prone to evil (13:23; 17:9) believed they could have been cured by something external like a change of laws. Only God could really renew human beings (31:33).

Later events in Jeremiah's life

Josiah was killed in battle, rashly trying to stop Egypt going to Assyria's help against the rising power of Babylon (2 Kings 23: 29–30). For a time Judah passed under Egyptian control, Josiah's successor being replaced by their man, whose name they changed to Jehoiakim (2 Kings 23:33–37). In 605BC the Babylonians, under their powerful king Nebuchadrezzar (the more accurate form of his name), defeated the Egyptians. Wisely, Jehoiakim submitted to Babylon, but three years later rebelled, bringing the Babylonian army down to besiege Jerusalem. Jehoiakim (conveniently) died, to be followed by his son, Jehoiachin. After only three months the city fell to the Babylonians in 597BC, who took the new king and many others into exile in Babylon. They placed Jehoiachin's uncle on the throne, changing his name to Zedekiah. Against the prophet's advice the king, who emerges as a weak man, easily swayed, rebelled in 589BC. The next year the Babylonians arrived and again laid siege to the city of Jerusalem. When Zedekiah tried to escape after a protracted siege, he and his sons suffered terrible punishment and the victorious Babylonians entered the city in 586BC, deported many more of its citizens, and placed a governor, Gedaliah, in charge. With Jerusalem devastated, he ruled from Mizpah. Even this was not the end, for he was assassinated by Ishmael who subsequently escaped to Amman. Many Judeans, fearing Babylonian reprisals, decided, against Jeremiah's strongest counsel, to flee to Egypt, taking the prophet with them. It is the last we hear of him.

These tumultuous events, described both in 2 Kings 24—25 and in the book of Jeremiah, form the backdrop of Jeremiah's life and ministry. Judah was to remain subject to Babylon until 539BC, when Cyrus led the Persians in the defeat of Babylon and allowed many Jews to return home.

The message of Jeremiah

The prophet's home, Anathoth, was in the area of Benjamin, part of the old northern kingdom of Israel. Perhaps it is not surprising, therefore, that Jeremiah's early preaching shows much of the influence of the northern prophet, Hosea. Like Hosea, he attacks mainly the religious apostasy of the nation, in which they deserted Yahweh and turned to the worship of other gods—although, as always, turning away from God had dire results in the social life of the community, where injustices of all kinds prevailed. Those whom God had appointed as 'shepherds' of his people—kings, priests and prophets—had betrayed their trust, while the people persisted in their ways in spite of all warning to the contrary.

All this laid them open to certain judgment, which the prophet saw as coming in the form of invasion and defeat by a 'foe from the north', clearly later to be identified with Babylon. No amount of empty temple ritual, no attempt to avert disaster by military alliances, could save the nation, since it was God himself who was their judge even though he employed human agents.

Jeremiah came to see that people were so wicked that they were rotten at the very heart, to the extent that no amount of outward reform could save them. It would need a renewal of the heart to change them radically and such a renewal was possible, not by human effort, but only by the grace of God.

Thus the prophet became certain that God intended to bring about the end of the current political and religious structures of Judah. Jerusalem must fall, its temple destroyed and its people taken into exile. Only on the other side of that disaster could the way be clear for the renewing work of God to be done. To this end, Jeremiah says that all armed resistance is useless. He even advises people to flee the city which is doomed anyway.

Such preaching was not popular and the prophet was often cold-shouldered by the community, denounced by other prophets, suspected by political leaders and imprisoned as a traitor. Yet it was he who was proved right by events, and his words were preserved and treasured, at least by some, and came increasingly to be seen as a source of hope and guidance for the post-exilic community whom God had preserved.

The book of Jeremiah

The book is divided into four main sections:

* Chapters 1—25, containing poetic and prose oracles which mainly attack the sins and apostasy of the nation.

* Chapters 26—36, containing mainly narrative material describing Jeremiah's ministry and the various responses it encountered.

* Chapters 37—45 narrate in some detail the events from Nebuch-adrezzar's siege of Jerusalem until its fall, and Jeremiah's role in them.

* Chapters 46—51 contain oracles against foreign nations.

The book ends with a brief historical appendix in chapter 52, narrating the last days of Jerusalem, but hinting at hope to come.

We know very little about the process by which the spoken words and deeds of the prophets were recorded and took their present written form. We are told in chapter 36 that Jeremiah dictated all his words to Baruch, who had them read and who, after they were burned, rewrote them. The same process is mentioned in chapter 45. The purpose of writing seems to have been to leave a clear record that the word God had given the prophet had been spoken, both as a warning to the hearers and those who came after them, and to show that, when the events predicted came to pass, they authenticated their speaker as a 'true prophet'.

There can be little doubt that these words became venerated and, as time passed, were found to have fresh meaning and new relevance in later circumstances. They might well then have been reissued and reinterpreted, even expanded, to bring out their meaning for that later situation. Many scholars believe that this has happened in the book of Jeremiah, especially in the long prose 'sermons' which are written very much in the style of the book of Deuteronomy and which bring out many of the theological lessons taught there. The Deuteronomic literature (Deuteronomy and the history books from Joshua to 2 Kings) seems to have been written to show why the disaster of the exile happened and to call survivors to learn the lessons of history and turn back to God so that they might know his covenant blessings again in the future. We refer to those who produced this type of literature as 'the Deuteronomists' and it may well be that, taking words and ideas of the prophet, they seek in these prose passages to bring home the lessons of the prophet for those in exile in Babylon after the predicted disaster had happened. They thus 'preached' the prophet's words to reinforce his warnings for a later generation and to assure them of the truth of his promises of future salvation. Finally, editors would bring it all together and arrange the material, preserving it and presenting it as a continuing word for those who, after the exile, formed the community of God's people in Judah.

That the prophetic tradition could remain open in this way is shown by the fact that we have two different versions of the book, the Hebrew one (the one in our Bible) and the one in the Greek translation of the Old Testament that we call the Septuagint. (The name means 'seventy', based on an old tradition that seventy scholars helped to prepare it, and so the sign for it is the Roman numeral for 'seventy', LXX). That version is shorter than ours, has significant differences in the text and places some material in a different order. Neither version can be said to be the 'right' or the 'original' one. They represent different Jeremiah traditions, but they do show that the prophetic tradition could be flexible and open for a long time.

While we may be sure that some such development of Jeremiah's preaching took place, detecting just which are the exact words of the the prophet and which have been added is not an exact science. This has led to varying opinions among scholars. A few, such as Robert Carroll, have been very radical, doubting whether we have any authentic words from the prophet or any reliable records of his life.

Carroll's opinion is that 'Jeremiah' is just a figure to give prophetic authority to the teaching of the later editors. This is unlikely, since there is enough individuality in the record to suggest that he is by no means just an 'identikit' prophet, entirely a later invention. Further, there would have been enough people around who knew of the times of the prophet's life to have detected a complete fabrication. Most scholars, therefore, take essentially the view of E.W. Nicholson that the book contains an authentic record of the prophet's teaching and activity, but that later (Deuteronomistic) editors added to, adapted, arranged and presented his words and deeds in such a way as to make them relevant to later times. That is essentially the view taken in this commentary.

That our prophetic book may contain material from hands other than and later than the prophet's should not disturb us. On the contrary, such material is witness to the living power of God's word which, once uttered, continues to speak for all times with fresh relevance and force. To read God's word is never to indulge in antiquarian research only. It is always a case of 'Today, if you will hear his voice...' (Hebrews 3:7).

Jeremiah's words may, then, have gone generally unheeded in his own day. But they continued to serve as an inspiration and source of hope for those who came later. Jesus himself drew on Jeremiah's idea of the 'new covenant' to depict his death and resurrection (Mark 14:24). And we, if we will, may still hear God speak through his 'suffering servant'.

A PRAYER

Lord as I read the words of your prophet from long ago,
may I hear what you want to say to me today. Amen

FOR FURTHER READING

Robert P. Carroll, *Jeremiah*, Old Testament Library, SCM Press, 1986.

William McKane, *Jeremiah*, The International Critical Commentary, T&T Clark, Vol. 1, 1986; Vol. II, 1996.

E.W. Nicholson, *Jeremiah 1—25*, The Cambridge Bible Commentary, Cambridge University Press, 1973.

E.W. Nicholson, *Jeremiah 26—52*, The Cambridge Bible Commentary, Cambridge University Press, 1975.

JEREMIAH'S CALL & COMMISSION

The appointing of a prophet

It is no coincidence that the book of Jeremiah, like the other major prophetic books, gives a prominent account of the call and commissioning of the prophet by God. As the book makes clear, there were plenty of people about at the time who claimed to be 'prophets', yet who were all saying different things. More than once Jeremiah finds himself in conflict with such people (as with Hananiah in ch. 28). It was therefore vital to show that a prophet who had such unpopular things to say as Jeremiah did was not acting on his own initiative. The promise to Moses that God would raise up 'a prophet like you' and 'I will put my words in the mouth of the prophet' (Deuteronomy 18:18) is exactly fulfilled in the case of Jeremiah (vv. 5, 9).

The divine compulsion

The sense of the call of God as a compelling destiny, reaching back even before birth (v. 5), is one that is well-known among those who are conscious that God has laid his hand upon them. It was true of 'the servant of God' in Isaiah 49:1, 5, and of Paul (Galatians 1:15), and it always brings a deep sense of one's own unworthiness and inadequacy (v. 6). This was also true of Moses (Exodus 4:10; 6:30), of Isaiah (Isaiah 6:5) and Paul (Ephesians 3:7–8). Jeremiah's complaint that he was 'only a boy' (v. 6) may not mean that he was still only in his teens at the time. Solomon used the same Hebrew word when he became king (1 Kings 3:7)—and he was already married! As well as age, it indicates a general sense of unreadiness for the task assigned. Such a sense is often, paradoxically, one of the indications of a person's fitness. To all who are fearful when God irrupts into their lives with a challenging call, God's response is always the same. The one who calls will supply all the necessary resources (vv. 7–9; compare Matthew 10:16–20; 1 Corinthians 1:26–30).

A prophet to the nations

Jeremiah's call was not just a cosy domestic one concerning Israel alone. Like the faithful servant of God who was told 'it was too light a thing' to be God's servant merely to Judah and Israel, but that he was to be 'a light to the nations' (Isaiah 49:6), so Jeremiah is told that he is to be a 'prophet to the nations' (vv. 5, 10). That is certainly fitting as a description of the book as a whole with its series of oracles concerning foreign nations (chs. 46—51). But, in addition, Judah's affairs were so bound up with those of other nations during Jeremiah's lifetime that no one could meaningfully speak to the people about God's relationship with Israel alone. Jeremiah is to be a sign that God is the God of all peoples and that his sovereign power runs throughout the whole world. The people of such a God have never been true to him in any age when they have sought to withdraw from the world and concern themselves only with church affairs or proclaim a gospel of individual salvation alone. To all such, it has always had to be said, 'Your God is too small.'

The prophet's task was 'to pluck up and to pull down' as well as 'to build and to plant' (v. 10). No one can build or plant until the site is cleared of debris or the plot of weeds. Hence Jeremiah, like the other prophets, brings a message of God's judgment on all that is at present corrupt and unjust. Only then can there be any real hope of the bringing in of God's new order.

God's word rooted in history

The events of Jeremiah's lifetime (vv. 1–3) have been mentioned in the Introduction (pp. 11–13). The fact that editors set the 'context' of a prophet's ministry in this way shows how God always speaks to particular people at specific times in a real historical situation. But the fact that, long after the prophet's day, editors were collecting and passing on the prophet's words shows also how that word of God, 'incarnate' in one period of human history, goes on speaking to all people in all conditions and at all times. The word of God is always both immediate and eternal.

A PRAYER

O God, give me the courage to respond to your call, believing that, in spite of all my limitations, your grace is all I need. Amen

TWO VISIONS

Verse 11 links the account of Jeremiah's two 'visions' with the commissioning we read in the previous section. That culminated in God saying, 'I have put my words in your mouth' (1:9). Now Jeremiah says, 'The word of the Lord came to me' (v. 11). This divine word took the form of a question-and-answer dialogue between God and his prophet, just as it did with Amos (Amos 7:8; 8:2). As with Amos also, the prophet sees two quite 'ordinary' sights—an almond tree in blossom and a cooking pot carelessly set aslant on the fire so that, when it boils, its contents will spill. Neither of these is what we would call 'visionary'. Nevertheless, the prophet, whose ear is attuned to what God is saying, sees deep significance in them. In fact, for people alert to God's presence and action, there can be no such thing as an entirely 'ordinary' event. Every event is pregnant with possibilities when we see God in it and are ready for the risk of seeing things as God sees them.

There is a play on words with the first vision, a frequent device of the Old Testament prophets, used doubtless to make their words more memorable. The Hebrew word for 'almond tree' is *shaqed*. The participle of the verb 'to watch' is *shoqed*. The sight assures the prophet that God is watching carefully to make sure his word is going to be fulfilled (v. 12).

A threat from the 'north'

Just what that 'word' predicts is made a little clearer by the second vision. The pot on the fire is tilted from the north so that, when it boils over, its contents will pour out towards the south, scalding all in its path. The threat is of judgment from God at the hands of an invading army. The identity of the army is not specified, nor does it need to be. The Hebrew word for 'north' is *zaphon*. In the Canaanite literature 'Mount Zaphon' was thought of as the abode of the gods, just as the Greeks thought of Mount Olympus. There is just a hint of this in Psalm 48:1 where Jerusalem is described as 'the mountain in the far north', that is, the dwelling place of the one, true God. So judgment 'from the north' means that, whoever the human agent, the judgment is really from God who can use any human instrument when it suits him (compare Isaiah 10:5–6). Whomever Jeremiah exactly had in mind, later generations could identify the threat in terms of their own situation. That is why, in the final form of the book, which was completed during the time of the Babylonian exile, the 'enemy' is identified with Babylon. The fact is that at all times and in all historical situations, the people of God find that the unchanging word of God is as true in their day as it was in the prophet's. The details and circumstances may change, but it remains true that to turn away from God is always to find frustration and defeat. 'Babylon' stands for all the chaos we create when we cut ourselves off from God's direction and God's help. Jeremiah brings this out in his diagnosis of his people's situation. Their sin is that they have turned from the worship of the only God, who created and redeemed them, and instead worship gods that they themselves have made (v. 16). The temptation to create our own gods is always with us.

The prophet's resources

The call to the prophet is a stern one, a call to conflict with the powerful and wealthy in society, all those in fact who have a vested interest in the status quo—kings, leaders and priests (vv. 18–19). In such a context it may be that the phrase 'people of the land' (v. 18) refers to landed property owners rather than to the 'common people'. But the God who called the prophet to this relentless struggle renews his promise of divine strength (v. 19; compare 1:8). Perhaps it is always true that we know as much of the reality and resources of God as we need for the jobs we are doing for him. Is that why we sometimes seem to experience so little of his presence?

A PRAYER

O God, teach me not only to look for you in the extraordinary and sensational, but to sense your presence and hear your voice in the humdrum routine of everyday events. Amen

ISRAEL'S APOSTASY

The influence of Hosea on Jeremiah

This opening oracle of the book is introduced again with the phrase, 'The word of the Lord came to me' (1:4, 13). Yet what follows is an illustration of the truth that God has many ways of speaking to us, and very often one of those ways is through other people. That is certainly the case with Jeremiah, for in this passage he shows strongly the influence of Hosea, his northern predecessor. For example, he uses a word that figures prominently in Hosea's vocabulary, the Hebrew word *hesed* (v. 2), which in various English versions and in different contexts is translated as 'loving kindness', 'devotion', 'loyalty' and 'faithfulness'. Hosea uses it of God's unfailing devotion to his people and the loyalty for which he looks from them in response (Hosea 2:19; 6:6). Also Hosea's is the picture of the relationship between God and Israel as a marriage, a marriage which began with an ideal 'honeymoon' period in the desert when Israel knew and worshipped only Yahweh as their God. This marriage between Israel and God, however, turned sour when the bride, Israel, entered Canaan and, confronted with the gods of the Canaanites, became unfaithful to Yahweh by worshipping them as well—especially Baal, the most active of them all (Hosea 2:15–16; see Jeremiah 2:2). So Jeremiah hears God's word to some extent through Hosea just as we often hear God speaking to us through others. However, like Jeremiah, we have to make that word our own and find its relevance and 'newness' for our own particular situation.

Israel as God's 'first fruits'

Jeremiah says that Israel was God's 'first fruits' (v. 3) in that God chose her before all others. He showed this particular care for her in delivering his people from Egypt, leading them through the wilderness and bringing them into the fertile land of Canaan (vv. 6–7; Exodus 4:22–23). But there is a double edge to this relationship. For all 'first fruits' were 'holy' to God: that is, they were to be specially dedicated to his service (Exodus 23:19; 34:26), and this included first-born children (Exodus 13:2, 13). So in describing Israel as God's 'first-born' the prophet is saying that not only did this involve God in the responsibility of caring for his children, but it involved them in the responsibility of being 'holy' to God, of being set aside for his special worship and service. And this makes all the more heinous the sharp contrast that runs through the whole passage between God's faithfulness towards his people and his people's disloyalty to him (vv. 4–8). God did not choose Israel because he has favourites, or because he does not care for people of other races, but because it was his intention to reveal himself to the world through his 'first-born' (Genesis 12:3; Isaiah 49:6). They forgot that the divine 'election' is election not to privilege only, but to responsibility.

The futility of rejecting God

Not only the enormity but also the futility of deserting God is driven home in this passage. Its enormity is that such a betrayal of one's God cannot be paralleled anywhere else (v. 10). From Cyprus in the west to Kedar in the east—that is, neither among the settled, cultivated people of the Mediterranean islands, nor the nomads of the desert—has such an action been seen. But it is also futile. The gods the Israelites have decided to worship are 'worthless'. Yet, in another play on words, the prophet maintains that the worship of the 'worthless' makes its devotees 'worthless' too (v. 5; compare 2 Kings 17:15). Indeed, it is always true that what we worship—that is, that which we love, devote our energies to, put at the pinnacle of our scale of values—always influences the kind of people we become. Deriding those who worship what they themselves have made, the psalmist says, 'They who make them grow to be like them' (Psalm 115:18, REB). The forceful contrast between a leaking, static water tank and a life-giving, perennial spring (v. 13) offers its own commentary on the life God offers his worshippers and the deadening, frustrating futility that even the most attractive things produce when we make them the sole end of our lives.

A PRAYER

Jesus, Thou joy of loving hearts,
Thou fount of life, Thou light of men;
From the best bliss that earth imparts,
We turn unfilled to Thee again.

Ray Palmer (1808–87), from Latin, 12th century

The FRUITS *of* APOSTASY

The sacrifice of 'first-born' status

This section is shot through with irony as it depicts the absurd consequences of forsaking God for other objects of worship. The opening question of verse 14, 'Is Israel a slave? Is he a homeborn servant? [better, NEB's 'Was he born in slavery?'] Why then has he become plunder?' ironically recalls 2:3. Of course Israel was not born a slave; he was God's 'first fruits', the first-born son, entitled to his Father's special protection. Far from allowing other nations to plunder Israel, God held all who attacked him guilty and saw that 'disaster came upon them'. So, by turning from Yahweh, Israel has forfeited this special status and lost the divine protection. Verses 15–16 show how this has happened. Memphis and Tahpanhes were Egyptian cities, but it is probably a mistake to try to set this highly poetic oracle in one particular historical context. 'Egypt' is a symbol for all the oppressors who, at one time or another, plundered Israel. So God can ask, 'Have you not brought this upon yourself by forsaking the Lord your God?' (v. 17). God's judgment is not usually to be thought of as his aiming to harm us in a fit of injured pique. 'Judgment' happens when we choose to turn away from God and so cut ourselves off from the love that longs to enfold us.

The ineffectiveness of alliances with foreign nations

The second irony is to be found in verse 18, for this vividly recalls 2:13. Verses 18–19 concentrate not on the worship of the gods of other nations, but on seeking military safety by forging alliances with them, rather than trusting, as a 'first-born' should, the protection offered by their Father. Having forsaken the 'fountain of living waters' (2:13), they have turned to the waters of the Nile and the Euphrates; in other words, they have sought alliances with Egypt and Assyria. Again, we should not look for one occasion when Israel turned to them both, for this is a familiar prophetic theme (for example, Hosea 5:13; Isaiah 30:1–3), and there were many points in Israel's history when such alliances were sought. To us, this prophetic theme may seem a trifle idealistic and impractical. How was a king to safeguard his people in times of military threat? The prophets may have thought that such alliances usually proved ineffective (and they very often did). But, more likely, they looked back to the great periods of their history—the Exodus, the entry into Canaan, the great days of David's reign—when Israel had no one to lean on but the God who had promised to be faithful to his 'first-born'.

The burden other gods exact

The final irony is that of the utter weariness that the service of other gods entails. Verses 20–25 stress not the political but the religious apostasy by which Israel turned to the worship of the gods of other nations; and because the Baal cult was a fertility, nature religion, often involving the use of ritual prostitution, a series of crude sexual metaphors is employed. Israel has been a 'prostitute' (v. 20), a 'vine' which failed to give good wine (v. 21; compare Isaiah 5:1–7), and an animal 'in heat' (vv. 23–24). Verse 25 shows the weariness that such a lust-driven pursuit can induce under the picture of the pain and hurt that befall the desert wanderer. What a profound psychology is shown here! 'I know the pain and damage I am inflicting on myself, but I must go on—I cannot help it.' That paraphrase of verse 25 is true by no means only of unbridled sexual passion. Any 'god' I worship can exact a terrible toll. People sacrifice health, peace of mind, family life, simple enjoyment of everyday things, to the pursuit of wealth, fame or power. And these all too often turn out, in spite of the price they demand, to be 'broken cisterns' (2:13).

A PRAYER

Thou hast made us for Thyself, and our hearts are restless until they find their rest in Thee.

Augustine of Hippo (354–430)

FALSE SOURCES *of* COMFORT

The absurdity of Israel's conduct

The vivid metaphors of the earlier part of the chapter continue in this section. When trouble suddenly bursts on them from the blue, Israel is found looking as defenceless and ashamed as a burglar caught in the act (v. 26). To have transferred their allegiance from the living God to the worship associated with sacred trees and stones is shown for the foolish and futile practice it always was (v. 27). They turned from the God who had shown himself to be their true 'Father' to inanimate objects which proved useless in a time of a crisis (vv. 27–28). Then, with a complete lack of consistency and logic, they called on God, blaming him for not doing more to help them (v. 29).

Continuing the rich range of metaphors, Israel has acted as improbably in forgetting her God as a girl forgetting her jewellery or a bride her wedding dress (v. 32). Yet God was far more essential to the well-being of his 'bride' (2:2) than any mere ornaments. Again, Israel is like a prostitute, promiscuous in her eager and willing indulgence in the fertility cults of the Baalim (the Hebrew plural of 'Baal', v. 33). Yet all her religious pluralism failed to show itself in the kind of 'righteousness' God desired, for the needs of the 'innocent poor' were neglected (v. 34).

Finally, the sheer superficiality of the people is exposed. If some prophets brought home to them unwelcome truths, the prophets were simply eliminated (v. 30). Any temporary lull in the troubles besetting them was interpreted as a sign that God's judgment had passed, and hence of their innocence and the 'rightness' of their present course of conduct (v. 35). And, lacking any deep roots, how quickly they veer about, following every new fad of political thought and fashion (v. 36). Such superficial judgment and action, however, will be shown for the inadequate thing it is. The very nations they trust to deliver them will subjugate them and lead them away in captive processions (v. 37). For those who appear so strong and attractive to superficial, human eyes are in fact the very people God has rejected.

God's faithfulness

Like a counterpoint running through a passage that denounces Israel's falseness, inconsistency and superficiality is the persistent faithfulness of God, who is still challenging them through the series of ironical, rhetorical questions from his prophet (vv. 28, 29, 31, 32). He has judged his people in every generation (which is what the term 'sons' or 'children' in verse 30 means). Yet even this has failed to bring them to their senses (v. 30; compare Amos 4:6–11). Has he at any point in his dealings with Israel been as inhospitable and cruel as a desert can be, or as remote as if he were cut off in deep darkness? (v. 31). On the contrary, their own tradition (which the questions recall) tells them how he fed them in the wilderness and led them through it as a pillar of fire.

The significance of the passage

The whole of this passage is, in effect, an exposition of the original questioning of the absurdity of Israel's ways in 2:11. It may all seem a little remote to us, for whom Baal worship is scarcely a burning temptation! Yet does not Jeremiah show profound psychological understanding of continuing relevance here? It often seems natural to us, still, to live our lives seeking selfish ends and short-term goals, and then turn round and blame God when not everything goes according to (our) plan. Too often for comfort, we regard God not as the very heart of all our being, but like some ornament or item of dress to put on when it suits us, something to add a little extra security and comfort at the margins of our lives. And, if ours are not the heinous sins of worshipping the Baalim, or deliberately oppressing the innocent poor, our lives, when not deeply rooted in God, all too easily tend to superficiality—superficiality of judgment, of aim, of appreciation of the needs of those around us, of shifting from one set of values to another and setting our sails to the latest winds of moral and intellectual fad. Perhaps Jeremiah has something to warn us about still.

FOR MEDITATION

We never better enjoy ourselves than when we most enjoy God.

Benjamin Whichcote (1609–83)

CAN SINNERS REPENT?

Both parts of this section (vv. 1–5 in poetry, and vv. 6–10 in prose) are connected by the theme of the marriage between God and his people; the infidelity of the 'wife' and her failure to return to God. Jeremiah himself may often have spoken in prose, but generally scholars believe that many prose passages in the book are expansions of his words by the Deuteronomistic editors. They echo closely the vocabulary and style of the Deuteronomistic literature (see Introduction, pp. 15–16). The passage as a whole illustrates just how difficult the interpretation of a biblical text can be—and how, sometimes, important theological issues hang on the way we do understand it. The issue in verse 1 depends on the law in Deuteronomy 24:1–4. That supposes a case where a husband decides to divorce his wife when she no longer pleases him because of some indecency, and this divorced wife subsequently remarries another man who, in his turn, also divorces her. In such a case there can be no question of a return to her first husband. She has been 'contaminated' and such a (re)marriage would 'bring guilt on the land'. So, Israel left Yahweh, her husband, for the Baalim (an ironic title since *baal* is one of the Hebrew words for 'husband'). If, for any reason, Israel were to abandon her worship of the Baalim, would it be possible for Yahweh to take her back? In the words of Deuteronomy 24:4, it would make the land 'greatly polluted' (v. 1).

This reading of our text presents us with a very pessimistic view. God will not return to his estranged wife, and the question, 'Would you return to me?' seems to underline this. Taken with verse 10 it seems to suggest that the sinners' position is hopeless. Repentance and forgiveness are doors that God slams in their faces. (Such a judgment fits the harsh, even crude language and imagery used.)

Yet the biblical text is not quite so simple to interpret. The Greek version of the Old Testament (the Septuagint: see Introduction, p. 15) reads, 'Will she return to him? Would not such a woman be greatly polluted?' That puts the onus for her failure to return on Israel, not on God. Further, the Hebrew of the last line of verse 1 is most easily read as a straightforward imperative—'Return to me!'—and that is how AV and RV have translated it. If we read it this way, then God is still pleading with his estranged 'wife'. True, all modern English versions, and most commentators, take it as an ironic question, for, in Hebrew as in English, one can ask a question by tone of voice.

Perhaps there is truth in both sides of the interpretative problem. In the context of the message of the book as a whole, it does seem as if Jeremiah thought it was impossible for pre-exilic Judah to repent and find salvation. The nation as a whole had made its choice. Judgment was fixed. Only on the other side of the exile could there be hope of a salvation which would be wholly the work of God's grace. Yet that does not necessarily mean that God ever abandoned his people. He continued to plead with them in many ways. He had warned them by sending a drought in judgment (compare 2:30 and Amos 4:7–8, ironic since the Baalim they worshipped were claimed as gods of fertility). The Judeans had seen what happened to the northern kingdom of Israel, so they also had the lesson of history (and to that extent were more guilty than their Israelite neighbours, v. 11). In such ways God had not been silent.

Words that disguise the truth

In both sections, however, there is the accusation that their response to such warnings, when it did come, was a matter of words only (vv. 4–5, 10). Their 'repentance' involved no intention to change their ways. The fact that verses 6–10 are described as being spoken in the 'days of Josiah' (v. 6) may be a reference to that king's worthy attempt at religious reform (2 Kings 22:8—23:24). If so, such reform was seen to be superficial and skin-deep at best.

So the question remains, is repentance possible or is it always beyond us? Later, as we shall see, Jeremiah insists that it is possible only by the grace of God working in human hearts (17:9; compare 31:31–34). So we are face to face with the great mystery, not only for Jeremiah and his contemporaries but for Christian experience as well. God calls us to respond to him and our responsibility is real. But God makes that response a reality by the gifts of his grace.

FOR PRAYER

Give what thou commandest, and command what thou wilt.

Augustine of Hippo (354–430)

7

GOD'S CALL *to* PENITENCE

For the first time in the book, a note of hope begins to sound, but it is to be heard only the other side of the judgment of exile, for both sections (vv. 12–14 and 15–18) presuppose an audience away from Zion/Jerusalem in 'the land of the north' (vv. 12, 14, 18; for the 'land of the north' as the place from which judgment will come and to which Israel will be exiled, see the comment on 1:13–15, pp. 20–21). Although the term 'Israel' in 3:11 referred only to the former northern kingdom, in verse 12 it refers to all the people of God, envisaged now as being in exile, but destined to be brought back and reunited in the land (vv. 14, 18).

The message is again made memorable by the device of play on words. The Hebrew verb 'to return' (*sub*) has a double meaning. It can mean 'to return' geographically, that is, from one place to another. It can also mean 'to (re)turn' in the sense of 'to repent', 'to turn back to God'. So the exhortation, 'return... Israel' (vv. 12, 14) means both to 'come back to God' and so to be in a position to 'return to your land'. And the play on words is further extended by the use of the word translated in NRSV as 'faithless' (*mesubah*, 3:11; *sobabim*, v. 14). Israel 'turned away' from Yahweh to worship the Baalim (v. 13), as a result of which they were 'sent away' into exile. Further, there is yet another ironic play on the word for Baalim, where God says to Israel, literally, 'I am your Baal', 'I am your husband' (v. 14).

God, the faithful husband, calls for faith

God is still, then, the faithful husband calling for his wife's return, and so the question of 3:5 is answered. God will not 'keep his anger for ever' because of his 'devoted loyalty', a word which recalls the faithfulness he called for from his 'bride' Israel (2:2; see the comment on pp. 22–23). The surprising statement in verse 14 that only some will return from exile suggests that the new community will be based on faith rather than nationality, a point that Paul was to make much later (Galatians 3:7). The same emphasis on 'faith' is suggested by the reference to the 'ark of the covenant' (v. 16). This had been placed in the temple and was apparently viewed as a footstool of the throne on which Yahweh sat among the cherubim (1 Kings 8:6–7; 2 Kings 19:15). Others, however, like the writers of Deuteronomy, had a rather 'Lower Church' view of it as simply a box in which the tablets of the law were stored (Deuteronomy 10:1–12). Presumably the ark was destroyed when the temple was burnt in 586BC. Verse 16, rather in the 'Low Church', Deuteronomic view, suggests that it will not be missed. God will now rule in Jerusalem in the hearts of his faithful people, and will need no special sacred objects or site. It is close to the view expressed in Jeremiah 7:4, and this whole prose section may be the work of those Deuteronomistic teachers who, in the exile, sought to bring the words of Jeremiah home to the exiles with new force.

God's future for Jerusalem

In the future God is going to renew his people and Zion/Jerusalem. Faithful 'shepherds' will be installed by God to replace the former false leaders (v. 15; compare 2:26). 'Shepherds' is a term used for rulers both in the Old Testament (for example, Ezekiel 34:1–23; Psalm 78:70–71) and throughout the ancient Near East. Hammurabi, king of Babylon, describes himself in his famous law code as 'the shepherd called by Enlil' (Enlil being a Babylonian deity).

Not only will all God's people be reunited once more in one kingdom centred on Jerusalem, but people of all nations will make their pilgrimage to the city to be enlightened and to worship (v. 17; compare Isaiah 2:2–4 and its parallel passage in Micah 4:1–4). So even the sins and failures that gave rise to the exile will be used and redeemed by the grace of God to forward his purposes. Israel's sufferings will prove to be, like those of the 'suffering servant', a means to 'enlighten the Gentiles' (Isaiah 49:6). In the end, God's grace triumphs over human blindness and sin.

A PRAYER

Lord, when I wander away from you, sometimes without realizing that I have done so, may a new realization of your unfailing love and constant readiness to forgive draw my feet back into your paths of truth and joy. Amen

FRUSTRATING GOD'S PLANS

A 'prophetic liturgy'

Several separate sections make up this passage, but they have been joined together in form and theme. In form they constitute what commentators have often called a 'prophetic liturgy', that is, a passage where the prophet brings together an appeal or accusation from God (3:19–20), followed by an outcry of lamentation from the people (3:21), a further appeal and assurance from God (3:22a), followed by an act of repentance from the community (3:22b–25). The whole liturgy ends with two further assurances from God which together form a kind of 'instruction' or even 'preaching' (as in Hosea 14).

The frustrated plans of God

Not only are these sections joined in form but there is a motif running through them, that of the frustration of God's plans. Chapter 3 verse 19 shows the plans of love God had for his people. He intended to give them a special place among the family of nations, living in a pleasant land and in a special relationship with him by which they would address him as 'my Father'. Again the 'turning' (Hebrew: *sub*) motif is heard. God thought that such love would mean they would never 'turn away' from him (v. 19; see comments on 3:12–18, pp. 30–31). But their apostasy, under the now familiar picture of infidelity in a marriage relationship, was a tragic frustration of his purposes. Yet now, a different response to the divine plea is heard from that in 2:4–5, with the people's cries of distress 'on the heights' (3:21), a reference to their worship of the Baalim on the 'high places'. So now the prophet provides them with words of penitence by which they could signal a true return to Yahweh (3:22b). The appeal from God, who, as the divine healer, wants to heal the very distress their own sins have caused (3:22), is a reminder of the way unhealed suffering can frustrate human potential.

God's promises for Israel and the nations

Israel's response is met by a most surprising promise from God (4:1–2). If their return is a matter of action and not just of words (unlike that in 3:4–5, 10), then God's frustrated purposes for the nations will be realized. The last two lines of verse 2 cite the promise to Abraham in Genesis 12:1–3. God will so bless him that 'by him shall all the families of the earth bless themselves'. Abraham and his descendants will become a kind of measure or yardstick of blessing when people wish each other well: 'May you be as blessed as Abraham has been'. And hinted at there is the thought that one day those nations will want to share the source of that blessing for themselves. That is why God has set Israel among his 'children' and given them a special relationship with himself (3:19). It is not just that Israel was his favourite, but that it was his purpose to reveal himself to others through them. And so, by denying their special status they were frustrating not only God's purposes for them but for all the nations as well. We can never keep the fruits of our own sins to ourselves. Others always suffer because of them and are denied what they might otherwise have enjoyed.

A call for new action

In the 'instruction' that follows in 4:3–4, Israel is called to break out of the circle of sin and frustration by brave and decisive new action. Let them now till land which has been allowed to lie fallow, so that it may realize its potentialities by becoming fertile. It is always worth the while of the people of God to ask themselves, 'What purposes of God for myself and others am I allowing to lie fallow? What bold new initiative might release the possibilities of this situation?'

Circumcision was one sign of Israel's distinctive relationship with God (Genesis 17:11). Jeremiah, like the other pre-exilic prophets, was impatient of religious rites which were a matter of form and show only. It can only be from the heart—that is, by the love they show for God in worshipping him alone and following his commands—that they can show truly that 'special' relationship of which circumcision was the sign (Deuteronomy 10:16). And that is true for the people of God of all times.

A PRAYER

Lord, show me what potential in me is lying fallow and help me to bring it to you to make it fruitful for you and others. Amen

SUPERFICIAL RELIGION

Flee for your lives!

A vivid series of metaphors in this highly poetic section describe the coming of the invading army 'from the north' (see 1:13–15). He is like a rampant lion (v. 7), or a sirocco, a devastatingly fierce, hot wind which blows in from the desert, scorching and covering in dust all in its path (v. 12). This wind is of no use for something profitable like winnowing; it is only destructive. So the moment for sifting out the grain from the chaff has gone. Only judgment now awaits. The advance of the enemy is as swift and unhindered as violent storm winds, or charging cavalry (v. 13), that early military equivalent of the tank column.

The prophet is instructed to sound the warning—and in no uncertain way, the Hebrew of verse 5 meaning 'proclaim it fully'. Those living in the undefended lowlands must make for the safety of the walled towns, of which Zion/Jerusalem is the most notable. To this end a 'standard' must be raised on the watch-towers and the alarm trumpet sounded, calling the people to safety (vv. 5–7). Not that even these fortresses are likely to provide protection for very long. Because Yahweh is bringing the invader to execute his judgment, no resistance will be effective (vv. 7, 16).

God has deceived his people

Verse 10 presents a problem that must not be dismissed too quickly. Elsewhere the prophet accuses God of deceiving him, and in the strongest possible language (see 20:7 and the comment on pp. 106–107). Undoubtedly, Jeremiah is referring here to the 'false' prophets who proclaimed 'peace', that is, assured the people of God's salvation and deliverance when the moral and spiritual preconditions for that 'peace' did not exist (see 14:13; 23:16–17; Micah 3:11). The allusion to 'Jerusalem' in verse 10 and in Micah 3:11 suggests that such prophets were seen to be basing their confidence on the promises God had made that Jerusalem was his dwelling place and that he would defend it against all comers (Psalms 46:4–7, 11; 48:8; 132:13–18). Further, there had been the divine promise that there would always be a descendant of David on the throne (2 Samuel 7:16; Psalm 89:35–37). Thus the prophets of salvation could, and doubtless did, claim to be basing their promises on the word of God himself. That is why Jeremiah challenges God. God himself has to some extent been responsible for the misleading of the people. It is a problem which continued to torment the prophet, as we shall see. Jeremiah alone, it seems, is convinced that when the king, priest, prophet and people have turned their back on God, religion can never be a kind of magic talisman offering automatic protection. That is why all those who see it that way will be confounded (v. 9).

A change of heart needed

The 'heart' is a recurring theme throughout the book (v. 14). Just as the 'heart' is the source of evil thoughts, so a change of 'heart' is what is needed now if the people are to change. In English usage we tend to set 'heart' over against 'mind'. The Hebrew word (*leb*), however, incorporates all that we mean by both the emotions and the intellect as well as the will. It represents the 'inner' part of human life and personality, as opposed to the outward matters of form and conduct, though Jeremiah sees clearly that the two are inextricably linked. It is what is happening 'within' that determines how people behave outwardly. The call to 'cleanse the wrongdoing from your heart', therefore, is a call for a response of the whole personality, and not merely for a superficial performance of 'religious' acts and duties. Not that the call seems to be uttered with much hope of success. The march 'from the north', represented by mention of the northern town of Dan and the hill country of Ephraim, continues (vv. 15–18). No doubt that is why Jeremiah came to see that if there was to be a 'change of heart', it must be achieved by God (24:7). It is he alone who can 'give them a heart to know me' (see also 32:39).

A PRAYER

O for a heart to praise my God,
A heart from sin set free…
Thy nature, gracious Lord, impart,
Come quickly from above;
Write Thy new name upon my heart,
Thy new best name of love.

Charles Wesley (1707–88)

The PROPHET'S ANGUISH

In Jeremiah 4:8 the prophet says, 'The fierce anger of the Lord has not turned away from us.' In one sense he is standing over against the community, announcing its forthcoming judgment and calling on its members to flee before the invader. Yet, in a real sense also, he is one with his people. He shares their fate and identifies himself with them. That attitude is seen even more clearly in the extraordinary outburst of anguish in verses 19–21. He hears the trumpet sound of alarm for which he has called (4:5) and sees in his vivid imagination the coming destruction of the people's houses (v. 20, 'tents' by this time being an anachronism, used perhaps to suggest impermanence). Yet these are '*my* tents… *my* curtains'. The prophet is suffering with his people as he sees what drives them into panic-stricken flight (vv. 19–21). Yet, in the next verse, he is speaking words of God (v. 22). He shares God's anguish over his people as well. So here the prophet is torn between the God he represents and the people who are 'his'. Perhaps this tension is something to which the people of God of all times are subject. They must be close enough to God to see with his eyes, love with his love, and burn with his anger against all corruption and injustice. Yet they must also be fully identified in love and compassion with their fellows.

Return to chaos

We have already had one allusion to Genesis in this chapter (4:2), to the promise to Abraham of Genesis 12:1–3. Now we have a remarkable series of allusions to the traditions of the creation story of Genesis 1. There, before creation, all was dark, shapeless chaos (Hebrew: *tohu wabohu*; see comments on p. 42). Now Jeremiah looks on the earth and sees it as *tohu wabohu*, 'waste and void' (v. 23; Genesis 1:1). In Genesis 1 we are told how in that primordial darkness 'God said, "Let there be light" and there was light' (Genesis 1:3). But now Jeremiah sees that the heavens 'had no light' (v. 23). God established the dry land by forcing back the chaos waters into predetermined bounds (Genesis 1:9–10), but now hills and mountains are tottering on their foundations (v. 24). God had created the birds of the air (Genesis 1:20), but now Jeremiah sees that the birds have flown (v. 25). God created humankind (*adam* in Hebrew) as the pinnacle of his creation, but now the prophet sees 'no *adam*' (v. 25). God had called on the earth to be fruitful (Genesis 1:11–12) but now the 'fruitful land has become a desert' (v. 26). Genesis tells how God created by his word, 'And God said… and there was'. But now the 'word' of God is spoken in judgment (v. 27).

In Jeremiah this is poetry, metaphor for the terrible sufferings he sees coming on his people and their land, in spite of the slight note of amelioration at the end of verse 27. But in our time we have seen how human sin can threaten the return of chaos to God's creation. The use of nuclear weapons and chemical warfare; a ruthless exploitation of the earth's resources which is blind both to the needs of future generations and to the ecological effect of the wastes we are producing; an unfair distribution of the earth's produce so that whole sections of the world's population are driven to despair and, sometimes, to extremist action: in all these ways we threaten the return of chaos.

A people blind to reality

Verse 29 graphically portrays the flight before the invader. Yet the people, personified as 'daughter Zion' (v. 31), carry on with their superficial way of life like partygoers on board a doomed ship (v. 30). And, most tragic of all, a child is born (v. 31), that greatest symbol of hope and new life—just as the killers close in. The worst consequences of our sin can be to rob our children of their heritage.

FOR MEDITATION

If, as the Christian faith proclaims, the deepest experience of God is to be found only through the fellowship of the cross, that fellowship must be no sentimental ideal, no esoteric and hidden desire, but something worked out amid the realities of life.

H. Wheeler Robinson, *The Cross of Jeremiah*, SCM Press, 1925, p. 46

HARDENED *to* GOD'S LOVE

This passage can be read as a conversation between God and the prophet, with God calling the prophet to look for even one righteous person in the city and accusing the people of blasphemy (vv. 1–2). The commands 'run', 'search' and the others are in the plural. Perhaps the prophet is seen as employing agents to make his search more thorough. Jeremiah's response comes in verses 3–5. He can find none righteous among the ordinary people in the streets, but a certain coarseness and ignorance might be expected among them. So he goes to the 'ruling classes', only to find them just as ignorant of God's ways. So in verse 6 God announces the coming judgment already threatened in the book, a threat reinforced in verses 7–9 as he accuses the community of religious apostasy and the kind of sexual licence which is one sign of the breakdown of society.

The hardened heart

The passage depicts a strange contradiction in human behaviour. People use the oath 'As the Lord lives' (v. 2; compare 4:2) but they live as though God did not exist. The 'reality' of God makes no practical difference to their lives at all. They ignore his commands; they live for their own ends; they do not call on him in their time of need. They even use his name to validate their lies. God is just not a factor to be reckoned with. This is a lasting phenomenon. We can all be guilty of it, at least at times. In worship we utter the profound words of the creeds; we join in prayer and praise; we hear and see God's truth proclaimed in word and sacrament. And then we live our lives just like everyone else, as though it were not life-shattering to be created, loved and redeemed, and accompanied through every vicissitude of life, by such a God. We too sometimes say 'God lives'—but then live as though he were dead or, at least, indifferent. The challenge of this passage is that those who go on denying God lose the capacity to hear and respond to him (v. 3).

The value of one good person

The Hebrew of verse 1 is interesting and challenging. The call is to see if one man (the Hebrew word is *ish*) can be found who acts justly and seeks truth, and the parts of those verbs used are masculine. That does not mean that Jeremiah is to seek out only men and not women. It is just the way Hebrew works and it means, as NRSV has rightly put it in more inclusive language, 'one person'. Yet God says not 'that I may pardon him', but 'that I may pardon her', the feminine pronoun referring to Jerusalem and the whole community of that city. It suggests that even one godly person can have a saving effect on others by his or her faith and example. Abraham found this to be true when he pleaded with God not to destroy the town of Sodom for the lack of 'five' righteous people (Genesis 18:22–33). So our passage shows that both our sin and our faith have effects beyond ourselves. Verse 7 shows how the 'children' of this sinful generation now forsake Yahweh and swear by 'no gods', so the sin of the parents affects the generations who come after them. But it challenges us also to believe that godly individuals, by their prayer, witness and example, can also have an influence for good far beyond themselves.

In spite of the totality of judgment threatened here, it is unlikely that there were no righteous people in Jerusalem in Jeremiah's time. It is the exaggeration of disappointment and despair, much as Elijah complained to God that he was the only faithful one left, only to be reminded by God that there were others as well (1 Kings 19:10, 18). The mere existence of the book of Jeremiah shows that there were at least some who listened to his words, treasured and preserved them, and applied them later to new situations. The fact that the fall of Jerusalem did not mean an end of God's plans for his people shows that some people of faith always endure, even in the worst times of trouble and crisis.

A PRAYER

Lord, make my faith and love for you firm enough today to help someone else to be strong in their hour of need. Amen

'DON'T RECKON WITHOUT GOD!'

Practical atheism

Often in the Old Testament, Israel is likened to a vine or a vineyard (Isaiah 5:1–7; Ezekiel 15:1–8; Psalm 80:8–13). In almost every instance the context is one of failure and judgment. Israel did not produce the fruit of 'righteousness' for which God looked and so now, in verses 10–11, he gives command (to the attacking nations?) to pull down her vines and strip them bare. Because of Israel's faithlessness (v. 11), the vines no longer belong to him and he no longer acknowledges them as his own.

This is the last thing the Israelites expected. They saw their calling to be God's chosen people as ensuring complete divine protection. Such false confidence is pilloried in verses 12–13. It is not quite clear whether these two verses show the people and their leaders first speaking falsely of the Lord (v. 12) and then condemning the true prophets like Jeremiah, describing them as empty windbags (v. 13); or whether it is the false prophets who are preaching a superficial message of assurance in verse 12, with Jeremiah attacking them in verse 13. Either way, it is a 'virtual atheism' that is being criticized. Such people 'speak falsely' of God by saying 'He is not', as the Hebrew of verse 12 has it. This can hardly mean that they deny his very existence, but that they assume he can be reckoned without. He is there to protect them: he will do nothing to injure them. In response to such 'false words' about him, God will give his words to his prophet, words which will be as effective as a raging fire (v. 14; compare 23:29). What an ironic contrast to the 'empty wind' of the false prophets, the Hebrew word for 'wind' and 'spirit' being the same (*ruah*). This is a reminder that it is always difficult to know whether a movement or a person who claims to be acting in the power of God's Spirit is really authentic or not. This passage, and others later in the book, tell us that we always have to 'test' the spirits (compare 1 John 4:1). The evidence for the genuineness of what is claimed as a 'word of God' is not in the external manner or form of its delivery, nor in the mere claims of those who speak, but in the contents and effects of the word.

God's enduring plan for his people

The content of Jeremiah's word in verses 15–17 continues the note of judgment sounded in verses 10–11, judgment merited by their 'false speaking'. The terror of what is to come is enhanced by the utter strangeness of the invaders (almost certainly the Babylonians are meant), characterized by their alien language (v. 15), and the knell-like tolling of repeated Hebrew words. Four times the word 'nation' (*goy*) occurs in verse 15 and four times the verb 'to devour' (*akal*) in verse 17. It will be a relentless march of terror in which all will be destroyed, even the cities to which they fled for safety (v. 17; see 4:5).

Yet, amid all the destruction, a pale glimmer of light appears. In verse 10, a 'full end' was not to be made to the vines, and the same note recurs in the prose of verse 18. The strong parallels between verse 19 and Deuteronomy 29:22–28 have suggested to many commentators that this 'mitigating' note is the work of Deuteronomists (see Introduction) in the exile who wanted to assure those who had survived that God still had a purpose for them. That may well be true but, in doing so, they would only be expounding a real element in Jeremiah's own preaching. He was called 'to plant' as well as 'to pluck up' (1:10) and the note of hope is by no means absent from his prophecy, even though he is quite sure that the whole present 'Establishment' of temple and nation is doomed. Hope can be fulfilled only on the other side of the exile and such fulfilment will be entirely a work of God's grace. This is what is hinted at in verses 10 and 19 (see also 4:27). As such, it is a note that was not only relevant to the prophet's contemporaries, but would bring encouragement and hope to the exiles later in Babylon. It assures us too that God's plans are never finally frustrated by human sin and failure.

FOR MEDITATION

*Who trusts in God's unchanging love
Builds on the rock which nought can move.*

Georg Neumark (1621–81)

ORDER & DISORDER

The order of God's creation

The appeal to the community in this passage is to reflect on God as Creator (vv. 22, 24). Just one stage in the process of creation is singled out, the act of God in setting the shores as boundaries for the oceans. Behind such a purely geographical phenomenon, however, an allusion to something deeper is being made. In the traditions of Israel and her neighbours, the original act of creation consisted of God's taming of the primeval waters of chaos (Genesis 1:1–10). In some forms of the story there was an actual struggle between the god and some monster representing chaos. In the Babylonian story, for example, the god Marduk fought and slew the dragon monster, Tiamat. He tore her dead body and from the pieces formed a firmament in the skies which kept the chaos waters at bay, so enabling the dry land to appear on which human beings, animals and vegetation could flourish. An annual ritual re-enactment of this battle in Babylonian worship was seen as a way of ensuring the annual gift of rain and renewed order and fertility in the whole created world.

There is nothing like that in Genesis, although the Old Testament shows that the Israelites knew various forms of this story, some in which the monster was called 'Rahab' (Psalm 89:9–11; Job 26:12; Isaiah 51:9) and some in which it was called 'Leviathan' (Isaiah 27:1). In Genesis, God created the firmament which kept the chaos waters at bay so that the dry land could be formed (Genesis 1:1–10). The Hebrew word for the waters is *tehom*, which may be related to the Babylonian 'Tiamat', but that is as far as any resemblance to the Babylonian myth goes.

In Jeremiah 5:22, then, more than just the making of the seaside is being alluded to. God, the God of creation, is the God who brings order out of chaos and who gives the rain which makes the land fertile (v. 24). There is irony in the restatement of this great truth, for the Israelites had turned to the worship of Baal as the supposed god of fertility. Indeed, even surrounded as they were every day by evidence of God's created order, they had no eyes to discern its significance nor ears to hear warnings about neglecting the giver of it all (v.

21). REB has a splendid rendering of verse 25: 'Your wrongdoing has upset nature's order, and your sins have kept away her bounty.'

Moral disorder

Just what form such 'wrongdoing' took is spelled out in verses 26–29. The people tolerate a lack of any sense of compassion and justice in society, charges familiar in the prophetic books (see Amos 5:10–12). Some grow rich by exploiting the poor and forcing them into slavery. They ignore the appeals of the weaker members of society who cannot win favourable decisions in the courts by bribes, or buy the intervention of those who could help them. And, ironically, it is these very ruthless, rich and powerful people who are supported by the institutions of religion, with both priest and prophet toadying to those who pay them well (vv. 30–31; compare Micah 3:5).

There is a surprising relevance about the whole passage. We too are learning that the very creation itself can suffer from the relentless exploitation of its resources and the reckless disposal of the wastes of over-consumption throughout its soil, seas and atmosphere. Further, the ever-widening gap between the 'haves' and the 'have-nots' in our global village can threaten wars and disorder of many kinds. Too many today, as in the time of Jeremiah, have a vested interest in turning a blind eye and a deaf ear to calls for conservation and justice. The great need of our time, as then, is 'respect' for ('fear' of) God, the Creator (vv. 22, 24).

A PRAYER

Thank you, Lord, for the order and beauty of your creation and all it provides for us. Help us to use its resources wisely and unselfishly, so that there may be enough for all, and a rich inheritance of its wealth for those who come after us. Amen

QUACK CURES *for* DEEP WOUNDS

The impending attack

This is a highly poetic and vividly dramatic passage in which the prophet, the invaders and God all speak. It predicts the coming judgment on Jerusalem at the hands of an invading army 'from the north' (v. 1) and explains why God will allow all this to happen.

In verses 1–3 the prophet warns his people of the coming disaster by calling on them to get out of Jerusalem while they can. Earlier they had been warned to flee into the walled towns (4:5–6). Now it is made clear that there will be no hiding place. The call to 'the sons of Benjamin' (*bene binjamin*) and to 'blow the trumpet in Tekoa' (*bitqoa' tiq'u shophar*) is governed by the poetic interests of assonance in Hebrew rather than concern to give an accurate itinerary of the enemy or to specify only one group of those living in Jerusalem. The few names mentioned are selected to show that nowhere will be safe. In verses 2–3, a cruel parody of what might otherwise be an idyllic pastoral scene warns that 'shepherds' (enemy kings and generals) are about to 'graze' Zion and her environs. Verses 4–5 depict the calls of the military leaders to precipitate attack, urging them to press home their assault by night if they cannot be ready in daylight. In verses 6–9 God speaks, encouraging the enemies and calling on them to fell trees to set up siege ramps. This is far from the assurances the people were used to, that Jerusalem is God's city where he dwells as protector (Psalm 46). The reason he turns from being protector to judge lies in the ever-continuing wickedness of the city's population. There is an irony in the description of the self-renewing nature of their sin as a spring of living water (v. 7), since they had rejected God, the true fountain of living waters (2:13). The final call from God is for a radical 'gleaning' (v. 9), indicating probably a total destruction rather than a sifting process to save a 'remnant'.

A people deaf to God's word

The prophet breaks out again in verses 10–11a, asking God how he can hope to warn anyone, since the people's ears are 'uncircumcised' (like their hearts, 4:4). Circumcision was the sign of the special covenant relationship between God and Israel (Genesis 17:9–14). But their ears have been tuned to different wavelengths, with the result that they are no longer capable of hearing God. Those who listen only to the clamour of the material and sensual world get to the stage when they can hear no other voice. The call of the spirit to love, the cries of the needy for help, the clamour of the oppressed for justice, all fall on deaf ears, whereas Jeremiah hears and must proclaim God's warning (v. 11a).

Verses 11b–12 paint a chilling picture of the nature of a military invasion before which all, including the very old and the very young, are victims, men 'disappear', women are raped and family homes are looted and burned. These days, such scenes are even more familiar than they were in Jeremiah's time because they flash across television screens in our own living-rooms. Perhaps today we need 'circumcised eyes' as well as ears.

Superficial 'cures'

Jeremiah complains that prophets, priests and everyone else were so bent on 'getting rich quick' that they had bothered to staunch a fatal wound only with a sticking plaster (vv. 13–14). They cry 'peace', one translation of the Hebrew word *shalom*. It can also mean 'salvation' or 'all is well'. McKane (p. 147) represents them as crying '"Health, health", where there is no health'. They were, of course, merely repeating the assurances given in the temple worship, but failing to remember the moral and spiritual conditions attached to those assurances. There comes a point where there is danger in merely repeating, parrot-like, the dogma handed on to us in the words of our 'fathers'. Even if that dogma expressed theological truth, if it is not thought through and worked out afresh by every generation in terms of its own situation, its call for discipleship interpreted in new social and political contexts, and relevant language found for its expression, it no longer has the reality to meet people in their deepest need. The truths of one generation can all too easily become the ineffective platitudes of the next.

A PRAYER

*O God, give me ears which are always sensitive to your
still, small voice. Amen*

OLD & NEW *in* RELIGION

Time to choose

This passage contains the last of the warnings of invasion by the 'enemy from the north' (vv. 22–26), a prominent theme in these early chapters (1:13–16; 4:5–8; 6:1–8). Small wonder that the prophet depicts the people as standing at a crossroads in their fortunes (v. 16). Again and again God has appealed to them, sending prophets who, like sentinels, warned them of impending disaster (v. 17). But their habitual, repeated refusal to listen is clearly driven home by the repetition of the phrases at the end of both verses 16 and 17: 'We will not walk'; 'We will not give heed'.

Jeremiah sees their choice as between continued drift on their present path of injustice (described in 6:13–15), an injustice they seek to cloak in a shallow veneer of ornate ritual observance (v. 20), or a return to the 'old ways'. What does he mean by such a general phrase? The context shows that he means a return to the commands of God's word, expressed through *Torah* (that is, God's law) and through the words of the prophets (v. 19). It was these words that spelled out the way in which they would find their true 'good' and real 'rest for their souls' (v. 16).

The 'old' and the 'new'

Calls to 'return to the old ways' often either come from the lips of old people, or are heard in times of insecurity and uncertainty. They reflect the kind of tension that individuals and communities often feel between loyalty to the 'old' and eager openness to the 'new'. Both law and prophets pointed back to the revelation God had made of himself in the past, through his saving acts and through the law given through Moses. These they saw as valid revelations of God, with abiding truth and relevance. Yet both were capable of development and adaptation as time went on. The law came to include regulations governing agriculture, regulations affecting life in settled towns, concerning monarchy and so on, none of which would have been relevant in Moses' day. Yet these new laws sought to work out in new circumstances the principles embodied in his law. Our passage here shows how words once spoken by a particular prophet in a particular situation could be seen to have new application and relevance to another time and a new situation. So, verses 22–23 are quoted again in 50:41–43, this time addressed against Babylon. The cry 'terror on every side' (v. 25) is found again in 20:3, applied to Pashhur, and yet again in 46:5 (of Egypt) and 49:29 (of Kedar). The 'old', once-for-all word of God is like a fountain of living waters, continually springing up with new life and force, and every generation has to hear it for itself and work out how it affects them in their own peculiar situation. This is the dynamic, creative tension between 'old' and 'new' in revelation.

Are human choices final?

The concluding section depicts the prophet in a new image, that of 'refiner' (vv. 27–30). As he proclaims God's word, he aims to sift out the silver from the dross. Yet the process proves futile. So great is the people's resistance that the furnace overheats the bellows and destroys the process by which something of value might be salvaged. God rejects his community.

So, was their choice at the 'crossroads' final? We know that Jeremiah's warnings were fulfilled. Jerusalem fell and was destroyed, large sections of the community were exiled, the state of Judah under the Davidic monarchy came to an end. Yet the book also shows that that was not the end, for God went with his people into exile. There he still pleaded with them. The present form of the book of Jeremiah shows how 'Deuteronomic' circles continued to preach and apply his message (see Introduction). And there, on the other side of judgment, God did bring some of his people back to form a new community with whom and through whom he could continue his purposes of grace. Our choices are of eternal significance. But the last word—such is the witness of this book—is with the redeeming grace of God.

A PRAYER

Lord, give me the strength to be faithful to your truth, once delivered to the saints; yet make me sensitive, so that your Spirit may guide me in showing how that truth may throw light on the paths I must walk today. Amen

JEREMIAH'S SERMON *in the* TEMPLE

False perceptions

A major theme of this sermon, delivered by the prophet in the temple, concerns false perceptions. The people entering the temple find a reassuring security ('trust', v. 4) in the mere presence of the place. Since it is God's home, he must dwell in it and defend it against all comers (Psalms 46:5–7, 11; 48:3, 12–14). They 'trust' in deceptive words (v. 8), that is, in the mere dogmatic formulae of their faith, unmatched by right living. They worship gods they do not know (v. 9). It is strange to put their trust in unknown deities rather than in the God who has proved his faithful love again and again in their history. They are convinced they are 'safe' (v. 10). In their perception the house of God has become a safe haven for those whose injustice to the poor and defenceless has turned them into 'robbers' (v. 11). Jesus quoted these words of Jeremiah when he cleansed the temple (Mark 11:17), adding further words from Isaiah 56:7 which insisted that God had intended his house to be a place for the worship and enlightenment of peoples of all nations, including the immigrants whom Jeremiah's hearers persecuted (v. 6).

God's 'true' perceptions

By contrast to the people's distorted insights, God 'sees' (v. 11) and he sees piercingly and truly. He sees their neglect of the basic requirements of the law for defending the rights of the weak and underprivileged, the kind of ethical behaviour called for in the Ten Commandments (vv. 5–6, 9). He knows that his 'presence' in the temple and the land is not automatically or ritually controlled and guaranteed. Only if they amend their ways, 'then I will dwell with you in this place' (v. 7). One way of reading the Hebrew consonantal text of verse 3 (there were no vowels in the original) makes the same point. It can be read either as 'I will cause you to dwell in this place' or 'and I will dwell with you in this place'. Whichever way verse 3 is read, God sees his presence with them in temple and land as conditioned by behaviour, not by rite and ritual.

The dangers of religious institutions

This sermon is not actually 'anti-temple' or 'anti-worship'. But it contains a stern warning of the dangers inherent in all the outward forms and institutions of religion. They may indeed be a valid means of expression of true worship and effective channels of God's presence and his grace. But equally, they may become empty husks in which any living kernel of meaning has shrivelled and dried. They can all too easily become substitutes, not channels, for the life of the Spirit—ends in themselves rather than means to an end. Even the sanctuary at Shiloh in which Eli and Samuel had ministered was destined to be destroyed in God's judgment (v. 12; see Psalm 78:60) and the same fate can as easily befall the temple in Jerusalem (vv. 14–15).

The prophet's word continues speaking

Many commentators have pointed out that this 'sermon', expressed in prose, shows much of the vocabulary and literary style of the book of Deuteronomy and the 'Deuteronomistic History' (see Introduction). We need not doubt that Jeremiah preached such a message (another version of it occurs in chapter 26). But in this, and other such prose passages in the book, the Deuteronomistic editors of the book, living later in exile in Babylon, found continuing truth for their own day and proclaimed it afresh in their own words. Jeremiah's message explained why God had allowed his temple to be destroyed. They realized that the exiles now in Babylon needed to heed the prophet's call to obedience to *Torah* just as much as those who heard it when it was first preached. And the same words have continued to be searchingly relevant for the people of God of all times and in all places.

A PRAYER

Lord we thank you for set places, times and forms by which we can worship you, and we thank you for all the structures that enable us to live and work together as your family. But keep us always vigilant and open to change so that they may remain living channels for your Spirit. Amen

17 JEREMIAH 7:16–28

A PEOPLE DEAF *to* GOD'S WORD

An ironic contrast connects the various sections of this passage. Although God has spoken to his people by his act in saving them from Egypt (vv. 22, 25) and through a long line of prophets (v. 25), they have never listened from the earliest days (vv. 22–26) and do not listen now (vv. 27–28). What they did claim to have heard, and acted on, was a distortion of his word (v. 22). So now God will not hear them (v. 16).

God tells the prophet to stop praying

The call not to pray for the people (v. 16) shows us that intercession was regarded as part of the double role of the prophet. A prophet represented God to the people and the people to God (Amos 7:1–7; 1 Samuel 7:5; 12:19; Jeremiah 14:7–9, 19–22). The Hebrew verb 'to pray' (v. 16) carries an overtone of 'interposing' one's words, or even oneself, between God and those for whom one is praying, an idea intensified in the later phrase in the same verse which might be rendered, 'Do not confront me'. This suggests an active, even energetic view of intercessory prayer. It is something to be borne in mind when the people of God today claim to have inherited a 'prophetic' ministry. How, then, do we explain God's call to Jeremiah to stop praying? Some say it is a graphic way of saying that in this instance judgment has been determined upon. Others have suggested that later, in the exile, it was necessary to explain why, while the prophets' words had been fulfilled, their intercessory ministry had proved ineffective. Whatever the reason, this specific instance should not be seen as a general truth that, when results do not appear to be immediate, the people of God should stop praying. In fact, as the rest of the book makes clear, Jeremiah never did give up his role of being spokesman of the people before God. He was so one with them and one with God that he continued agonizing before God throughout his ministry (for example, 8:18—9:1).

Whom does betrayal really hurt?

Two kinds of zealous and punctilious worship are described. The first (vv. 17–19) concerns the worship of the 'queen of heaven' (perhaps the goddess Ashtarte) in which whole families enthusiastically take part. The practice is more fully described in 44:15–23, where perhaps we get a hint of the reason for it. In chapter 44, those who have fled to Egypt after the fall of Jerusalem attribute the disaster to their neglect of the worship of the 'queen of heaven'. They must have felt, unlike the prophet, that their suffering was due not to their own sins but to the failure of Yahweh. But in turning to the worship of the deities of neighbouring powers they were indeed playing with fire, for it was at the hands of these very nations that they suffered. Perhaps that explains verse 19, where God says, 'Is it I whom they provoke? Is it not themselves, to their own hurt?' Sometimes what we see as 'the judgment of God' may in fact be the consequences of our own foolishness. Perhaps, most often, we judge ourselves.

God does not want sacrifice

Others, no doubt the majority, were busily engaged in all the minutiae of the sacrificial system of the temple (v. 22). Verse 23 joins the chorus of prophetic voices questioning the value of all this (Amos 5:25; Hosea 6:6; Isaiah 1:11; Micah 6:6–8), with a flat statement that God did not command them (v. 22). Then what of all the ritual law to be found in Exodus, Leviticus and Numbers, which ascribes the whole elaborate system to God's instructions to Moses? It is true that most Old Testament scholars think that many of the detailed instructions about sacrifice come from the later temple period. Even so, it is hard to think that there was ever a time when the Israelites offered no sacrifice of any kind. Perhaps verse 22 means something like, 'Do you think I brought you out of Egypt only, or mainly, so that you could offer me sacrifices?' To which the answer is, 'No! The most important part is to "obey my voice and walk in my way"' (see v. 23). Such a word would have had special relevance later for those in exile when they could offer no sacrifices.

FOR MEDITATION

We know that our sin grieves God (Jeremiah 2:5–8) but do we not inflict its consequences on ourselves and others too?

'Lo, all things fly thee, for thou fliest Me!'

'The Hound of Heaven', Francis Thompson (1859–1907)

A CALL *to* MOURN

The prophet utters a call to 'daughter Jerusalem' to mourn (v. 29). The 'you' is feminine in Hebrew, and the thought is of the city, collectively personified as a woman (4:31; 6:23). Cutting off the hair was one accompaniment of mourning rites (Job 1:20). So the call is not now to express sorrow and repentance for sins (they have resisted invitations to do that) but to mourn the 'death' of those rejected by God whose sentence has already been passed.

Unspeakable abominations

The charges against the people in the verses that follow include idolatrous worship in the temple itself (v. 30). Its nature is not specified but presumably it involved bringing cult objects of other gods into the sanctuary and worshipping them. These were the very things King Josiah ordered to be removed from the temple and burned (2 Kings 23:4) but which were probably reintroduced in the crisis in the reign of Jehoiakim (see Introduction, p. 12). No doubt the untimely death of Josiah was taken as evidence that his (to many) unwelcome reforms had not been in accordance with God's will.

Further, the Israelites have been offering children as human sacrifices at a 'high place', named here Topheth in the valley of Hinnom (v. 31). The consonants of Topheth probably mean 'fire' or 'oven', but the editors have inserted the vowels of the Hebrew word *bosheth* ('shame'). Hinnom was a valley to the south-west of Jerusalem where, in times of crisis, child sacrifice was practised (see 2 Kings 21:6). Such a cult was widespread in the ancient Near East and was dedicated to gods like Baal and Molech, probably a god of Phoenician origin but, again, given the vowels of the word 'shame'.

God's judgment

Acts of judgment against such 'abominations' are described in horrific detail. The general picture of the return of the fertile land to a 'waste' (v. 34) is sharpened with the announcement that there will be no weddings. These are not only occasions of personal, family and clan happiness but give hope for the renewal and continuance of life. There will be neither joy nor life. Indeed, so many will be slaughtered that there will be no room for more burials in the valley of Hinnom (the site of many graves), which will be gruesomely renamed (v. 32). Further, the tombs of kings and national leaders will be rifled and desecrated (vv. 1–3), a threat of total extinction in an age where, with no belief in an afterlife, it was important to be commemorated by an honourable memorial. The worst Amos could say of the Moabites was that they had burned the bones of the king of Moab (Amos 2:1). The only crumb of comfort Ahijah offers to Jeroboam is that one of his sons will be decently buried (1 Kings 14:13).

What kind of God spoke to Jeremiah?

Such bloodcurdling threats inevitably raise questions about the nature of the God who seems to show such petulance, even vindictiveness. The prose passages that follow the poetic call to mourning (v. 29) probably come from the Deuteronomistic editors and preachers in the time of Babylonian exile. That is suggested by the vocabulary and style in general and by the almost exact parallel between 7:33 and Deuteronomy 28:26 in particular. These men have lived through the kind of horrors they describe here and believe passionately that they have seen the fulfilment of Jeremiah's warnings that to turn from God would be to court disaster. They attached the blame to those who, dismayed by the crisis, had felt that Yahweh had failed them and so turned to the worship of foreign deities and persevered in that indifference to justice which had so fatally divided and weakened the community. We can understand, perhaps even admire, their zeal and sincerity, while believing that their view of God does not convey the whole truth. Jeremiah himself, while warning of judgment, never gave up his intense yearning for and identification with his people, so portraying a God who also continues to identify himself with his people in their distress, and even in their sin. That was why his message expressed hope as well as threats. The possibility of redemption, however, in no way denies the darkness of turning away from God, the true source of 'joy' and 'life' (v. 34).

MEDITATION AND THANKSGIVING

He came to this poor world below
And wept, and toiled, and mourned, and died,
Only because He loved us so.

W.W. How (1823–97)

The FOLLY of this WORLD'S WISDOM

Israel's unnatural stubborness

Verses 4–7 contrast Israel's persistence in apostasy with all the norms of reasonable behaviour. If we trip over, we get up. If we find we've taken a wrong turning, we go back to the crossroads where we missed our way (v. 4). Migrating birds know the season to fly. Such is the 'order' (*mishpat*) of the Lord (v. 7). *Mishpat* indicates a way of life based on God's way or rule, and the appeal to the 'orderliness' of nature is not infrequent in the Old Testament (Isaiah 1:3; Jeremiah 5:22–23). By contrast, the persistence of Israel's stubborness is underlined by the repeated use of the Hebrew verb *sub*, which means 'to turn' or 'return'. 'If they go astray, do they not turn back? Why then has this people turned away in perpetual backsliding... (and) refused to return? ... All of them turn to their own course' (vv. 4–6). That is why, even when God has listened intently, he has heard no straight word from them (v. 6). It is this long period of rejection of God that has led to their sentence being passed.

The foolishness of the 'wise'

Verses 10–12 substantially repeat 6:12–15 (see comments on p. 45), showing that the same word from God could be seen, either by the prophet or his editors, as relevant in more than one situation, a theological truth which has led to the production of the prophetic books over long periods of time. Now, to the earlier attacks on prophets and priests is added a diatribe against the 'wise', who are further described as 'scribes' (v. 8). Just who these people were and what exactly is being attacked here is not spelled out. It seems as though, in addition to priests whose job was to teach *Torah* (18:18), as the law was more and more enshrined in writing, a professional group appeared whose task it was to commit it to writing, add fresh legal adjudications in new cases and expound it (rather like someone attempting to write a commentary on the Bible today!). Jeremiah speaks of their pens as 'false' and the results of their scholarly labours as distorting the true meaning of the law (v. 8). Perhaps what is being attacked is that kind of punctilious concern with detail that gives fussy attention to the correctness of tiny details of procedure while ignoring the fundamental moral dimension of *Torah*. This would be in line with just the kind of attacks on frenetic ritual activity found elsewhere in Jeremiah (6:20; 7:21–23). There is a kind of erudition that can all too easily get buried in details, a point Jesus made in his graphic simile of those who, while trying to strain out gnats, managed to swallow camels (Matthew 23:24). It is all too easy to focus on the details of religious life (for example, the use of incense, the ordination of women, forms of church government), or of doctrine (for example, predestination or free will), and miss what it is really all about.

On the other hand, it is just possible that Jeremiah thought the 'written' law second best anyway! Certainly he envisages a time when there will be no need for it (31:33). He knows that external obedience to a written code is not enough. It is the heart that needs changing (4:4; 17:9–10).

No harvest

With such leaders and with such persistence in evil, no wonder God says that when he comes to harvest his 'vineyard' and gather fruit from his 'fig tree' (Israel) he finds nothing (v. 13). Isaiah's 'song of the vineyard' makes the same tragic point (Isaiah 5:1–7) and there is a further poignant comment on this in Jeremiah 8:20.

FOR MEDITATION

If God were to come for his harvest in my life today,
what would he find?

The PROPHET SHARES the GRIEF

No peace or healing

Verses 14–16 constitute a lament by the people bewailing their condition. To this, a response by God has been added (v. 17) which brings no consolation. The opening ironically takes up the prophet's earlier call to flee from the invading army to the safety of the fortified towns (4:5–6). Now, nowhere is safe. The statement that God has given his people 'poisoned waters to drink' may be merely metaphorical, like the 'cup of judgment' mentioned in 25:15. But there may be a more specific allusion. In Numbers 5:16–28 the ancient, and appalling, custom of submitting a wife accused of adultery to a trial by ordeal is described. She was given a cup of poison from which to drink which, if she were guilty, it was believed, would cause disease and barrenness. If that is the allusion here, it would have a special force since Israel has been described as God's 'unfaithful wife' (3:1–5).

In vain (v. 15) the people have looked for the 'peace' promised by their prophets (v. 11) and for the 'healing' that tradition assured them was God's promise to his people (Exodus 15:26). On the contrary, earlier threats of the 'enemy from the north' ('from Dan', v. 16) are renewed.

Verse 17 is the divine response to the people's lament, rejecting any implied call for help based on a frank confession of their sin (v. 14). Again, the picture of 'snakes' being let loose among the people may be merely a metaphorical description of the invading army, or it may be more specific. Numbers 21:4–9 preserves a tradition from the time of Israel's wandering in the wilderness. It tells how, in judgment for their lack of faith, God let loose poisonous serpents among them. On that occasion, healing was provided by Moses' bronze serpent. On this occasion, God makes no such provision.

The prophet's agony

Verses 18–19 express the agonized words of the prophet in response to this terrible message of judgment he has to bring. He hears the people's cry of distress, 'Is the Lord not in Zion? Is her King not in her?' (v. 19). They recall all the promises of the psalms that God dwells in the city, ready to defend her against all those who would attack her (as in Psalms 46; 48; 132:13–18). The assurances of their temple worship have failed them. 'The harvest is past… and we are not saved' (v. 20). Any agricultural community is in severe trouble if the harvest fails and there are no supplies in the barns for the winter. Some scholars believe that there is here also a more specific allusion to a supposed autumnal festival in the temple (autumn being the time when, with the return of the rains, the new agricultural year began), a festival celebrating God's original victory over the forces of primeval chaos in the acts of creation and the exodus from Egypt. Psalms like 74:12–17; 89:9–14; 93; 104:1–9, together with those celebrating the kingship of God (for example, Psalm 95), are seen as its liturgy. Its proper observance guaranteed fertility of the soil and peace and order in the community for another year. If that occasion had passed with still no signs of fertility or deliverance ('peace'), then they were in trouble indeed.

There is an unattractive religious characteristic in which some who feel themselves on the inside of the circle, the 'elect', take a certain grim satisfaction in contemplating the fate of the poor sinners outside the circle. Jeremiah did not share such feelings. He yearned over his wayward people with an agonized love that led him to identify himself with them in all their sin and the suffering of its consequences. It is true that he often harshly condemns their sins. But the same prophet who can do that also knows a suffering love that those sins can wound (9:1) but not annul. Perhaps here he is in himself foreshadowing the fuller revelation of the Incarnation. The God who condemns and judges sin still loves sinners with a suffering love which will not give up and which will itself ultimately prove to be the redeeming 'balm in Gilead' (v. 22).

FOR MEDITATION

See from his head, his hands, his feet,
Sorrow and love flow mingled down:
Did e'er such love and sorrow meet,
Or thorns compose so rich a crown?

Isaac Watts (1674–1748)

The BREAKDOWN *of* TRUST

The prophet longs to escape

Both 9:1 and 9:2 open with the same Hebrew words, 'Who will give (me)…?' This is an idiomatic way of expressing a longing, which most English versions rightly translate as 'O…'. Perhaps that is why verses 2–6 were added to verse 1 when the book was edited. The effect is startling. The prophet who has just been identifying himself with his people, weeping over their sins and the state to which they have come, now turns from them with revulsion and longs to escape from the whole turmoil of the social scene. He longs to get away to the desert and live a hermit's life in an overnight traveller's lodge. Perhaps the modern equivalent of the urge to get away from it all is the country cottage!

Such a violent transition of mood has led some commentators to believe that the speaker of verses 2–6 cannot be the same as the one who poured out his heart for his people in 8:18—9:1. But that is to show a misunderstanding of the conflicting emotions that can torment even the most dedicated servants of God and those most committed to serving their fellow human beings. There are times when it all seems too much to cope with. The psalmist expressed exactly this mood when he cried, 'O that I had wings like a dove! I would fly away and be at rest; truly, I would flee far away; I would lodge in the wilderness' (Psalm 55:6–7).

Elijah, after the violent yet triumphant drama with the prophets of Baal on Mount Carmel, fled to the wilderness and longed to die (1 Kings 19:4). It is a perfectly understandable human response to times of crisis and stress, and perhaps there are times when it is right to withdraw—for a while. God dealt gently with Elijah in his despair, but soon commissioned him for more active service (1 Kings 19:15–16). And, as we shall see, God always answered Jeremiah when he brought his complaints. But always the servant is sent back to the arena (as in Jeremiah 12:5). There is no retirement in the service of God and his world.

The consequences of forgetting God

Many of Jeremiah's oracles are concerned with the people's apostasy, their betrayal of God. This passage concentrates much more on the breakdown in human relationships. Within the community of family and society, their tongues are like stretched 'bows' (v. 3), ready to shoot their arrows of deceitful and wounding words (v. 8). Falsehood makes truth look weak (v. 3). Each man is a 'Jacob' to his brother (so the Hebrew of v. 4). The name 'Jacob' is related to the Hebrew verb 'to deceive' and its mention recalls Jacob's double-dealing towards his brother, Esau (Genesis 27). Smooth words cloak self-calculating intentions to wound (v. 8), a situation the poet Wordsworth depicted as 'Greetings where no kindness is'. One commentator has forcefully described it: 'Speech... is no longer a method of communication, but a smoke-screen behind which motives and objectives are concealed' (McKane, p. 201). A good deal of modern advertising and government and corporation 'spin-doctoring' illustrates that truth all too well.

Yet running through this dreadful diagnosis of the breakdown of social relationships is the persistent note that relations with God have broken down. The people are 'adulterers' (v. 2)—as elsewhere, probably a reference to their religious apostasy. God interjects, 'They do not know me' (v. 3), and again, 'They refuse to know me' (v. 6). In a convoy, each ship is given a bearing on the flagship. If individual ships veer off station in relation to that, they begin to run foul of each other. Just so, our passage says, it is when individuals lose sight of God and turn away from him that order in society begins to break down. Free from restraint, individuals career across the path of all who get in their way.

A corrupt society needs remaking

The only hope when there is so much counterfeit moral coinage in circulation is to call it all in and refine out the dross (vv. 7, 9). This is what God intends to do with the nation/state of Judah. For the whole 'Establishment' of that nation there is nothing left but lament over its utter downfall (vv. 10–11). The ground will have to be broken up for hope to be seeded and new life to grow again (see 1:10; 4:3–4).

A PRAYER

Lord, speak to me, that I may speak,
In living echoes of thy tone.

Frances Ridley Havergal (1836–79)

The GROUND *of* CONFIDENCE

The wisdom that can diagnose ills

In this section two prose passages (vv. 12–16, 23–24) are loosely connected by the theme of 'wisdom' (vv. 12, 23). They are separated by two poetic passages (vv. 17–19, 20–22) connected by the theme of mourning. An obscure final prose section (vv. 25–26) rounds off the whole and paves the way for what is to follow in chapter 10.

The first passage (vv. 12–16) asks who is wise enough to make sense of all the terrible things that have happened. Why has the land promised to their ancestors been devastated and their descendants exiled among aliens? The word God gave to his prophet offers the true explanation. Jeremiah has shown again and again that all that has happened is judgment from God upon a people who have ignored his law and turned to the worship of other gods. That is why God has given them 'wormwood', a poisonous drink made from bitter herbs, and poisoned water (8:14).

This is a fair summary of the prophet's message but it is expressed in strongly Deuteronomistic language (see Introduction). Almost every phrase can be paralleled in the book of Deuteronomy or in the historical books that the Deuteronomists have edited (see 2 Kings 17:7–17 on the reason for the fall of the northern kingdom, and 17:19–20 on the similar fate of Judah). Thus, in exile, the preachers are using the message of Jeremiah to explain to their hearers why all these sufferings have overtaken them. They are asserting the divine authority of the prophetic word and its continuing relevance. True insight ('wisdom') is gained by listening to God's word.

Mourning in a time of bereavement

The poetry of verses 17–19 and 20–22 speaks for itself. It is a call to mourn for the coming death of the nation. In Old Testament times there were professional mourners who were summoned to lead the obsequies (v. 17), although perhaps the suggestion is that death will be so widespread that others will need to be instructed in the arts (v. 20). There is a hint of a link with the two 'wisdom' prose passages in that the Hebrew depicts these mourners as 'wise' in the art (NRSV 'skilled women', v. 17). These passages offer no explanation for the terror. They speak only of the human misery involved in a time of national calamity.

Wisdom that discerns the cure for ills

The second 'wisdom' passage (vv. 23–24) shows that the true ground of any real, lasting human security lies not in the accomplishments of human sagacity, power or wealth, but in the spiritual and moral discernment of the true nature of God as a God of faithfulness, justice and moral and ethical 'rightness'. If a nation sets its mind to know God and puts him at the heart of all their life together, the treachery and oppression described in 9:2–6 will have no place. The 'cure' for their ills lies in looking at God in worship, in listening to his word and making that word the guiding principle of all their life. It is an enduring message. There is a place, of course, for human accomplishments. Human skill, strength and even wealth can be of enormous benefit to humankind if they are dedicated to the service of God and if those who possess them have the spiritual insight to know God and what he requires (see Micah 6:8). One wonders if Paul had this passage in mind when he wrote about human 'wisdom' to the church at Corinth (1 Corinthians 1:19–31).

Be different in life

Verses 25–26 present difficulties for interpretation but their main drift seems clear. Other nations besides Israel practised circumcision. The Babylonians, however, apparently did not, and so, in exile, many Israelites increasingly felt that this was a true sign of their own distinctiveness. But circumcision, just as an external rite, will not save those nations whom God intends to judge, any more than the equivalent practice of a certain kind of 'tonsure' (v. 26). And it will not save Judah any more than other peoples. What is needed is circumcision 'of the heart', that is, a real dedication and commitment to God in worship and service, a point Jeremiah had already made perfectly clear (4:4).

A PRAYER

Lord, we thank you for your many gifts to us, gifts of mind, of health and strength, of opportunity and material blessings. Give us the wisdom to use these gifts for you, and in the service of others for your sake. Amen

ONLY ONE TRUE GOD

This diatribe against the gods of the nations and their makers and worshippers is without parallel in the book of Jeremiah (although vv. 12–16 are repeated at 51:15–19). Jeremiah accuses the people often enough of infidelity and betrayal of Yahweh by their worship of the Baalim, but this logical analysis of the non-reality of other gods is unique. There are parallels elsewhere in the Old Testament, however, especially that part of the book of Isaiah (chs. 40—55) which seems to come from the time of the Babylonian exile, particularly 40:19–23 and 44:9–20. Two almost identical sections in the Psalms (115:3–8; 135:15–18) suggest that such passages may have been part of the worship of Israel. Such parallels to other biblical passages, the fact that the Septuagint version of Jeremiah here has a shorter text with a different verse order, and that an Aramaic comment has appeared in the Hebrew version (v. 11), have all suggested to most commentators that here we have a reflective and probably liturgical passage later than Jeremiah, which yet brought Jeremiah's warnings against apostasy with special relevance to the time of the exile.

The folly of apostasy

The differences between idols, with all their related superstition, and the true, living God are brought out in a series of stark contrasts. The astrology which was so marked a feature of Babylonian religion ('the way of the nations', v. 2) made religion a matter of fear when it was thought that one's fate was immutably fixed in the movements of the stars. By contrast, the God of Israel, whose love had made the Israelites his own people, was a never-ending source of joy and hope (v. 16). The gods had to be made by the expense and labour of humans (vv. 3–4, 9). Even the silver had to be transported from Tarshish (on the Spanish coast) and the gold from 'Uphaz', an unknown place of legendary wealth. By contrast, God is the one who redeems Israel by his own effort (v. 16). The idols have to be hammered into position so that they stand firmly and so cannot move (v. 4). God is the creator of the whole earth (v. 12). The idols cannot speak (v. 5) whereas God subdues the waters of chaos when 'he utters his voice' (v. 13a). The impotent idols cannot effect anything, for good or ill (v. 5), whereas God subdues the hostile nations (v. 10) and makes the created order fertile (v. 13). The 'instruction' of the idols is mere 'wood' (v. 8), whereas the 'wisdom' of Yahweh is above that of all others (v. 7). The idols do, perhaps, have one effect on their worshippers, who become 'stupid and without knowledge' (vv. 8, 14). As the NEB renders Psalm 115:8, 'Their makers grow to be like them and so do all who trust in them.'

A faith that sees beyond appearances

All this sounds very fine. But in the time of the Babylonian exile 'appearances' must have tested such faith to its core. Some were tempted to say of Yahweh, 'The Lord will not do good, nor will he do harm' (Zephaniah 1:12; see Jeremiah 10:5). The very pagan worshippers of these idols could ask their Jewish captives, 'Where is their God?' (Psalm 115:2). With Yahweh's temple destroyed, his king and people exiled and the city of Jerusalem, his dwelling place, in ruins, it must have seemed to some that the gods of the nations were indeed stronger.

All God's people know times when he seems far away or impotent, and then the temptation to turn to other sources of hope and help is strong. It is then that we need to be reminded what God has done for us in the past, how he has spoken in love and redeemed, both in our own personal experience and that of the whole fellowship of his people over the centuries. In the time of the Babylonian exile, God was still at work among his people at the very time he appeared to be most distant. His work for them and with them did not stop because Nebuchadrezzar's armies had captured Jerusalem in the name of their god, Bel. No one has heard much of Bel lately. But the God of Abraham is still at work.

A PRAYER

Lord, keep me trusting you, even when you seem far off
and false gods are near at hand. And may I continue to grow to be
more and more like the One I worship. Amen

A PROPHETIC LAMENT

Renewed warnings

Again the prophet is called to announce the coming judgment of God on his people. He does it by issuing another summons to the beleaguered inhabitants of the city (vv. 17–18) to gather their few possessions together and join the pitiable trek of the homeless and helpless victims of the Babylonians. Again the note of an assault from a 'foe from the north' is sounded (v. 22), but there is no doubt that this foe is merely the instrument of God, since it is God who decides on the fate of the nations (v. 18).

The anguish of prophet and people

The pitiable spectacle of columns of helpless and homeless refugees, victims of war (vv. 17–18), tragically familiar to us as well, evokes the response of an outpouring of grief (vv. 19–20), to some extent parallel to that found in 4:19–22. As there, it is not altogether clear whether the speaker is the nation, personified as the mother of its inhabitants, or the prophet. Perhaps the distinction is not a great one, for we have seen that Jeremiah feels so acutely the suffering of his people, even though he sees that suffering as due to their own sin, that he identifies with them and speaks for them. So great is the devastation that now no 'sons' will be left to rebuild what has been destroyed. Such an identification of the prophet with his people contrasts starkly with the self-seeking, superficial leadership shown by their official 'shepherds' (v. 21). This is a term widely used in the ancient Near East to describe their kings, but in the book of Jeremiah the term is broadened to include all their so-called leaders, including prophets, priests and wise men.

A change of heart is needed

The first-person speech continues in the prayer of verses 23–24, presenting the same question of just who is speaking. Again we must assume it is the prophet, acting in his capacity as representative of his people before God. What a contrast with the 'shepherds' of verse 21 who did not 'inquire of the Lord'. The prayer is a strange one. It opens with a general kind of statement that mere men and women cannot control their destiny, a statement of a kind that we find in the Wisdom literature (as in Proverbs 16:1; 21:30). In all of human life there is a good deal that is 'given' to us, which we cannot control. This includes our birth, the environment in which we grow up, our temperament, the gifts and talents we have, the 'fortune' of good or bad health, of fame or anonymity, of success or failure. Some of the cards of life are just 'dealt' to us.

But the prayer includes a request not for a change of fortune, but for a changed heart, with its 'Correct me, O Lord' (v. 24). It is a profound insight to see that what we need is not so much a change of 'luck' but a change of heart so that we offer all our 'given' circumstances to God and seek to find his way for us in and through them.

It seems a little strange to ask God to deal with us in 'justice' (as the Hebrew reads) when sin has been confessed. But the suggestion is that God might act in a way which justly reflects his own nature, and that nature is to show mercy and forgiveness to those who repent (see 3:22; 14:7–9). That is why the prophet calls on God's mercy for the penitent, rather than his anger, which brings the obdurate sinner 'to nothing' (v. 24).

A cry for judgment

Verse 25 almost exactly echoes Psalm 79:6–7. It is probably an editorial addition from the time of the exile, when its bitterness would be understandable. It calls on God to deal with the nation's oppressors in the way in which Jeremiah had just said he dealt with sinners who did not repent.

A PRAYER

Lord, we often call on you to change the events and circumstances that befall us. But, most of all, we ask you to change us, so that we may seek your will through every chance and see how we may serve you in every condition in which we find ourselves. Amen

A CALL *to* COVENANT LOYALTY

Jeremiah, God's spokesman

It is interesting that the opening of this passage describes God's word coming to Jeremiah, and yet what is said is in the plural. 'Hear' is plural in the Hebrew, as is the 'your' in the phrase 'your ancestors'. The whole message is in fact addressed to the community with whom, as we have seen, Jeremiah is so closely identified. Yet he is also close to God, as his response 'Amen, Lord' in verse 5 shows. It is this 'two-way' role that makes him ideally suited to be mediator of the divine word to his contemporaries. Those who are to be effective spokes-people for God in every age must be close to God and yet, at the same time, truly alongside their contemporaries. It is in the second of these qualities that most religious people fail. Much church activity and constant use of religious language may often cut us off from other people and reduce our opportunities of communicating effectively with them.

Preaching the covenant

'Covenant', the theme of this sermon, is very prominent in the book of Deuteronomy (see Deuteronomy 4:13; 5:2), where it describes the relationship between God and the people of Israel. Like all good sermons, Jeremiah's has three points! Verses 3–7 proclaim what God did for his people and the obligations this placed upon them; verses 8–10 describe Israel's persistent failure to meet those obligations; while verses 11–13 pronounce God's sentence of judgment. Scholars have pointed to the similarity between the biblical portrayal of covenant and many ancient treaties between nations. In those, where one is the stronger party, the treaty usually begins with a pre-amble of all the benefits the patron state has conferred on the other; it lays down stipulations which must be observed by both parties and ends with a series of sanctions enforcing those terms. This is exactly the way covenant is described in both Exodus and Deuter-onomy. First, God states what he has done for his people (Exodus 20:2; Deuteronomy 1—4). There follow all the obligations imposed upon the people (Exodus 20:3—23:33; Deuteronomy 12—26) and

God's promises to keep faith with his subjects (Exodus 6:6–9; Deuteronomy 26:16–19); and, finally, the sanctions of 'blessing' or 'cursing' with which these obligations were to be enforced on the people (Leviticus 26; Deuteronomy 27—28).

As with Jeremiah's 'temple sermon' (ch. 7), this is in prose and full of Deuteronomic vocabulary and phraseology. Verse 3 can be compared with Deuteronomy 27:26; verse 4 with Deuteronomy 4:20, verse 5 with Deuteronomy 11:9, and so on. Yet there are also close connections with the poetic oracles of Jeremiah: verses 11–13 can be compared with 2:27–28; the Hebrew of verse 12, which speaks of their 'offering incense' to their gods, echoes 1:16; and indeed the whole theme of their sin and folly in turning away from Yahweh to other gods is, as we have seen, one of Jeremiah's major preoccupations.

The explanation for all this is most likely that Deuteronomistic editors in the time of the Babylonian exile took the message of Jeremiah as a 'text' for their preaching to their own contemporaries who were perplexed by what had happened. The answer lay in the very word God had spoken through his prophet, Jeremiah. It is the people's unrepented sin and their failure to respond to God's care for them that have brought the 'curse' of the covenant upon them.

A source of hope

Yet if the exiles had ears to hear it, there was a ground of hope in this very word. The recital of God's goodness to their 'fathers' would remind them of a God who can and does deliver his people from the 'smelting-furnace' of oppression (vv. 4–5). When he did so, he told them that they would continue as his covenant people and he as their covenant God, mindful of all his obligations to them, if they would 'listen to my voice' (v. 7). If, even now in the bleak environs of Babylon, they were to take up their covenant responsibilities, God would still show himself powerful and faithful (Exodus 34:6–7). In times of failure and distress it is always good to recall past evidence of God's unfailing mercy.

FOR PRAISE

Fear not, He is with thee, O be not dismayed;
For He is thy God, and will still give thee aid:
He'll strengthen thee, help thee, and cause thee to stand,
Upheld by His righteous, omnipotent hand.

Attributed to Robert Keane in *Rippon's Selection of Hymns*, 1787

REJECTING GOD & HIS MESSENGER

How tragic a fall

Verses 14–17 contain a threat of judgment against Israel, typified by the command to Jeremiah not to pray for them (v. 14; compare 15:1). But against what a background this tragic state of affairs is set! Israel has been God's 'beloved' (v. 15) and his own special 'planting', destined to produce the fruit in their lives which would reveal God's own nature (vv. 16–17). Born and nurtured in the grace of God, Israel was destined to be a 'light to the world' (Genesis 12:3). Now, however, the evil she commits and tolerates makes her a barren, dead tree fit only for burning (as in Ezekiel 15:1–8).

Perhaps the most tragic thing about sin is its sheer waste—its denial of our true potential as sons and daughters of God, destined for his service in the world. For what is at risk is not only what we ourselves might have become but all the joy and help we might have given to others if we had really served them with the love God meant to show to them through us.

The prophet's lament

Verses 18–20 introduce us to the first of the so-called 'confessions' or, better, 'laments' of Jeremiah, to which, as to others, is added an answering word from God (vv. 21–23). 'Lament' better describes these passages because of their striking parallels to the 'laments' in the Psalter. Those, too, often describe the suffering of the psalmist which may include, as here, threats from enemies (Psalm 54:3), the false accusations of others (Psalm 27:12) or more general distress of mind or body (Psalm 6). Often in such psalms there comes a point where the sufferer becomes convinced that God has heard his prayer (Psalm 22:22).

It is widely believed that many of these psalms were used in the temple worship and that they would have been presented by a temple priest or prophet who would act as spokesperson for the worshippers before God and bring God's answering word to them. This, therefore, raises the question of how we are to understand such passages in Jeremiah. Are they the personal outpourings of his own grief, and do they thus afford a window into his own inner spiritual autobiography? Or is the prophet acting as spokesman for the community? The answer seems to be that they reflect both dimensions. There are some things intensely personal to the prophet and yet, as we have seen, the prophet identifies himself so closely with his people that their suffering becomes his, and his reflects and expresses theirs. If we really love other people, prayers for ourselves and prayers for them become inextricably woven together.

The prophet's rejection

This first lament, surely, expresses mainly Jeremiah's own sufferings. His call from God has cut him off from even his closest human relationships as he comes to realize that his hearers, to use a modern psychological term, 'transfer' their hatred of the message to the messenger. His was a personality that clearly felt this deeply (15:17). In the face of such hatred and acute personal danger, the prophet has nowhere to turn but to God, and that is exactly what he does in these remarkable passages. Indeed, there is a striking description of prayer in the Hebrew of the last line of verse 20 which reads, 'I have laid bare my case before you.' In these prayers Jeremiah really does 'strip bare' his own situation and that of his people. He almost streaks naked into God's presence with all his doubts and fears, even with his accusations against God himself. Such 'honesty' in prayer, for all the doubts and inner struggle it reveals, is really a remarkable confession of faith in the love, the understanding, the grace and the power of the God to whom we pray. The issue is whether we believe that God loves and accepts us as we are, or only as we, and others, think we should be.

Such prayer does bring a response from God (vv. 21–23), who assures the prophet that his enemies will prove no match for the God who is always with him as he promised (1:8).

A PRAYER

Lord, your grace is such that there is no part of me that I cannot lay bare before your loving and accepting gaze. Take me as I am now, but realize in me all that for which you have destined me. Amen

The PROPHET'S QUESTION & GOD'S ANSWER

Honesty before God

This is the second of Jeremiah's 'laments' (see pages 68–69 for comments on the first at 11:18–23). The opening words, 'You are in the right, O Yahweh', use law-court language to express conventional, orthodox piety: 'God is just and all his ways must be good.' The small Hebrew word that follows should, however, be given a much more strongly adversative sense than some modern English versions provide—'nevertheless' or 'but I am going to speak of justice with you', a daring expression which elsewhere in the book is reserved for the judgment God himself speaks against sinners (1:16; 4:12). The question troubling the prophet is the age-old problem for faith: 'If God is righteous, how is it that evil and its perpetrators so often triumph in his world?' (Psalm 73:1–14; Job 24; Habakkuk 1:13). The constant success and prosperity of those who exploit the poor and innocent behind a façade of religious piety and sanctimonious worship suggests not just that God is indifferent, but that he actively supports them (v. 2). Yet their evil affects God's creation (v. 4), a cause-and-effect connection between human sin and its consequences for the natural world made elsewhere in the book (4:23–28). It is a truth all too often confirmed in the ecological effects of human greed and evil in our modern world. The prophet's natural reaction is that God should assert his 'justice' by giving the wicked their just deserts (v. 3).

This expression of orthodox faith followed by its 'but' (v. 1) suggests the same kind of integrity in the prophet as informs all the prayers in which he brings his doubts and fears to God. Two extremes are possible to people of faith when their faith is sorely tested. One is to deny the doubts and questions and retreat into a strident orthodoxy which pulls down the shutters on the real world of contradictory experience outside. The other is to give way to cynicism and renounce faith. A third way is to have the courage to open up all our inner tensions to God in the faith that he will come with us and lead us through our particular 'valley of the shadow'.

God's unexpected answer

The trouble with letting God in on a situation is that he does not always act as we expect him to. His reply to Jeremiah is no offer of quiet escape or 'easy' answer that solves all the problems. In the prophet's discharge of the mission God has entrusted to him, he is going to face far sterner challenges ahead (v. 5), of which increased hostility from his own family is but one example (v. 6; see 11:21). God's answer to prayer is not always to remove the circumstances that daunt us, as Jesus, supremely, was to find (Matthew 26:39). The call he gives his people, in which alone our true destiny and fulfilment lie, will always evoke all we have to give. A student with examination nerves might well ask God to give him or her some excuse for missing the examinations! The degree these tests bring, however, may well open the way to a much fuller career and life of service, something which was the inspiration for the study all along.

So what God offers is not escape from the circumstances, or immediate light in every dark corner, but the strength to face all that lies ahead (something the 'wicked' fail to realize, v. 4) and to triumph over and through it. Only because Jesus drank the cup that God gave him was he able to offer it to others as a means of salvation and say, 'This is my blood of the covenant which is poured out for many' (Mark 14:24).

A PRAYER

Not for ever by still waters
Would we idly quiet stay;
But would smite the living fountains
From the rocks along our way.

Be our strength in hours of weakness,
In our wanderings be our guide;
Through endeavour, failure, danger,
Father, be thou at our side.

Love Maria Willis (1824–1908)

WHO ARE GOD'S ENEMIES?

God uses the nations to judge his people

The description of Israel in verse 7 sets the whole passage that follows in terms of the starkest tragedy. Israel is 'my temple', 'my heritage' and 'the beloved of my life'. Such was her status and her calling. The picture of the people as God's 'temple' suggests God's desire to live in her midst, making himself continuously known to her. (The same idea occurs in the New Testament: 1 Corinthians 3:16; Ephesians 2:21). The term 'my people' recalls the covenant (Exodus 6:7), while the Hebrew of the phrase 'the beloved of my life' suggests the strongest intensity of love—'with my whole being'. Yet this status has been tragically betrayed as they have rounded on God like wild beasts (v. 8, and possibly v. 9, which speaks either of Israel attacking God like a hyena or herself being attacked by the nations). Certainly she is going to be invaded by the kings ('shepherds') of powerful neigh-bours (v. 10). Such attacks are really the judgment of God himself, for the invaders wield 'the sword of the Lord' (v. 12). So the land is ravaged to the point where there is no harvest to reap (v. 13) and yet no one has the 'heart' to do anything about it (v. 11).

We may get used to such passages in the prophets, but it is diffi-cult to imagine the scandalous horror with which such threats would have been heard. In the convenient covenant theology of the 'holy war', their enemies were seen as God's enemies, and God's help in overcoming them in time of war could be assumed (Judges 5:31). By their treatment of God, however, his own people have made them-selves his enemies and their prayer for vengeance on his enemies rebounds on themselves.

On a lesser scale, it is easy to look outside ourselves for our 'enemies', but often our real need is for a change within ourselves so that we can develop the character to triumph over circumstances and the love to break down barriers with other people.

The true hope of restoration

Verses 14–17 take up the theme of Israel's relations with other nations, but from quite a different perspective. The passage differs from verses 7–13 in that it is in prose, its language and style are much more those of the Deuteronomistic editors, and it seems to presuppose the exile. Nevertheless it also takes up the prophet's theme of the nations as instruments of God's judgment, as well as his role as a prophet to the nations, one called to 'pluck up' as well as to plant (1:9–10; and see how often the verb 'pluck up' occurs here). These later verses see the threat from neighbouring nations to be not only that of military assault (v. 14) but also from the example of idolatry by which they led Israel into the worship of Baal (v. 16). Isaiah had predicted that although Assyria was God's chosen instrument of judgment against his people, yet she herself would in turn be judged for her arrogant pride (Isaiah 10:5–16). So here, the nations are to be 'plucked up' and Judah released from their bondage (v. 14). Yet God's plans for the restoration of his people extend even to their former enemies. If the malign religious influence they had formerly extended over Israel were to be reversed, and they learned from Israel to worship Yahweh, the true God, then these former enemies could learn to live together in peace and share a common prosperity with Israel (v. 16). Otherwise, they too will be judged (v. 17).

If this section, while being based as we have seen on Jeremiah's teaching, actually came from the time of the Babylonian exile, then it represents a remarkably positive point of view. Israel would indeed prove to be 'a light to lighten the Gentiles' (Isaiah 49:6). It casts a ray of light even down to our own time. The only true hope for reconciliation among warring nations lies in a reconciliation with God, a truth expressed even more potently in the New Testament (Ephesians 2:14).

PRAYER

Lord, I often pray for a change of circumstances, or for a change in other people. Today I dare to pray that you will so change me that I may find your strength to cope with the circumstances you have given me and your love to transform my relations even with those people I find most difficult. Amen

The SIGN *of the* LOINCLOTH

A symbolic act by the prophet

This is the first passage in the book in which the prophet is told to do something, rather than simply to speak the words he has heard from God. Such acts of 'prophetic symbolism' play a prominent part in Jeremiah's ministry (as they do in that of other prophets). Other instances are found at 16:1–4; 19; 25:15–29; 27—28; 32:1–15; 43:8–13; 51:59–64. To understand them, we must realize that they are intended as much more than mere 'visual aids'. They are rooted in the Old Testament theology of the prophetic word. For the word the prophets spoke was also seen as much more than merely announcing something, but as actually achieving something. One primitive example of this is seen in the story of Balaam (Numbers 22:1—24:25). Balak, the king of Moab, anxious to defend his territory against the Israelites, hired a local 'seer', Balaam, to utter a curse against them, 'for I know that whomever you bless is blessed, and whomever you curse is cursed' (Numbers 22:6). God, however, directs Balaam to bless Israel instead, and so they prosper. Such a view of the effectiveness of the spoken word may well have its roots in magic. In magic, however, human beings are trying to harness supernatural powers to their own ends. When the prophets spoke, it was believed, *God's* word spoke through them so that God could achieve his own righteous ends, which, far from serving human self-interest, might well bring judgment on those who heard it. Prophetic actions were regarded in the same way. They were visible words of God. It was this belief that could lead to attempts on the prophet's life (11:21) or his imprisonment (38:1–6), because his predictions that Jerusalem would fall consti-tuted a real danger, bringing about the very thing they dreaded most.

The fatal consequences of sin

This first 'visible word' of Jeremiah involves his buying a waistcloth and wearing it unwashed. According to verse 11, it is a symbol of the originally pure covenant relationship between God and Israel. The command to take it to the 'Euphrates' and bury it there seems strange, not only because it was some 400 miles away from Judah (the journey one way took Ezra four months, Ezra 7:7–9), but because it meant his Judean audience would have been small or non-existent. So some scholars have suggested that perhaps he drew a map of the river, as Ezekiel drew a relief map of Jerusalem (Ezekiel 4:1–4); or that he went to a village a few miles from Anathoth whose name, Perath, would have recalled the Hebrew name for the Euphrates. What is clear, however, is that the loincloth, abandoned and interred for a long time, was utterly ruined and useless. So, Israel's exile in Babylon or, perhaps, the religious consequences of her attempts at military alliances with that region (v. 10), would utterly ruin the 'pride' of Jerusalem. That is, all its buildings would be destroyed, its wealth taken away as spoil, and their covenant relationship with God ended in shame and disgrace (v. 11).

It is strange that such a totally negative picture of the exile is painted here, for there is a persistent note of hope running through the book that God would redeem Israel after judgment. However, such a future hope (for some) in no way lessened the enormity of their sin or the horrors they would have to endure in the years ahead.

God's redemption is a wonderful miracle of grace, but is it perhaps possible for us to jump too lightly over sin and its consequences in our sometimes rather glib and triumphalist celebrations of that grace? It is miraculous that, by God's grace, the worst of sinners can be reconciled to him. Yet the consequences of our sin, for ourselves and even more for others, are not easily and glibly erased. Perhaps it is good for us, as it was for Jeremiah's hearers, to ponder deeply the sin which, in our case, led to Good Friday, before we celebrate that release from 'exile' that we proclaim with such joy on Easter Sunday.

FOR MEDITATION

I know my transgressions,
and my sin is ever before me.
Against you, you alone, have I sinned,
and done what is evil in your sight…
Create in me a clean heart, O God,
and put a new and right spirit within me.

Psalm 51:3–4, 10

APPEARANCES PROVE DECEPTIVE

The wine of destruction—not of joy

Three short passages (vv. 12–14, 15–17, 18–19) are connected by the general theme of 'appearances that prove deceptive'. The first begins with a surprisingly banal statement to be credited with the status of a 'word of God': 'Wine jars should be full of wine.' The prophet's hearers respond with the equivalent of a sarcastic 'Of course', implying that they hardly need a prophet to tell them something as obvious. For people of all times, even a bottle of wine (let alone a jarful!) can be a promise of pleasure to come, perhaps at a shared meal—even something 'sacramental' of the fellowship which joins us together. But, as any teetotaller will remind us, wine is double-edged. It can also make people drunk and, when drunk, aggressive. It is in this sense that God is going to make the whole community, from king to commoner, drink a destructive draught of his judgment. They will become a mutually hostile community, riven, divided against each other as they blunder and stumble, out of control, to destruction. This image of God's judgment as a 'cup' to be drunk is fairly common in the Old Testament (see Jeremiah 25:15–27; Isaiah 51:17, 21; 63:6).

We can receive life from God that sparkles with joy, like wine. But when we turn from him, life can be experienced as menacing and destructive. We can, with the psalmist, 'lift the cup of salvation' as 'we make our vows to God' (Psalm 116:13) and find it overflowing with life and joy (Psalm 23:5), or experience it as a 'cup of judgment' (Psalm 75:8).

The light that fails

The same note of choice sounds in verses 15–17. The hearers who so sarcastically dismissed the prophet's previous word as beneath their attention (v. 12) are urged not to feel themselves above this one (v. 15). Either they find the true light of God in acknowledging his 'glory' (Isaiah 60:1) or they will find themselves like sheep (v. 17) doomed to stumble dangerously on steep mountain tracks when the apparent half-light of a new dawn turns out to be the twilight heralding the approach of night—appearances once more proving deceptive. The prophet sees what will happen if they reject this word and weeps secretly for the disaster into which the flock will blunder.

The power that falls

The king and queen mother have also been enjoying the trappings and appearances of pomp which are destined to prove false. Monarchy, where it exists, is always the keystone to the whole edifice of the political and social 'Establishment'. Their power and symbols of power thus represent the wealth and success of society as a whole, or, at least, of those who have a vested stake in it. Splendid royal palaces and the pomp and circumstance of royalty are all forms of state propaganda. The fall and debasement of monarchy, which Jeremiah here (vv. 18–19) predicts, is therefore an ironic symbol of the collapse of the whole state. The enemy, already successful in the Negeb to the south, will sweep victoriously over the whole territory. This saying is often taken to refer to King Jehoiachin who reigned for only three months and was, with Nehushta the queen mother, then taken captive to Babylon (29:2; 2 Kings 24:8, 12, 15). As usual in the book, however, specific historical details are lacking, and the saying serves as a general warning to the community of all times.

A PRAYER

Lord, give me the reality and not only the appearance of faith.
Make me truly your own so that my character may reflect
the genuineness and beauty of your Spirit in whatever
circumstances I happen to be. Amen

ONLY GOD CAN CHANGE PEOPLE

The enormity of sin

There can be no denying the harsh severity of this passage in its description both of the community's sin and the judgment that is to come because of it. In addition, there is the almost offensive crudity of its sexual imagery. In general, it is yet another allusion to the threat from the 'foe from the north', the ruthless invader who comes at God's bidding to despoil Judah (v. 20). While the whole community is indicted, it seems to be the leaders, as representatives of the 'flock' and responsible for its well-being, who are particularly addressed. It was a 'beautiful' flock entrusted to them by God, and the contrast between that 'beauty' and the lewd lustfulness of both the sin and its judgment that follows could not be starker. The word 'beauty' can be applied in the Old Testament to the splendour of a high priest's apparel (Exodus 28:2); to the honour of the royal house of David (Zechariah 12:7); and to the temple made beautiful by God's presence (Psalm 96:6). Of course, it is also a quality of God himself (1 Chronicles 29:11, where, as often, NRSV renders it 'glory'). So the 'flock' was destined to represent the 'beauty' of God himself as he dwelt among them and sanctified them for his work in the world. But Israel has exchanged such 'beauty' for the lust and commerce of a prostitute (v. 27) and will suffer the public disgrace of a woman found guilty of adultery (vv. 22, 26). The flock will no longer graze in the fertile land of promise but will be driven, like chaff before the wind, into exile (v. 24).

If we find such language and imagery offensive, can we nevertheless begin to catch in the intensity of the prophetic word something of the sheer horror and enormity of sin, with its tragic frustration of God's loving purposes of the best for his people? Many times we have heard the indignant throb of Jeremiah's heart as he sees the people putting themselves into alliances with other nations and taking on the worship of their gods. The very term 'sin' tends to embarrass us. We are ready with our 'psychological' explanations for it, or we employ euphemisms, preferring to speak of 'lapses', or 'slips', or 'errors of judgment'. Perhaps occasionally we need to be shocked by such a passage as this into realizing again the sheer enormity of sin and its awful consequence in breaking our relationship with the God who has called us to share and reflect his 'beauty'.

Judah's suffering self-inflicted

Verse 21 is very difficult to translate, and to interpret when we have translated it. That is why the English versions differ considerably in their renderings. But NRSV seems near its sense with the idea that it is the very nations whose military support Israel sought in defensive alliances who will now turn on Israel and make her their subject. For the very attempt to shield under the might of the nations and to find help from their gods has been a denial of Yahweh's power and care. As in the case of 'the young lady of Riga, who rode with a smile on a tiger', the smile, ultimately, turns out to be on the face of the tiger. It is often the case that alluring secular sources, which promise us that their only business is our joy, prosperity and freedom, turn out to be acting far more from motives of self-interest than from real concern for us. We often make a bad bargain when, like the Judeans, we 'forget' God and place in others that trust which is safely vested only in him (v. 25).

How can sinners become clean?

Verse 23, with its two striking pictures of circumstances that cannot be changed, answers the question with which the passage ends in verse 27, 'How long will it be before you are made clean?' The prophet's answer is, 'Never, if you rely on your own efforts.' Jeremiah knew that only the grace and love of God could make the human heart clean in a new covenant relationship (31:33–35). It is a lesson proclaimed anew every time Christians celebrate the Eucharist: 'This is my blood of the covenant, which is poured out for many for the forgiveness of sins' (Matthew 26:28).

A PRAYER

Lord, give us the faith truly to believe that only in you are all our best hopes for ourselves truly founded. Amen

A CRY *to* GOD *in* DISTRESS

Events beyond human control

This section provides a classical example of what is often called a 'prophetic liturgy', recalling as it does many of the psalms of lament and other such passages in the prophetic books. The form often includes a lament over the present suffering of the people (vv. 2–6); a cry from the people to God for help, often acknowledging sin (vv. 7–9); and an answering oracle from God, either expressed, as here (v. 10; or Psalm 12:5), or implied (as in Psalm 22, between vv. 21 and 22). The psalms of lament are often very general in their language, speaking figuratively of drought, famine, threat from enemies, illness, malicious gossip and so on, so that their words could be used by many worshippers in varying times of their own need. Clearly the situation here depicted in verses 1–6 is that of drought, but its suffering is also portrayed in vivid poetic imagery which tends to make the prayer more general in scope. The picture of the nobles sending their servants to fetch water (v. 3) brings home the general suffering described in verse 2. These are the men of affairs and substance who are used to getting their own way and ordering things to their own convenience, and they employ staff to see that this is achieved quickly and effectively. But even the most powerful are helpless. The 'hind' (NRSV 'doe') was proverbially noted for her affection for her own (Proverbs 5:18–19), yet even she is powerless to care for her fawn (v. 5). Farmers, used to coping with all weathers and subduing the most barren of soil, are totally defeated, and the wild ass who 'can live where the crows would starve', to quote the old Welsh saying, are helpless.

We are all, rightly, brought up to accept responsibility for ourselves, our dependants, our community, our environment and our circumstances. All our training and education is devoted to this end. But it is always worth reminding ourselves that in the face of some of the greatest realities of our lives we are often powerless. We all need help 'beyond ourselves'.

Is God a 'visitor' or a 'resident'?

The intercession of verses 7–9 acknowledges past sins but contains a number of ironies. People acknowledge that God has proved a deliverer in times past, but go on to ask him if now he is going to be only a stranger, someone passing through who just calls in for the night (v. 8), or someone who really is 'in the midst of us' (v. 9). But only they themselves can determine the answer to that. If they address God only at rare moments of crisis, how can he be other than a stranger? Is God to act as 'a mighty warrior' or be one who can 'give no help'? (v. 9). Everything depends on how they trust him. The answer to their prayer is that they will know God as one who truly dwells with them and acts for them if they will acknowledge that 'they are called by his name' and act accordingly.

This poses a searching question for all of us. Do we admit God into our political, social, civic and individual lives only as an occasional visitor, or invite him in as a permanent resident?

God's rejection of their prayer

The normal 'oracular response' to such 'prophetic liturgies' was, as we have seen, an assurance of deliverance from God. The shocking climax to this one is that God repudiates their prayer and denies Jeremiah the role of intercessor and mediator (vv. 10–12; see 7:16). It is this awful climax to the whole section that probably explains its introduction in verse 1 as a word of God to Jeremiah when, in fact, what follows is largely a communal lament of the people. All relationships have to be kept alive and active. It is desperately important that ours with God is such that, when we call on him in moments of crisis, we are coming to a known friend and not summoning a distant stranger. For us, God is the one who, in the Incarnation, has come among us as resident and who is always seeking admission as constant guest (Revelation 3:20).

FOR MEDITATION

I know thee, Saviour, who thou art,
Jesus, the feeble sinner's friend;
Nor wilt thou with the night depart,
But stay and love me to the end;
Thy mercies never shall remove;
Thy nature and thy name is Love.

Charles Wesley (1707–88)

WHEN PROPHECY FAILED

True and false prophecy

Jeremiah's deep sense of isolation from family (11:18–23) and society (15:17) extends to the circle of prophets. It was the unpopularity of the word he believed God had given him that proved divisive, for there were plenty of prophets going round preaching the exact opposite (2:8; 4:9–10; 5:12–13; 6:13). It is this of which he complains to God now (v. 13).

Having different prophets preaching different things was clearly a source of confusion, for several Old Testament texts grapple with the issue (Deuteronomy 18:18–20; Micah 3:5–6, 11; many places in Jeremiah and Ezekiel 13 are among key texts). We should not assume that we ourselves would have been able instantly to detect the difference. The false prophets did not walk round in false beards and with obviously evil intent. Indeed, could not those who proclaimed in God's name, 'I will give you true peace (*shalom*) in this place' claim the authority of God's own promises? He had promised David a throne which would be 'established for ever' (2 Samuel 7:16). Had he not also promised to make Jerusalem his 'dwelling place for ever' (Psalm 132:13–18)? Did they not proclaim in their worship that 'the Lord of hosts is with us' (Psalm 46:7, 11) and had they not been instructed to tell the next generation 'that this is our God for ever and ever' (Psalm 48:13–14)? For a prophet to announce that God had rejected his people and would allow king, temple and city to be destroyed by pagans must have seemed well-nigh blasphemous. Of course, events were to prove such prophets as Jeremiah right, which is why their words were preserved, preached and written down. Further, history was to show that God did prove to be 'their God for ever', although this meant that he led them in ways they could not have divined. The explanation that Jeremiah, and those who preserved his words, gave for the disaster—that all along the promises had been conditional—offered to those in exile some theological rationale for the apparent breach of such promises. But to see all that cannot have been easy at the time.

In fact, this raises one of the profoundest issues for faith, the nature of authority in religious belief. How do we know and perceive the truth about God? We shall see some of the attempts to wrestle with that question in Jeremiah as we read through it, but there are no easy, external rule-of-thumb devices by which we can gain certainty. Here, God tells Jeremiah that these other prophets have not been sent by him (v. 14). Nevertheless, how could their hearers have known that? In truth, these charlatans had not wrestled in the presence of God to discern the mind of God (a factor hinted at by Paul in 1 Corinthians 2:14 where he says that the true gifts of God can only be discerned spiritually). Their 'prophecy' is nothing but their own thoughts and ideas received second-hand (v. 14).

But perhaps there is one external factor aiding recognition of what is truly from God and what is not, and that is the ethical dimension. Does this 'truth' that some claim to be from God result in greater 'God-likeness' of character? Or are its spokespeople characterized, as here, by 'wickedness' (v. 16)? This was a point Jesus made when he said, 'You shall know them by their fruits' (Matthew 7:20).

The care of the true prophet

Perhaps another sign of the true prophet is to be seen in verses 17–18, in the sheer care of the prophet for his people and his utter involvement with them. He is grieved to the point of tears when he sees the suffering which is to befall them when the invader tramples all over them. While the official prophets and priests, swept by reality out of their depth, run round in demented circles, not knowing how to interpret what is happening and with no words profound enough for such a situation, Jeremiah shows himself to be, as well as to speak, a true word of God expressing something of the divine care and pity for his people. Perhaps that is why his expression of grief is described as a 'word' of God (v. 17a).

A PRAYER

Lord may I show something of your true nature
in my care for those in need. Amen

GOD REJECTS *an* IMPENITENT
PEOPLE

One more chance of turning

Verses 19–22, like verses 7–9, offer another prayer, lamenting the community's present sufferings, acknowledging again their sin and confessing that God is their only hope. They appeal to that established ground of all God's gracious dealings with them, for the sake of his 'name' (v. 21), by which is meant that he acts in grace and mercy in order to show his true nature (Exodus 9:16). They acknowledge his supreme power, he who sits on his 'glorious throne' (v. 21), a 'throne' symbolized in the Jerusalem temple where 'God sits enthroned upon the cherubim' (Psalms 80:1; 99:1). Only he can send 'rain', that symbol of all the blessings of his creation and salvation (Psalm 68:7–10). And they take again upon themselves the obligation of their covenant status with this creating and saving God; they acknowledge him alone among all other gods (v. 22; compare Exodus 20:3).

Sadly, such an expression of a real return to their covenant God remains the words of the prophet alone. The nation as a whole does not take the opportunity the prophet dares to provide in spite of God's word to him in verses 11–12.

A sad reversal of salvation

Jeremiah had already been told not to pray for the nation (7:16; 14:11–12). Perhaps his deep attachment to and longing for his people led him to persevere nevertheless. Now God's rejection of intercession is even more sharply expressed. Moses and Samuel were not only regarded as the founders of the prophetic movement as such (Deuteronomy 18:15; Psalm 99:6), but tradition recorded their effective intercession for the people on several occasions of crisis (Exodus 32:11–14; 1 Samuel 12:19–25). Things have now reached a state, however, where even their prayers would no longer move God (15:1). Indeed, the role Moses played when God delivered his people from bondage in Egypt is recalled in a tragic and ironic reversal of such an act of salvation now. As Carroll points out in his commentary (p. 320), God's words now about his own people, 'Send them out of my sight and let them go' recall his words to Pharaoh in Exodus 5:1, 'Let my people go'. The kind of disasters then visited on their enemies, the Egyptians, are now to be visited upon them (15:2–3). The great salvation act of God in redeeming his people from slavery in Egypt was often spoken of as an act of God's 'mighty hand and outstretched arm' (Deuteronomy 4:34). Now he has 'stretched out [same Hebrew verb] his hand' against his own people (v. 6). Verses 7–9 spell out in piteous poetic images what this means, in terms of women put in a powerless position in society when bereft of the protection of husbands and sons.

A strange note is heard in verse 4, where all this is said to be because of the sins of King Manasseh. This may reflect the conviction of later Deuteronomistic editors (see 2 Kings 23:26–27). For Jeremiah to have told his contemporaries that all that they were about to undergo was because of the sins of someone who had lived and reigned nearly half a century before would appear to blunt the sharpness of his challenge to his hearers. Whatever he thought of Manasseh, we have seen that Jeremiah left his hearers in no doubt of their own full responsibility.

Perhaps two points therefore arise for us today. One is that when people in Jeremiah's time, or in any time, deliberately choose to turn their backs on all that God offers in love, they strike a very poor bargain indeed. The other is that while we are all influenced to some extent by those who have gone before us and we all suffer from the harmful effects of the sins of others, in the end each of us is responsible for our own choices and our own decisions.

A PRAYER

Lord, today may I be open to all that you wish to offer me in love.
Amen

35 JEREMIAH 15:10-21

The LONELINESS *of the* LONG-DISTANCE PROPHET

The prophet's distress

The whole passage before us is one of the most moving in the book, depicting as it does the real inner cost of being true to God when that loyalty sets us over against all that, as human beings, we hold most dear. Unfortunately it is beset by problems of interpretation, especially in verses 11–12. The Hebrew text is difficult, and the different Bible versions offer such diverse variations that they only make matters more confused. As a result, we cannot even be sure whether the speaker in verses 11–12 is God (NRSV) or the prophet (RSV), nor whether what is said offers promise or threat, or a mixture of both. Verses 13–14 also occur at 17:3–4 and seem to have been added at this point by an editor who saw the words 'from the north' in verse 12 as a threat to the nation. Perhaps it is best to see the passage therefore as consisting of two 'complaints' by the prophet (compare 11:18–23; 12:1–6) in verses 10 and 15–18, and two responses from God in verses 11–12 and 19–21.

The isolation of remaining loyal to God

In both passages Jeremiah tells God of the price he is paying for his obedience to the call to be a prophet and for being faithful to a message which was so widely unpopular. He has not tried to exploit his neighbours in any way, yet they all revile him (v. 10). He accepted God's message and made its words part of himself because they pointed the way to life and the joys of salvation (v. 16; compare Ezekiel 3:1–3). Yet this very scale of values shut him off from the warmth of human fellowship he so craved, for others found their pleasures from very different sources (v. 17). In his distress he even wishes he had never been born, a longing he expresses in graphic language (v. 10; compare Job 3:3–26). The worst thing of all is his sense of isolation from God, who seems to let him down just when he needs him most. The earlier Jeremiah had confidently proclaimed that God was a 'fountain of living water' (2:13). Now, in an almost shocking complaint to God, he says that God is like a deceptive wadi, one of those stream beds which in winter are raging torrents, but in summer, when most needed, are arid and empty (v. 18).

Deliverance, but not escape

Verses 11–12 are difficult to interpret. Somehow God seems to promise both good and yet constant hostility, with the ultimate promise that those weakened by mixed motives and aims (bronze and iron) will not be able to prevail over the one who is wholly firm for God (iron). That is certainly the nature of the stern promise of verses 19–21. There will be no let-up in the constant struggle with those who reject God's words and God's ways, but the one who has 'eaten' them and found them a trusty source of joy will prevail over those who shift and drift about from one goal to another. Again, however, these 'confessions' of Jeremiah show the deepest dimensions of prayer. He comes to God just as he is, and pours out to him all his inner agonies and doubts in a way that we might almost term blasphemous. He comes as well with his real limitations, seen in an outburst of hatred against his persecutors and desire for revenge on them (v. 15). Perhaps we, for our part, often try to hide this side of ourselves from God with our rather more conventional and pious type of devotions. God met Jeremiah at the deepest point of his need. It is very hard to accept that we do not have to make believe, even just a little, in God's presence.

FOR PRAYER

Lord, help me to believe that your love is deep enough to meet me, accept me and help me exactly where and as I am now. Amen

SHARING *the* PEOPLE'S LONELINESS

Jeremiah forbidden to marry

We have seen enough of Jeremiah to know just how deeply involved with his compatriots he felt himself to be. Envisaging their coming suffering is inner torture for him. He has already spoken of his sense of isolation from all that gives them joy because of what he sees lies ahead of them (15:17–18). Now, this loneliness is intensified as God forbids him to marry (vv. 1–2). Ostensibly this is because of the dreadful fate that awaits all the families of the land (vv. 3–4). But this is more than just the kind of pessimism about the national or international situation which leads some, even now, to believe it would be unfair to bring a family into such a world. It is a personal identification with his people, a sharing at the deepest level of the anguish and loss they are destined to experience. Just as Ezekiel was told not to indulge in any kind of public display of mourning when his wife died, because his private grief was nothing compared with the national suffering that was to follow (Ezekiel 24:15–24), so Jeremiah is forbidden to share any of the joys of marriage and family life which are to be so short-lived.

Verse 4 makes it clear that all that is to come is the result of God's judgment, since, for the Hebrews, who had no real idea at this time of life after death, for bodies to lie unburied was the final ignominy for commoner (7:33) and royal (1 Kings 16:4) alike.

Mourning and celebration are meaningless

There will be no time for the normal mourning rituals, so many will be the dead (vv. 5–7; compare Amos 8:3). It is strange that those mourning rituals mentioned here were actually forbidden by the law (Leviticus 21:5; Deuteronomy 14:1). Either this suggests that it was a later law, or one not generally known in Jeremiah's time, or that the widespread use of such practices was yet another instance of the people's neglect of God and their calling as 'a people holy to the Lord' (Deuteronomy 14:2). Equally pointless are occasions of human joy and celebration such as weddings (vv. 8–9) since all joy is about to be overtaken by disaster (as in Amos 8:10).

Indeed, the end of the celebration of such 'covenant' ceremonies as weddings, already foreshadowed by the command to Jeremiah not to marry, is only symptomatic of the end of the deeper 'covenant' relationship between God and his people. All the accompanying blessings promised in that covenant relationship are to be taken away (v. 5)—'peace', or 'salvation' as the Hebrew word *shalom* is better rendered; 'steadfast love' (Hebrew *hesed*); and 'mercy' (as in the great covenant promise of Exodus 34:6). The only people to go on holding out promises of such blessings to this rebellious people now are the false prophets (6:14). Indeed, there is irony in the statement that no one will be offering 'the cup of consolation' to those who mourn (v. 7), for the only 'cup' God is going to hold out to his people is the cup of judgment, to be meted out to them at the hands of the Babylonians (25:15).

Is there anything but gloom and disaster in this passage? Perhaps the fact that there is a prophet who cares enough to be brutally honest and to avoid all false comfort and superficial cure, and enough to involve himself in all their suffering, is a sign of hope. In the darkest times God, it seems, does not leave himself entirely without human witness.

FOR MEDITATION

We are still left with only the narrow way, a way often hardly to be found, of living every day as if it were our last, yet in faith and responsibility living as though a splendid future still lay before us. 'Houses and fields and vineyards shall again be bought in this land,' cries Jeremiah as the Holy City is about to be destroyed… It is a divine sign and pledge of better things to come, just when all seems blackest. Thinking and acting for the sake of the coming generation, but taking each day as it comes without fear and anxiety—that is the spirit in which we are being forced to live in practice. It is not easy to be brave and hold out, but it is imperative.

Dietrich Bonhoeffer, *Letters and Papers from Prison*,
SCM Press, 1953, pp. 24–25

WHY GOD IS JUDGING HIS PEOPLE

Their sins and those of their ancestors

It was not unnatural that Jeremiah's contemporaries should have rounded on him as he made predictions as dire as those in 16:1–9, and asked him 'Why?' But the reason they had no idea of 'why' is itself an indication of their predicament. They could not 'see' that which, ironically, would unfold 'before your eyes' (16:9). Their eyes would be opened, but too late.

No doubt it was not only those who lived in the days of the prophet who would have asked 'Why?' Once the disaster had fallen on them, those left at home and those taken into Babylon ('the land of the north', v. 15) would also have asked the same question. That is why Jeremiah's words in this chapter are expressed in the kind of prose that often characterizes the Deuteronomists. We see the same kind of account in their writings in Deuteronomy 29:22–28 and 1 Kings 9:8–9.

The response to their question raises interesting issues for us as well as those who heard them. For it states that this judgment comes because of the sins of their 'ancestors' (v. 11) and because of their own sins (v. 12). There is no doubt that what we are and, to some extent, how we act is conditioned by those who have gone before us. We inherit our genes from them and we experience the consequences of their actions, whether for good or bad. Deuteronomy itself makes this point very firmly, that we do influence those who come after us and that this gives an awesome responsibility (see Deuteronomy 5: 8–10). Yet, for all that, we cannot just hide behind their skirts and say, 'It wasn't my fault. I couldn't help it.' No doubt, God in his infinite wisdom and grace understands what is beyond our control and makes due allowance for it. Yet all of us, within the limits of the circumstances which are 'given' to us, do have responsibility and freedom to act for ourselves. Jeremiah makes this clear when he modifies the old law of Deuteronomy by rejecting the false comfort that some drew from it (31:29–30).

The warning of the prophet is further extended in verses 16–18 with their forceful imagery of the fisher dredging for fish hidden in the water and the shepherd rounding up his flock when they have been grazing over many miles of heath and mountain land. Similar pictures are used elsewhere by the prophets (Ezekiel 12:13; 29:4–5; Amos 4:2; Habakkuk 1:14–17).

To reveal himself to his children

Verses 14–15 and 19–21 appear to interrupt the flow of this section by introducing a totally different note. Verses 14–15 look into the time of exile in Babylon ('the land of the north') and promise a glorious return. Indeed, it will be so wonderful that it will eclipse even the mighty act of God's redemption in bringing his people out of slavery in Egypt. A prophet of the exile makes exactly the same promise (Isaiah 43:14–21). Verses 17–19 are even more remarkable. They envisage a complete change of heart when people will call on God in truth as their 'strength' and their 'stronghold' and acknowledge the absurdity of ever having tried to make gods for themselves (v. 11). Indeed, it is possible that the 'nations' spoken of in verse 19 refer not only to the scattered and exiled Israelites returning with a complete change of heart, but even to the people of other nations as well (see Isaiah 45:22–23). Yet these passages are not out of harmony with the rest of 16:10–21, whoever is responsible for placing them just where they are. For they too answer the question, 'Why has God done this to us?' Since the people were blind to all his actions and deaf to his words, the disaster of exile was the only answer. But even this calamity is aimed at the further goal of teaching them his 'power and might' and revealing his nature of love to them (v. 21).

FOR MEDITATION

Perhaps this passage should lead us humbly before God to (a) a sympathetic understanding that the acts of others may not always be fully under their control; (b) accepting responsibility for our own actions; and (c) being aware of the influence for good and evil that we exercise over those who come after us.

FAITH & FAITHLESSNESS

Sin, a matter of the heart

A number of themes weave and interweave through this passage. While each is developed in a particular way in each section, we may see a community of theme linking verses 1–4 with 9–10 and verses 5–8 with 11–13, with a certain degree of continuity between both groups.

Verses 1–4 graphically depict the way repeated sin becomes ingrained in our very nature. Each time, a deeper mark is etched in our hearts, minds, habits and affections, so that it becomes continually easier to follow this groove habitually. Repeated here is the familiar charge of religious apostasy, the Israelites' worship of the gods and goddesses of Canaan being described in language very reminiscent of the vocabulary of the Deuteronomists (Deuteronomy 12:2; 2 Kings 17:9–12). As in both those two references, the nation here is warned with the loss of the land which had been promised to their ancestors and into which God had led them by his grace, and so this is yet another passage in the book where we can see that Jeremiah's warnings would have been recalled later in the time of the exile to explain why the disaster had overtaken them. A link to verse 11 occurs with the warning that they will lose all their carefully amassed wealth and possessions (v. 3). The reference to the 'horns of the altars' in verse 1 is interesting because these were associated in the temple worship with the sacrificial blood by which expiation for sins was attained (Leviticus 4, especially vv. 7, 30, 34; 8:15). Their mention here means either that the mere manipulation of the sacrifices gives no automatic forgiveness for sins which are unrepented of and still indulged in, or perhaps that the people are taking even their worship of foreign gods into Yahweh's own temple.

These verses also link with verses 9–10 through the theme of the 'heart'. Sin becomes engraved on the 'heart' (v. 1) so that the heart itself becomes twisted and devious (v. 9). It is the 'heart' that is open to the searching gaze of God who can read all its subterfuges and deceits (v. 10). Jeremiah does attack the people for specific sins. But he sees clearly that 'sin' is more than a series of actions, to be put right just by outward changing of the acts themselves. Just as a disease manifests itself by certain symptoms, the disease itself needs to be cured, not just the symptoms palliated.

Two sources of trust

The prophets have plenty to say about those who look to human beings for their help in times of trouble (for example, Isaiah 31:1–3). In fact, human beings often let one another down just when their help is most needed, either by proving faithless or, even when well-intentioned, because their powers to help are futile. The contrast between the godly as trees planted by water and the ungodly as shrubs shrivelled and parched in the desert is naturally familiar in the writings of those who lived cheek by jowl with the wilderness (see Psalm 1). It is a picture that lends itself to describing a peace and stability which are not dependent on outward circumstances alone, or just good luck. The times of drought will surely come and affect every living thing. But those whose roots run deep to the source waters of the One who is the 'fountain of living water' (v. 13) will be able to withstand them. Indeed, the theme of verses 5–8 is taken up in verses 12–13 and developed in a counterpoint which reverses the order of the earlier verses. An outburst of praise to God, whose presence in the temple was symbolized by the ark of the covenant, the 'throne' upon which God sat in glory and power (Exodus 26:34; Psalm 99:1–12; Jeremiah 3:16–17), expresses the very trust called for in verses 7–8. This trust is contrasted with the folly of those who turn away from him, those said to be 'cursed' in verses 5–6.

In the end, what matters is not perhaps how much faith we have, or how great our faith is, but in whom we are putting such faith as we have.

A PRAYER

Lord, may my roots strike so deep into you that I have resources to face times of spiritual drought and aridity. Amen

39 JEREMIAH 17:14–18

The PROPHET'S PRAYER

The prayer that is also praise

This is another of the 'confessions' of Jeremiah' (see 11:18–23; 12:1–6; 15:10–21). Like many of the prayers of personal lament that we find in the Psalms, this opening prayer is at the same time an expression of praise and of confidence (see Psalms 4:1; 18:1–3). We should not try to compartmentalize 'praise' and 'prayer' too much, for to cry out to God in our times of need is to confess that he is someone who is compassionate enough to hear and powerful enough to act. Intercessory prayer therefore is itself an act of praise. Jeremiah prays because he has no doubt that when God acts to 'heal' and to 'deliver', then both healing and deliverance are real (v. 14). It is interesting to note that elsewhere in the book both these verbs are used of the sickness and distress of the nation (8:22; 14:8, 19). In the light of what follows, there can be no doubt that Jeremiah is voicing his own inner conflict before God. Yet, even here, the prophet is so much one with his people that his needs are also theirs, and theirs his.

Rejection of God—and his messenger

As in the earlier 'confessions', it is the pain of the people's rejection of God's word, and therefore of the prophet as the bearer of that word, that hurts the warm-hearted, outgoing Jeremiah (vv. 15–16; compare 15:10, 16–17). He has been commissioned by God to warn of certain coming judgment if the nation persists in its ways and fails to turn back to God. Such a message, overturning, as it appeared to do, the very certainties of their faith in their election as God's own people, was in their eyes monstrous. To make matters worse, God had not authenticated his prophet by doing anything to fulfil the dire warnings. So they jeeringly mock Jeremiah by asking where God's 'word' is. In Hebrew, the same term (*dabar*) means both 'word' and 'deed' or 'act', hence God's statement in 1:12, 'I am watching over my word to perform it'. But he does not appear to be watching over it to perform it now, hence their sarcastic question, 'Where is the word of the Lord? Let it come!' (v. 15).

Faithfulness—and humanity

It is very difficult to discern the exact meaning of Jeremiah's word to God in verse 16, since the Hebrew is capable of more than one translation, as the differences between versions of the Bible, ancient and modern, testify. The same word in the first line of the verse can mean either 'evil/trouble' or 'shepherd', according to which vowel signs are put into it (the original text having no written vowels). So Jeremiah could be saying either that he has not sought to run away from his role as 'shepherd' (as in NRSV); or that he has not been unfaithful to all that God intends to do as the divine 'shepherd' of his people; or that he has not actively sought a day of evil. The first is unlikely, since it offers poor parallelism with the next line and nowhere else in the book is Jeremiah described as a 'shepherd'. The second is possible, but the third is the most likely in the light of what follows. Jeremiah has not taken a kind of malicious delight in proclaiming trouble. Rather, it was his love for his own people that made him hesitant to take on the task. All his words and inner motives have been open to God. God knows he has been faithful—and what that faithfulness has cost him.

Verses 17–18 must be seen as a further prayer that God will vindicate his word, rather than simply an outpouring of vindictiveness against the very people he claims to love. Yet it reminds us that it is difficult to keep our motives always clear and pure. McKane says of this that, if this is a 'mark of Jeremiah's fallibility, it also demonstrates the authenticity of his humanity' (p. 414). God has always used imperfect human instruments for his work, and does so still. Yet, while he calls us 'where we are', his purpose of grace is not to leave us there.

A PRAYER

O Lord, keep me faithful in your service, both when that service is joyful and encouraging, and when it is hurtful and costly. Amen

---

A SERMON *on* SABBATH OBSERVANCE

The call to keep the sabbath

Verses 19–23 represent another of the prose sermons that occur throughout the book of Jeremiah, like the 'temple' sermon in chapter 7 and the 'covenant' sermon in chapter 11.

There are two problems about the sermon. The first concerns its location. The Hebrew of verse 19 reads, 'the gate of the sons of the people', usually rendered, as in NRSV, 'the People's Gate'—but this place is not mentioned anywhere else. Some amend the text to read 'the Benjamin Gate', which is mentioned again in 37:13 and 38:7. However, the content of the sermon matters more than its location.

But it is here, in fact, that a deeper mystery lies. There can be no doubt that the law to keep the sabbath was old and well-known before the exile (Exodus 20:8–11; Deuteronomy 5:12–15). It was mentioned by the eighth-century prophet Amos (8:5). There is no reason, therefore, why Jeremiah should not have called for obedience to it. Yet this 'single-issue' sermon, concentrating on one specific law and elevating it to the one issue that decides their national fate, seems to come strangely from the prophet who saw apostasy as the main symptom of a people's perversion of the heart (4:4; 17:9) and their failure as a failure of love for God (2:2, 13).

On the other hand, we know that sabbath observance became of much greater importance during the exile when, in Babylon, sacrificial worship was no longer possible and obedience to the law became the test of the people's devotion and a sign of their distinctiveness from those around them (Isaiah 56:2; Nehemiah 13:15–22). This, coupled with the fact that the prose of the sermon is strongly Deuteronomistic in tone, suggests that this is another example of the special application of Jeremiah's words to a later generation. However, Jeremiah did see that a right, loving relationship with God would manifest itself in specific acts of obedience (4:1–2) and he did call for obedience to *Torah* (6:19; 16:11). Further, the Deuteronomists themselves saw no real contradiction between their call for obedience to the law and the need for a right attitude of the heart towards God (Deuteronomy 10:16; 30:6). The sermon therefore presents us with the challenge that love for God is not just a matter of fine feelings and warm words. It will show itself in obedience to him in the specifics of life.

Continuing relevance of the sabbath

To say that God continues to speak to later generations through the prophetic word raises acutely the question of whether what the Old Testament has to say about sabbath observance has any relevance for Christians today. Only Seventh Day Adventists take it all so literally that (with some logic) they keep Saturday as a day of worship. Perhaps there are three values in keeping a day of worship. In our worship we are reminded constantly of our relationship to God and that this relationship is founded on his great deeds of love for us. The sheer joy of such worship is stressed in verse 26. The 'bringing in of burdens' and doing 'work' (vv. 24, 27) speak mainly of economic activity, as does the passage in Nehemiah 13:15–22 (and the reference in Amos 8:5). The wholesale opening up for business and profit of the day traditionally set aside for worship obscures that vision of God which needs constant renewal if it is to remain fresh. But there is also an element of hope about it. Verse 26 looks forward to the time when people will come from all places to celebrate their relationship with God, and in Isaiah 56:6–8 this promise is extended to peoples of other nations as well. Worship can fire and enthuse us by a vision of all that God in his love has in store for us, and for all the peoples of his world.

FOR MEDITATION

There was a man that could look no way but downwards, with a muck-rake in his hand. There stood also one over his head, with a celestial crown in his hand... but the man did neither look up, nor regard, but raked to himself the straws, the small sticks, and dust of the floor.

John Bunyan, *The Pilgrim's Progress*

The SIGN *of the* POTTER

God's power to remake

Verses 1–6 tell of another occasion when the prophet was instructed to act rather than simply to speak, as in 13:1–11 (see comments on pp. 74–75, especially concerning the nature and purpose of acts of 'prophetic symbolism'). Here he is given the rather passive role of going to the potter's house and watching—a reminder that anyone who is going to speak with the authentic accents of God has to listen and wait first. He sees the potter turning clay on the wheel, but the casting and shaping go wrong. The potter stops, remoulds the clay and starts again until he gets a result that seems 'good' to him (v. 4). God can act like the potter. If Israel fails to allow itself to be formed according to God's design, then he can start the process all over again.

On the face of it, this 'sign' is one both of warning and of hope. It would have been quite natural for Jeremiah and his hearers to think of God as a 'potter'. The Hebrew verb from which the noun 'potter' comes is *yasar*, and Genesis 2:7 tells how God 'formed' (same verb) human beings from the clay of the ground and breathed into them the breath of life. And God, in his grace, can 'form' people to become all that he, in his love, wants for them. So the Servant says that God 'formed me from the womb to be his servant' (Isaiah 49:5) and God can tell Israel how precious they are to him for 'he created them for his glory and formed and made them' (Isaiah 43:7). Understood like this, the sign of the potter is one of hope, fitting in with much of the message of the book as a whole, that God, after the judgment of the exile, can take Israel and 're-form' them according to his good pattern and purpose.

God's sovereign power

At first sight, verses 7–12 bear little relationship to verses 1–6. However, all signs or 'symbols' share two characteristics: they are of limited application in that not every detail in them can contain the whole truth and, related to this, they are susceptible to more than one interpretation. The 'sign' of the potter in verses 1–6 could be interpreted another way, namely, that if one instrument fails to serve God's purpose he can dispense with it and use another. If the clay had hardened into an unsuitable finish, then the potter would simply smash it and start with more clay. This is a truth that gets vivid confirmation in the book of Esther, where Mordecai tells Esther that if she fails to help God's people in her moment of destiny, then deliverance will come to them but 'from another quarter' (Esther 4:14).

These verses remind the prophet and his people that God is not the God of Israel only, but of all nations—a fact which was implicit in Jeremiah's call (1:5). If Israel fails, God can choose any nation that proves responsive to his call. For, and here is the paradox and limitation of the image of the potter, God does not use his sovereign power to force people into his way. He waits for them to respond, and so the picture of the potter becomes a symbol of judgment against Israel for refusing his way (v. 12).

Turning away from God

Jeremiah has already contrasted the erratic behaviour of Israel with the constancy of nature (see 8:7). He does so again in verses 13–17. The upper slopes of the Lebanon range of mountains are always snowcapped. 'Sirion' (an emendation of the Hebrew text) was its highest peak. Streams that have their source in inaccessible places do not fail to bring down waters to the plains. But God's people have forsaken the 'ancient roads', that is, the ways that God showed them in his laws (see 6:16), and have been led astray into blind alleys by the gods to whose worship they have turned. Their suffering, like that of a land ravaged by the scorching sirocco east wind, will be so devastating that it will become an object of amazement to all who see it. Let them, then, learn the lesson of the potter, and allow God to mould them anew to his design.

FOR PRAYER

Lord, by your Spirit, continue to form me into all you want me to be, and make me responsive material in your hands.

The PROPHET'S COMPLAINT *to* GOD

The hostile reaction of the 'Establishment'

The Hebrew links verse 18 to Jeremiah's proclamation of judgment in verses 13–17 with an 'and', rightly rendered by NRSV as 'Then'. Whether it originally followed that particular passage or not, the verse gives us a window into the hostile reaction of those most affected by Jeremiah's preaching, namely, the religious and civil 'Establishment' (as in 6:13–15; 23:9–40). Their reaction is that of such figures of all times in all societies—to 'rubbish' him, for the Hebrew of the phrase rendered by NRSV 'let us bring charges against him' is 'to lash him with the tongue'. By calumny, innuendo and subtle distortion of his message, an awkward figure is discredited—something more easily done now than then, with many of the means of the mass media available to those who control them or who can buy their support. Indeed, an interesting variant in the Septuagint drops the negative and renders the last phrase, 'Let us pay careful attention to all his words' (that is, in order to trap him).

'Paying close attention' to the words of a prophet might sound very commendable, but the motive is everything. To listen to God's messenger mainly in order to criticize, and to judge what is said by insights already held dear by us, is to elevate our existing knowledge and our preconceived opinions above any possible judgment of them by God. Equally reprehensible is to listen in such a way as to make the messenger's performance our chief interest, praising the art but failing to come to grips with its truth, an experience that befell another prophet, Ezekiel (Ezekiel 33:30–33).

Verse 18 is a classic statement of the roles of the three main groups of those who were seen as 'messengers' of God. The priest's role was to give expert direction in all matters relating to *Torah* (the very word means 'Instruction'). The 'wise' were skilled in giving 'counsel', ranging from advice on ethical matters—including those affecting court policy, such matters as correct family life and even 'good manners'—to theological teaching. All such themes can be found in the books of Proverbs, Job and Ecclesiastes. Of one 'wise man', Ahitophel, it could be said that his advice was 'as if one consulted the oracles of God' (2 Samuel 16:23). 'Word', 'oracle' or 'vision', that is, some communication seen as being directed from God to a particular situation, was the province of the prophet (Ezekiel 7:26). The argument of Jeremiah's opponents seems to be that if Jeremiah is silenced they still have plenty of 'safe' men to protect the national and religious life of the community.

Jeremiah's response

As other 'confession' passages show, Jeremiah obviously felt rejection by his contemporaries keenly (11:18–23; 15:10–11). It was the harder to bear since he loved his people and had done all he could to intercede on their behalf, in spite of the message of resolute rejection that God had vouchsafed to him (v. 20). What an utter contradiction appears between verse 20 and verses 21–23! They express the harshest expression of hatred by Jeremiah anywhere in the book. It is not that the curses he utters against his people differ from the very things God has shown him would happen (and indeed did happen). It is that, here, Jeremiah seems to call for such disasters on them because of the treatment they have meted out to him. Perhaps the most dreadful thing is the last phrase of verse 23, where he calls on God to strike while the iron of his anger is hot. He seems to be afraid that, given too much time, mercy might temper God's judgment.

There is no way of dressing all this up and pretending it is any better than it is (see comments on 17:14–18, pp. 94–95). It is a long way from the prayer of Jesus, 'Father, forgive them; for they do not know what they are doing' (Luke 23:34). But do we not all sometimes show more of the spirit of Jeremiah here than the Spirit of Jesus?

FOR PRAYER

'Love your enemies and pray for those who persecute you'
(Matthew 5:44). Lord, may the realization that this is how you
have treated us move us to respond to you by treating others
in the same way. Amen

The SIGN of the EARTHENWARE JUG

The useless discarded

At the core of this passage is another act of 'prophetic symbolism' (compare 13:1–11; 18:1–11). Again, Jeremiah is commanded by God to go a particular place, this time to the Potsherd Gate, taking representative 'Establishment' figures (elders, senior priests) as witnesses, and perform a symbolic act. The Potsherd Gate was presumably on the southern side of the city, as it is linked with the Valley of Hinnom (v. 2). Later Jewish tradition said that it contained the city's rubbish dumps, and this would suggest that the gate got its name from the broken and discarded earthenware that was carried through it. Thus it was a symbolic location for the symbolic act of breaking the narrow-necked earthenware flask. The Hebrew name for this vessel is *baqbuq*, an almost onomatopoeic noun, linked to the verb 'to empty' or 'to gurgle', a connection which will be immediately apparent to any reader who has ever had liquid poured into a glass by an attentive host.

To compare this action with that of the potter in chapter 18 is to underline what was said there, that all 'symbols' are limited in their application and often of ambivalent meaning. The potter's reworking of what had been spoiled in chapter 18 (see pp. 98–99) could have been either a sign of hope, that God would start again with Israel, or of judgment, that he would start with other material. No such ambiguity attaches to this sign. Here we have to do not with malleable clay, but with a flask that has already been fired. It can therefore not be changed but, if it is misshapen, can only be smashed and discarded. Are the two actions therefore contradictory? This is where we have to remember who Jeremiah's witnesses were—representatives of the civil and religious 'Establishment'. It is this that has become hardened and unsusceptible to change. There can be hope for individuals—God in his mercy can even renew the kingdom—but not before the whole political and religious structure represented by these witnesses and the 'kings' of verse 3 has been brought to an end. Institutions that harden into machinery for maintaining the vested interests of their own élite rather than those of the people they have been called to serve are doomed to die. This is the message of Jeremiah and all the Old Testament prophets, and it is of relevance for political and ecclesiastical institutions of all times.

God's frustration of human sin

It is clear from the Old Testament that the Valley of Hinnom became a place where human sacrifice was carried out, even if only in times of extreme crisis. The place where this happened was called 'Topheth', a word linked to 'burning' (see 7:31 and comments on p. 52). The expansion in verses 3–9 of Jeremiah's prophetic action there attributes the cause of the coming destruction of the nation that it announces (and helps to bring about) to their apostasy in general and their burning of their children in particular. It is full of Deuteronomic terminology (compare v. 3 with 2 Kings 21:12; v. 4 with Deuteronomy 13:6; 28:64; v. 5 with 2 Kings 17:16–17; v. 7 with Deuteronomy 28:26; v. 9 with Deuteronomy 28:53, 55, 57) and so the whole passage may be the result of the Deuteronomists' preserving and developing the original message of the prophet. Certainly those in the exile knew only too well the fulfilment of the terrible prediction in verse 9 of what could happen during a siege (see Lamentations 4:10).

Even if this is so, however, the Deuteronomists have linked their expansion firmly with Jeremiah's original action. In verse 7, the Hebrew verb used to depict God's coming judgment of Judah is the verb from which the noun *baqbuq* comes, namely 'to empty', happily caught by NRSV in their rendering, 'I will make void the plans of Judah and Jerusalem'. If they had had ears to hear, they would have taken to heart the words of their worship: 'The Lord brings the counsel of the nations to nothing; he frustrates the plans of the peoples. The counsel of the Lord stands for ever… Happy is the nation whose God is the Lord' (Psalm 33:10–12).

FOR PRAYER

O God, inasmuch as without you we are not able to please you; mercifully grant that your Holy Spirit may in all things direct and rule our hearts; through Jesus Christ our Lord. Amen

Book of Common Prayer

The REJECTION of the PROPHET

Jeremiah proclaims his message publicly

Verses 14–15 tell how Jeremiah returned from 'Topheth', where he had performed his act of prophetic symbolism before some senior officials, and pronounced its significance to the people in general 'in the court of the Lord's house'. It is really a brief summary of the 'temple sermon' recorded in chapter 7, which also specified the sins committed at Topheth (7:31) and warned of judgment in very similar terms (7:20).

Confrontation at 'the Gate'

Such words, spoken within the courts of the temple itself—that seeming tangible evidence of God's dwelling among his people and his promise to defend them (Psalm 46:5–7, 10–11)—would have appeared to many as blasphemous. Small wonder that the priest charged with the maintenance of order in the temple, Pashhur, felt that enough was enough and signified official rejection of Jeremiah's words by having him beaten and put in the stocks (v. 2). Amos, over a century earlier, had been thrown out of the sanctuary of Bethel in the north for saying similar things there (Amos 7:10–15). As well as this Pashhur, son of Immer, we also read of a Pashhur who was father of Gedaliah (Jeremiah 38:1) and another who was the son of Malchiah (21:1; 38:1). Jeremiah tells his opponent that his name will be changed to 'Terror-all-around', the very term he uses to describe the 'foe from the north' sent by God in judgment against his people (6:25). In other words, he is 'the enemy within', and so we have the irony of one who was called to be a guardian of the life of the temple, and so of the people, being one of those primarily responsible for the destruction that is to come. Pashhur probably did not literally act as a 'prophet' (v. 6) but, like them, he was one of those false 'shepherds' who betrayed their sacred trust.

Perhaps this is the place to note how prominently 'gates' figure in the book of Jeremiah, to an extent equalled, and surpassed, only in the book of Ezekiel. Jeremiah addressed his temple sermon to those entering the gates of the temple (7:2); his sabbath sermon was delivered at the Benjamin (or People's) Gate (17:19); he broke the earthenware jar at the Potsherd Gate (19:2); he was imprisoned in stocks at the Benjamin Gate of the temple (20:2); he was said to be deserving of death by the royal princes at the 'New Gate' (26:10); at the same gate Baruch read the scroll on which Jeremiah's words were written (36:10); he was accused of desertion at the Benjamin Gate (37:13); Ebed-melech appealed for his life at the same gate (38:7); Zedekiah and others fled from the city before the Babylonians by the 'gate between the walls' (39:4; 52:7); and, on capturing the city, the chief royal officers of the king of Babylon came and sat in the 'Middle Gate' (39:3).

Of course, it was natural that people should enter and leave a city by its gates, and we know that the open concourses around the gates were places where crowds gathered and often judicial cases were heard. Yet one wonders if they have achieved almost something of a symbolic significance for the final editors of the book of Jeremiah. Gates are places of decision, where it is decided whom should be included and whom shut out; or one decides for oneself whether to enter or leave the city. Perhaps the fact that Jeremiah's words are recorded as having often been uttered at gates suggests that there were those who believed that, through the prophet, God had been knocking at the door of his people's life as an appeal to be allowed entry. The fact that Jeremiah was humiliated and judged at a gate signified the people's rejection of God's word, while the faithfulness of Baruch and Ebed-melech at the 'gates' suggests that there were, nevertheless, those who wanted to respond to what God was saying through his prophet.

FOR PRAYER

'Listen! I am standing at the door, knocking; if you hear my voice and open the door, I will come in to you and eat with you, and you with me' (Revelation 3:20).

O Lord, may I hear your knocking today and open the door to all the limitless possibilities you have for me. Amen

45

The PROPHET'S DESPAIR

The complaint

Verses 7–10 give us the last of the 'confessions' or 'laments' of Jeremiah (for the others see 11:18–22; 12:1–6; 15:10–12, 15–21; 17:14–18). It is the most bitter and extreme of them all. Indeed, it is hard to believe that a prophet could say what Jeremiah does to God. The Hebrew verb used twice in the opening words, rendered by NRSV as 'O Lord, you have enticed me, and I was enticed' means basically 'to be open', and then 'to be simple' or even 'naïve'. It may well be a reference to Jeremiah's youth at the time God called him (1:6) and the prophet is blaming God for taking advantage of his innocence and inexperience in forcing him into a vocation with which he is now at odds. NEB's 'you have duped me' catches the meaning well and seems better than the suggestion of sexual harassment which some critics have seen here and which lies behind the NRSV rendering. The immediate cause may have been the experience of the prophet's conflict with Pashhur (20:1–6) but it may relate more generally to his continuing suffering. The source of his hurt is the fact that he has become a laughing-stock in everyone's eyes because of the deep unpopularity of his message, and that the threats he has uttered have not materialized. Indeed, his message is mocked even by his friends as they repeat it (v. 10) and they try all means to trap him (v. 10; compare 12:6; 18:18–19). Even when he tried to escape from his mission, the inner compulsion of the divine call would not let him go (v. 9; compare Amos 3:8).

The prophet's confidence

It seems strange that, immediately following so bitter a complaint to God, the prophet can speak so confidently in verses 11–13. But we have seen that some, at least, of these 'confessions' are marked, like the psalms of individual lament, by a remarkable change of mood, following an answer to the complaint from God (see 15:19–21). If the complaint did contain an echo of Jeremiah's call, with its suggestion of his gullible youth at the time, certainly the assurances of that call are repeated now (1:7–8). God is stronger than all those who are ranged against him—an assurance given once, long before, to another young prophet (2 Kings 6:15–17). Verse 12 is almost identical to 11:20 and contains the same remarkable picture of prayer which is open, frank, and entirely honest before God (see comments on p. 69). This is the kind of prayer, from the depths of human need, that is met from the depths of God's grace. The call to praise God in verse 13 is, again, characteristic of many of the psalms of lament where the worshipper has been assured of God's answer to his or her needs. This does not mean that this whole passage is liturgical in character, as some have suggested. It is natural that individuals, accustomed to the language of corporate worship, should use that language in their own devotional life. This is one reason why corporate worship is so essential for the individual life of devotion.

The reaction

Whatever the relation of the terrible cry of bitter dereliction in verses 14–18 to what has just preceded it, it is remarkable that this book contains the desperate prayer of verses 7–10, the assurance of the divine response in verses 11–13, and yet such a moment of utter despair as this. The passage, with its deep sense of isolation and estrangement from life and the world, is one of the most terrible in the whole Old Testament, matched only by Job 3:3–26. It reminds us that all human beings, even the finest saints and servants of God, know violent swings of mood, and that not all the life of pilgrimage is lived on sunny uplands of faith and assurance. Yet God was there with his servant, even when he had no assurance of the fact. For Christians, the cry of dereliction of Christ on the cross (Mark 15:34) reminds us that God has entered even into our times of blackest despair.

A PRAYER

Lord, do not leave me in my darkest moments of despair, when I cannot even find the faith to believe you are there. Amen

STERN WORDS *to* KING & PEOPLE

A message for times of crisis

With chapter 21 a new section of the book begins, extending to 24:10. Until now, incidents and oracles have seldom been dated or linked to specific events. Now this changes and the following chapters relate in one way or another to periods when Jerusalem was under siege by the Babylonians (for the historical events, see the Introduction, pp. 12–13). Yet they are not in chronological order. The setting of chapter 21 occurs ten years later than that of chapter 24. This suggests that there is a theological theme which the final editors considered more important than mere historical information. And this theme is that Jerusalem fell because of the sin of all its people but, in particular, because of the sins of its leaders, the kings and prophets. Only on the other side of this terrible judgment could there be a new beginning (24:4–7).

The temptation to manipulate God

Zedekiah, appointed king by Nebuchadrezzar (2 Kings 24:17), sends a delegation to Jeremiah during the time of the second siege of Babylon, which lasted from 589 to 587BC. The Pashhur mentioned is not the same as the one whose challenge to the prophet is described in chapter 20. The priest Zephaniah (not to be confused with the biblical prophet of the same name) is recorded as undertaking a similar mission in 37:3 and as reading to Jeremiah a letter sent him by Shemaiah, rebuking him for not silencing the prophet (29:25–29).

When the king asks Jeremiah 'to enquire of the Lord' (v. 2), he is not asking merely for a polite prayer request but for the securing of God's help by means of some decisive prophetic word or deed. He wants the same kind of prophetic intervention that the king of Moab hoped to secure when he hired Balaam (Numbers 22:4–6). In this case, divine help is needed against the menacing Nebuchadrezzar (a better rendering in Hebrew of the name of the Babylonian king, 'Nabu-kudurri-usur', than the form 'Nebuchadnezzar' used in some other texts). Indeed, he asks for a 'wonderful deed' (NRSV) by God, using a word which often describes God's powerful intervention against

Israel's enemies (for example, against Egypt in Exodus 3:20, or the Canaanites in Joshua 3:5). In their worship they were accustomed to praising God for such 'wonderful deeds' in their past history (Psalm 105:2, 5). So Zedekiah is claiming their status as God's covenant people, a people entitled to expect his covenant mercies.

A discouraging reply

The reply is frightening. Instead of waging a 'holy war' on their behalf against their enemies, God is going to wage it against his own people, turning their own weapons against them and bringing their soldiers back into the city, glad to have even their lives as their only 'booty' (v. 9). The besieged city will know the customary diseases of such situations, but even those who survive plague will die by the sword of the enemy. The only hope (for the people—there is none for the royal entourage) is that they might desert a city doomed to God's judgment and seek the mercy of their enemy (vv. 8–10). The situation is hopeless, not merely because of the military might of the Babylonians, but because God has decided on the fate of the city (v. 10). Verses 13–14 hardly seem to fit the geographical location of Jerusalem, but they fill out the general theme of the utter inadequacy of the inhabitants' attempts at defence in the face of the divine judgment.

The obedience God requires

Verses 11–12 show why Zedekiah's desire to manipulate the power of God to secure his own survival, and that of his throne and city, are doomed. God is not there to serve human ambitions for power, success and security. Rather, it is he who makes demands on his servants. In this case, it was the role of the Davidic king to secure God's justice throughout the kingdom in the interests of the poorest and weakest of the community (Psalm 72:1–4). That alone is the way to secure the kind of victory that God alone can give (Psalm 72:8–11).

FOR MEDITATION

True worship consists in my offering myself to God for his service. Idolatry consists in seeking to secure God's help for my own interests. For sure he offers all his promises to us in love. But such love has its own imperatives.

47 JEREMIAH 22:1–9

The COVENANT *with* DAVID

The conditions for its continuance

This passage continues the 'royal' theme already found in chapter 21 but, unlike that, it is undated and the particular king addressed is not specified. We are simply told that Jeremiah was instructed by God to go to the royal palace and deliver his message, just as he had been sent to preach at the temple (ch. 7). Perhaps it is deliberately left general. The divine word applies to the whole Davidic dynasty, and it was the failure of the royal line as a whole that led to the disasters of 586BC. For here the king is charged with maintaining 'justice and righteousness' (v. 3) and this is seen in the way he maintains a just and fair social and legal order throughout the kingdom. If the poor and weak members of society are nearly always specified in contexts such as this, it is not only because of the need for what today we might call 'positive discrimination' towards those on the margins of society, but because they lacked wealth and influential patrons who might secure favourable manipulation of the legal system on their behalf. Thus it was the king who, as the final court of appeal, must uphold their cause (Psalm 72:1–4).

Some versions of God's covenant with David in the Old Testament stress most its unconditional nature (2 Samuel 7:12–16; Psalm 89:29–37). Others, however, insist that the continuation of the line depends on obedience to God's ethical and moral requirements (Deuteronomy 17:18–20; 1 Kings 2:2–4; Psalm 132:11–12). It is the Deuteronomists who, in their presentation of Israel's history, show that the fortunes of the whole nation depended on the obedience or, more often, the disobedience of the king (for example, 1 Kings 16:18–19). They saw the failure of the royal line as responsible for the state of the nation that led to the fall of dynasty and city. Thus this word of Jeremiah's becomes for them a kind of text to explain to their contemporaries just why God's promises to David and Jerusalem seem to have been broken. Note the reference again to the 'gates of this house' (v. 4) and see the comments on 19:14—20:6 (pp. 104–105) concerning the way in which they symbolize the need for choice.

The end of the royal line

Gilead (v. 6) was the rather rocky and hilly terrain to the east of the river Jordan between Galilee and the Dead Sea—much of the territory of the modern kingdom of Jordan. Its valleys, however, sheltered fine plantations of trees, famous for their grandeur as well as their medicinal properties (8:22; 46:11). The cedars of the lower slopes of the mountain range of Lebanon, to the north of Israel, were renowned for their height and splendour. There is irony in the threat (vv. 6–8) that, just as they are felled for their timber, so God will fell the royal house and cities of Judah, for the royal palace and temple had been built with timber from just these trees (1 Kings 5:6; 7:1–2). An earlier prophet had seen the cedars of Lebanon as a symbol of all that is falsely pretentious in human pride and self-esteem (Isaiah 2:12–17). The royal house of Judah had forgotten its God-given task and its utter dependence on his power, and made its own wealth and splendour its chief end.

Jerusalem, an object of derision

The prediction of the amazement and scorn that the sight of the ruins of the formerly great and beautiful city will evoke (vv. 8–9) echoes almost exactly the words of 1 Kings 9:8–9, and has already been hinted at in Jeremiah 19:8. The city that had been sought by God as his own dwelling (Psalm 132:13–18) will be abandoned by him. There is nothing sadder than the waste of a life, or an institution, which has the potential to be of service to God.

A PRAYER

To serve the present age,
My calling to fulfil;
O may it all my powers engage
To do my Master's will!
Help me to watch and pray,
And on Thyself rely,
And let me ne'er my trust betray,
But press to realms on high.

Charles Wesley (1707–88)

The WRONG KIND of ROYAL GRANDEUR

The fate of Shallum

The 'royal' theme is continued throughout this passage, which contains three poetic passages relating to unnamed individuals (vv. 10, 13–17, 18–19), while two prose sections (vv. 11–12, 18) link them implicitly or explicitly to particular kings. 'Shallum', son of Josiah, is called 'Jehoahaz' in 2 Kings 23:31–33. Perhaps Shallum was his personal name and Jehoahaz his throne name. 2 Kings 23:30–33 tells us that Jehoahaz became king on the death of his father at the hands of the Egyptians. The 'people of the land' put him on the throne, but for some reason the Egyptians deposed him and carried him away into exile after only three months' reign.

Attack on King Jehoiakim

The Egyptians replaced Jehoahaz with his older brother, Jehoiakim, named by them as a sign of his dependence on them (2 Kings 23:34–35). The same passage tells us that Jehoiakim had to levy huge taxes to pay the indemnity laid on him by the Egyptians, and governments which have to raise heavy taxes are seldom popular. However, this passage also charges him with grandiose building schemes which must have imposed still heavier burdens on his subjects. It is of great significance that verse 13 speaks of Jehoiakim's forcing his 'neighbours' (so NRSV) to work for nothing, for in Israel the king was not meant to be a grand overlord bearing down on his 'subjects'. He and his people were 'kinsmen' (Deuteronomy 17:15), and this is underscored in verse 18 in which it is said that Jehoiakim will die unlamented. No one will say 'Alas, my brother (or sister)', for his treatment of his subjects has not been as though they were members of the same covenant family of God. What a contrast he posed to his father, Josiah, who had lived well enough but for whom the interests of his people came first.

Destined for exile

In the Hebrew of verses 20–23, the one being called on to 'go up' and 'cry out' is addressed in the feminine second person singular. It would seem therefore that this section is a call to the whole community of Jerusalem, rather than to any particular king. They are to cry out in Lebanon, to the north of Israel; in Bashan, which is a rich, fertile area to the east of the Jordan; and in Abarim, also across the Jordan, but further south, in the territory of Moab. Just why these regions were singled out is not clear. Both Lebanon with its cedars and Bashan with its lush pastures (Amos 4:1) were areas of great riches. The mention of Lebanon here may link it with the false pomp of Jehoiakim (v. 15) and the threat to the community in verses 6–7. Thus its name might evoke thoughts of reliance on foreign powers and of human claims to riches and power, as might the mention of that other source of riches, Bashan. The Israelites had once encamped at Abarim (Numbers 33:47–48) and it was from there that Moses had viewed the promised land (Numbers 27:12; Deuteronomy 32:49). So perhaps all three places symbolize elements in their history of which they were proud. They would speak of that 'prosperity' in past times when God 'spoke' to them (v. 21). Now, however, Israel will have only their bitter fate to lament there because they had not listened to God's voice when they enjoyed the fruits of his works on their behalf.

The 'royal' theme of this whole section is maintained in the threat to their 'shepherds'—that is, 'kings' (v. 22)—now themselves to be 'shepherded' away in a veritable whirlwind of judgment. The 'lovers' referred to in verses 20 and 22 may refer to their worship of other gods (compare 2:23–25), or to the other nations, such as Lebanon, whose protection they had sought in alliances. But Lebanon, where the exiled Israelites are called on to cry out in distress (v. 20), will itself be destroyed and will 'groan' (probable reading) in anguish (v. 23).

A PRAYER

Lord, may I see all I meet today, who are in need, as my family, and serve them in your name as Parent. Amen

The END of the LINE of DAVID

God rejects Jehoiachin

It is difficult to exaggerate the emphasis given to the divine rejection of King Jehoiachin (like Jehoahaz, 22:11, he seems to have had another name, Coniah). God affirms it with a solemn oath taken on his very existence (v. 24). Jehoiachin was the son of Jehoiakim, who had been installed by Nebuchadrezzar as his puppet-king but who had rebelled (2 Kings 24:1–7). On his father's death, Jehoiachin succeeded him to the throne, but ruled for only three months before Nebuchadrezzar arrived to avenge Jehoiakim's rebellion. In view of all that had gone before, Jehoiachin wisely submitted without a fight once Nebuchadrezzar himself had arrived, and was taken away captive into Babylon with his royal family and many of the leading citizens, this being the first major deportation into exile in the year 597BC (2 Kings 24:10–17). As we have seen, Zedekiah was then placed on the throne (see Jeremiah 21:1–10 and comments on pp. 108–109).

Perhaps because he had submitted without a struggle to the end, Jehoiachin seems to have been treated generously by the Babylonians, ultimately being released from prison and given some kind of royal honour (2 Kings 25:27–30; Jeremiah 52:31–34). This may have led some to regard him as the 'real' king—a kind of 'king-over-the-water', as it were. Certainly, Hananiah was one prophet who voiced hopes for his ultimate return and the renewal of the rule of the Davidic line (28:1–4). Even after the exile, the appointment of Zerubbabel, a grandson of Jehoiachin (1 Chronicles 3:17–19; compare Haggai 1:1), as governor of Judah seems to have aroused great hopes for the post-exilic prophet Haggai, who applies to him the very term 'signet-ring' which is used in our passage of Jehoiachin (v. 24; Haggai 2:20–23).

Verses 24–27 reject such hopes as emphatically as Jeremiah was to do again later in reply to Hananiah (28:12–16). God will reject Jehoiachin in the way he would tear a signet-ring from his finger. A signet-ring was used to engrave in wax the seal of a document or letter, so stamping it with the authority of the sender. Jezebel had sealed up letters with her husband's signet-ring, so apparently giving them King Ahab's authority (1 Kings 21:8). So the image is a powerful expression of the divinely appointed role of the Davidic king who is said, thereby, to rule in God's name and with his authority, commissioned to carry out God's purposes for his people. But Jehoiachin will be discarded. No longer bearing God's authority to rule, he will be given into the power of the Babylonians along with the queen mother (2 Kings 24:12) and exiled, an exile from which they will never return (vv. 26–27).

Why was Jehoiachin rejected?

Considering that Jehoiachin reigned for only three months, such threats from the prophet must have led to some ask, 'Why?' Why should someone who can hardly have done much wrong in such a short timespan be thrown out like a broken pot? (v. 28). Both the reference to the queen mother (v. 26) and the strong assertion that none of his descendants would ever sit on the throne (v. 30) suggest that God was rejecting not only Jehoiachin but the whole Davidic line, for the evils it had committed and the right action it had failed to produce (22:13–17). The passage is, therefore, really an illustration of the truth already proclaimed by the symbolism of the potter (18:1–11). If a royal line, or any institution, fails to serve God's purpose, then God can discard that instrument and begin again with another. This gives the clue to understanding the promises concerning a renewal of the Davidic line elsewhere in Jeremiah (23:5–6; 33:14–16). Any such line in the future will mark a new beginning. The old one will have been discarded. It is in this sense that verse 30 must speak of Jehoiachin as 'childless'. He did in fact have children, as we have seen. But, from the point of view of the continuing historic Davidic succession, he might just as well be regarded as 'childless'.

FOR MEDITATION

I have given myself, all that I am and have, to God…
Now henceforth I am not to act in any respect as my own. I shall
act as my own, if I ever make use of any of my powers to anything
that is not the glory of God.

Jonathan Edwards, diary entry for 12 January 1723

GOD, *the* GOOD SHEPHERD

The failure of Israel's kings

This whole passage rounds off the section of the book dealing with the kings of Israel and Judah which began in chapter 21. It opens with a general indictment of them all collectively, rather than identifying any specific individual as in the preceding chapters. The term 'shepherd' was a natural and widespread way of referring to kings in times when the king embodied in his own person and role all that is now vested in 'government'. The link between David's two roles as 'shepherd' is made in Psalm 78:70–71.

Verse 2 contains a play on the Hebrew word *paqad* which means 'to visit' in both a good and bad sense. It can mean 'to take care of' in the sense of watching carefully over another, but it can also be used when one 'visits' another in punishment. Because the 'shepherds' failed 'to take care' of God's flock, God now 'will take care of them', as the modern English idiom has it. They have treated as their own and for their own profit those whom God describes as 'my people'.

God will take care of his flock

With the failure of the historical line of Davidic kings, the break-up of the kingdom, and the exile to which this failure led, the way is open for hope, but a hope now rooted in God alone. He will gather his people from all the lands to which they have been taken, and to which they have fled in panic, and bring them back to experience a new era of peace and prosperity (v. 3). He will provide shepherds who will truly care for them (v. 4). This evocative picture of God as 'the good shepherd' has always exercised enormous power. It is the theme of Ezekiel 34, which elaborates the central theme of this passage at much greater length. Psalm 23, which begins 'The Lord is my shepherd', must be one of the best-known and best-loved of all the Psalms, and has itself influenced some of the finest hymns. And the theme is taken up in John 10 where it provides one of the most striking in the series of 'I am' sayings of Jesus in the fourth Gospel.

A new Davidic line

The promise of a 'shoot' (vv. 5–6) springing from a tree that has been cut down influenced a good deal of hope after the failure of the historic Davidic line. It occurs in Isaiah 11:1 (where a different Hebrew word is used), and the term was applied to Zerubbabel after the exile (Zechariah 3:8; 6:12). The promise here is that this new Davidic line will govern with exactly the kind of 'right' and 'just' rule that the first one was called to exercise (21:12; 22:13, 15–16), but in which it so lamentably failed (10:21; 22:22). It is just possible that there is an ironic allusion to Zedekiah in verse 6, for his name means 'Yahweh is my righteousness'. The future king will be in deed that which such earlier kings were only in name.

A promise of a new work by God

Verses 7–8 appear in almost the same form at 16:14–15 (see comments on p. 91). It is a daring picture, since the deliverance of their fathers by God was, for Jews of every age, the great theme of Israel's faith and worship. They are challenged, however, to believe that a 'new Exodus' will take place, in which they will experience God's power and grace for themselves in a new way. This is the theme of the great prophet of the exile who gave us Isaiah 40—55 (see especially Isaiah 43:16–21). God's great saving acts in the past are the foundation on which all faith is built. But the challenge in every age is to be open to what he is doing now. The historic Davidic line was not to be renewed after the exile, however, so passages such as this inspired the hope of a future 'Messiah' ('anointed one').

A PRAYER

O God, I thank you for all that you have done for your people in every age. But may I be so open to you that you will become new to me every day, and give me eyes to see all that you are doing in the world now. Amen

SIGNS *that* BETRAY FALSE PROPHETS

Rottenness at the nation's heart

The opening words of verse 9, 'Concerning the prophets', form a heading for the remainder of the chapter which, after the section dealing with the kings (21:1—23:8), brings together a number of sayings about the prophets. Jeremiah was not the only prophet active at the time and the problem for his hearers, as for those who came afterwards, was, 'When different prophets say different things, how can you tell who is telling the truth?'

Jeremiah sees the false prophets as both symptom and cause of the nation's malaise. It is rotten at its very core, for nothing could be more central than the temple, itself the place of God's dwelling among his people, where worship was supposed to maintain an open channel between God and nation. Yet its divinely appointed guardians, both priests and prophets, are morally and spiritually rotten. Their 'adultery' (v. 10) is probably here a reference to the religious apostasy by which they practise Baal worship alongside that of Yahweh (compare v. 13; 3:1–5). Ironically, the Baal cult was one of fertility, designed to produce plentiful crops and prosperity. Yet the opposite has happened. The land appears cursed and its pastures withered (v. 10).

In these verses one striking sign of the true prophet appears— Jeremiah's intense suffering for his people and his sense of the burden of God's word (v. 9). It is exactly the opposite of the charge Amos brought against leaders indifferent to everything but their own enjoyment and well-being, when he said of them, 'They have not made themselves sick over the destruction of Joseph' (Amos 6:6, my translation).

Unholy lives

Verses 13–15 introduce another 'test' by which to differentiate between true and false prophecy. That is, 'What kind of lifestyle do they follow?' Too many of the prophets of his time Jeremiah saw as living lives of open immorality (the 'adultery' of verse 14 must here be literal) and, by their own example and easygoing preaching, encouraging wrongdoing in others. The result is that people are as indifferent to calls to repent as were the inhabitants of Sodom and Gomorrah, those legendary examples of wickedness (Genesis 13:10–13; Isaiah 1:10). Jesus was later to say, 'You will know them by their fruits' (Matthew 7:20), the exact message of these verses in Jeremiah.

Inventing their own message

We have seen more than one instance when Jeremiah felt at odds with the heavy message he had to bring (15:17–18; 20:8). Small wonder that some were not prepared for such a cost and found it easier to trim their sails to the wind of popular feeling (vv. 16–17). They could always cite God's electing, covenant mercy by which he had chosen Israel as his own people, and had made eternal promises concerning the Davidic king and the holy city of Jerusalem (Psalm 132:11–18). What they forgot was that such promises were conditional upon their obedience, and that the covenant contained threats as well as promises of blessing (Deuteronomy 28:1–68). It is always tempting to adapt the message in order to be a popular messenger.

Not seeking God

One reason why prophets speak only their own ideas is that they have not listened to what God is saying; they have not 'stood in the council of the Lord' (vv. 18, 22). This is a picture of God in heaven, surrounded by angelic messengers who listen to what he says and then go and discharge his mission on earth. One example of a true prophet being admitted to the council is that of Micaiah (1 Kings 22:5–23). The range of meaning of the Hebrew word *amad* ('stand') is significant here. It can indicate 'standing still' (Joshua 10:13); 'waiting', as opposed to rushing in headlong (Joshua 10:18–19); 'abiding', or 'enduring' (Psalm 102:26) and 'sticking to a task' (Ruth 2:7). All these qualities are needed by those who would truly interpret God to their contemporaries. A quiet listening in the depths of silent communion with God can save a great number of ill-considered words and rash, harmful actions.

FOR MEDITATION

Breathe through the heats of our desire
Thy coolness and Thy balm;
Let sense be dumb, let flesh retire;
Speak through the earthquake, wind, and fire,
O still small voice of calm!

J.G. Whittier (1807–92)

GOD'S WORD IS LIKE *a* HAMMER

Everything is open to God

Verses 23–24 appear to interrupt the section on prophecy that began at 23:9 with its heading 'Concerning the prophets'. Nevertheless, with its powerful statement that everything on earth is open to God, even the inner thoughts and motives of the mind and heart (compare 17:10), it asserts that God is not fooled by the correct formulae and plausible words of 'false' prophets, however hard it may be for their listeners to distinguish between 'true' and 'false'. Verse 23 might seem to suggest that God is not near at hand but only far above all human affairs. It probably means that God is both, in fact. He is not only near at hand but is also transcendent, enthroned above all the earth and able to see everything that is going on.

That God is both the Sovereign Lord, in whose hands are all the affairs of the universe, and yet also the close, intimate friend of each individual in their daily life, has always been a source of great comfort for faith. To emphasize only his nearness can be to overstress a familiarity which dispenses with true reverence and trivializes God. To overstress his loftiness may be to lose the warmth and inner experience of the One who has created and redeemed us individually and draws near to share our innermost life with us.

Fancy dreams

After the warning of verses 23–24, we return to the theme of 'false prophecy'. In this case the charge is that such prophets have 'dreamed dreams' (v. 25). Is the charge against them that dreams are always false substitutes for the 'true' word of God? This would be strange because some traditions in the Old Testament do reckon that God can reveal insights through dreams. Joseph's own dreams came true and he had the skill to interpret Pharaoh's dream, just as Daniel's skill in the same art was believed to have been given him by God (Daniel 1:17; 2:20–23). Even in New Testament times it was believed that God could sometimes make his mind known through a dream (Matthew 2:12). One passage that deals with the issue of false prophecy is Deuteronomy 13:1–6, where it is the content and consequence of a prophecy, whether given by word alone or by dream, which determines its truth or falsity. If it leads its hearers away from God, then it is false. That is what is being said here. These 'false' dreamers 'plan to make my people forget my name' (v. 27). Not the form but the substance of the prophecy is what counts. All true revelation will make God more real to those who hear and bring them closer to him. This test of the claims of those who maintain that God has revealed something to them remains relevant and necessary for the people of God in all ages. The authentic word of God has a power to burn up evil and hammer home the conviction that leads to repentance and faith. Mere fancies serve no purpose but that of ornament or titillation.

Second-hand words

Verses 30–32 bring yet another test of the false prophet. Whether they utter oracles ('words' in v. 30) or recount 'dreams', those who have not heard the word of God for themselves have to fall back on the second-hand peddling of truths they have heard from others but never made their own. That does not mean that even God's messengers do not learn from each other. We have seen how much Jeremiah gained from Hosea, and most of the prophets reveal a debt to those who had gone before, just as Ezekiel did to Jeremiah himself. Furthermore, 'tradition' is a bedrock of faith for the people of God in every age. But the words of others who have gone before us, the great words of the creeds from the past, have to be made our own in our personal experience if they are ever to be sounded with authority from our lips. Merely to repeat the dogma and words of bygone generations is to reduce God's truth to the counterfeit coinage of cliché and parrot-cry.

FOR PRAYER

And make us to go on to know,
With nobler powers conferred,
The Lord hath yet more light and truth
To break forth from his word.

George Rawson, based on words of John Robinson
and others about to sail in the *Mayflower*, 1620

HUMAN WORDS & GOD'S WORD

Who is the burden?

The section 'Concerning the prophets' that began at verse 9 ends with this passage, perhaps one of the most difficult to understand in the whole book. Certain textual difficulties, together with problems of knowing always who is speaking, or who is being addressed or spoken about, combine to make interpretation hazardous. How hazardous is demonstrated by the variety of translations of the text to be found in different English versions, and in the diverging exegesis offered by various commentators. It may be that the passage has developed a good deal in the course of transmission, and that various points have been developed at different times connected with the theme of 'the burden of the Lord'. All we can do is to try to disentangle certain strands in the text as we have it, but humbly recognize that, in the end, the passage may well preserve some of its secrets.

The theme begins reasonably clearly with the question asked of the prophet, 'What is the burden of the Lord?' (v. 33). The Hebrew word *massa* is a term often used of prophetic oracles. It comes from a verbal root meaning 'to lift', and the noun means 'what is lifted', hence 'a burden'. Given the context of the chapter as a whole, it may well be that the question is being asked sneeringly of Jeremiah by those who were used to hearing, or uttering, oracles assuring the community of God's promises of protection and victory (23:17). By contrast, Jeremiah's repeated warnings of judgment were seen as a gloomy and burdensome message, and one that they could safely mock because his dire predictions never seemed to come to pass (20:7–8). The term was used quite often to denote oracles of judgment (2 Kings 9:25–26; Habakkuk 1:1; Isaiah 14:28–31), although not always (Zechariah 12:1). The context of the section on prophecy as a whole, however, makes such an understanding intelligible here. The question is thus a mocking one, which denies true prophetic authority to Jeremiah and rejects warnings of God's judgment for their sins. The prophet's response is forthright. It is not God who is putting a burden on them but they who are 'burdening' God by their stubborn wilfulness.

This makes verses 35 and 37 intelligible. The people should, instead of sneeringly making fun of the prophet and his robustly unpopular message, be asking in all seriousness, 'What is God really saying to us in this situation?' A sincere and true openness to the word of God is the only way of ceasing to be a burden on him and of allowing themselves to be truly 'carried' by him (23:3).

False 'messengers' of God

Interspersed with these warnings to the general public, as it were, are words which seem more fittingly directed at those who claim to be 'prophets' and claim to be true bearers of the 'burden' of God's word. These false claimants (v. 34) should stop their activities immediately (v. 36), for their easygoing messages of assurance to evildoers (compare 23:17) are nothing but their own 'word' (v. 36; compare 23:16). Their claim to be bearers of the *massa* of God is false because God has not commissioned them (v. 38; compare 23:21–22). Ironically, God's judgment on them is that he will indeed 'bear them up' (with a slight emendation of the text) but, far from carrying them home as the true Shepherd promises to do (23:3), he will cast them and the people who followed them away into the darkness of judgment and exile (vv. 39–40).

If we thus disentangle these two strands in the passage, seeing one as being addressed to the wider public who heard Jeremiah's preaching but mockingly rejected it, and the other as concerning the false prophets who wrongly claimed to be bearers of the prophetic *massa*, we can see that the section on 'false prophecy' ends with a reminder that 'preaching' is a two-way enterprise. Authentic preaching involves the openness and sincerity of those who proclaim God's word, but, to become God's living and effective word in the life of a community, it depends on openness and sincerity in those who hear it.

A PRAYER

Lord speak to me, that I may speak
In living echoes of Thy tone.

Frances Ridley Havergal (1836–79)

GOOD & BAD FIGS

The setting for the vision

The vision of Jeremiah recorded in this chapter recalls those of the almond tree and the boiling cauldron in 1:11–17. All show similarities to the visions of Amos (Amos 7:1–9; 8:1–3). In each, God 'shows' the prophet something, quite possibly a perfectly ordinary scene, and questions him on what he sees. The prophet's answer is followed by an insight into the deeper significance of the scene or event. The setting of this vision is said to be after Nebuchadrezzar had taken King Jehoiachin and his entourage into exile in 597BC (v. 1; see 22:24–30; 2 Kings 24:10–17). Zedekiah was placed on the throne as a puppet-king but, before long, was induced into rebellion against Babylon by a pro-Egyptian party who believed that Egypt would help the Israelites to throw off the Babylonian yoke. In the event, the Egyptians offered no effective help and Babylon's revenge was swift and savage (v. 8; 21:1–7; 2 Kings 24:17—25:7). This was to lead directly to the further siege of Jerusalem, its capture, destruction and more extended exile in 586BC. Even so, there were those in the pro-Egyptian party who remained hopeful, but, when their policies proved futile, they too had to leave and chose to go to Egypt (v. 8; 2 Kings 25:22–26; Jeremiah 41:1–12; 43:4–7).

Misplaced confidence

What Jeremiah 'sees' are two baskets of figs placed before the temple, which is to say before God himself, since that was his dwelling place. They had been sorted so that in one basket was fruit of great delicacy while in the other only that which was unfit for consumption. Israel had already been likened to a fig tree in Hosea, where God says, 'Like the first fruit on the fig tree, in its first season, I saw your ancestors' (Hosea 9:10). Here the good figs are 'like first-ripe figs' (v. 2), which suggests that they represent the 'true' Israel, whereas Jeremiah has already seen Israel as under God's judgment because they had failed to produce the fruit on the 'fig tree' for which he looked (8:13). So, the people who went into exile with Jehoiachin are the 'true Israel' (vv. 4–7), while those who remained in Judah or went to Egypt would prove to be the 'false Israel' which fails to produce the fruit for which God looked, and which will therefore be judged (vv. 8–10).

If we ask what lies behind such a distinction of fate for the two groups, then we must set this vision in the context of the prophet's teaching as a whole. Then we see that there is more here than a purely arbitrary exercise of divine 'predestination'. Jeremiah was convinced that, because of the nation's sin, judgment was inevitable. The present state would fall and Babylon would be God's instrument in bringing about that fall. The only sensible course therefore was to submit to the inevitable. Only then, on the other side of judgment, would there be the chance of a new beginning, this time a beginning made possible by the divine initiative alone, when God would intervene to give his people a new heart (v. 7) and bring them back in both a literal, geographical sense to the land he had promised their fathers, and in a spiritual sense—that they would come back to him and serve him alone. That is why, from the first, his ministry was to be one of 'pulling down and plucking out' as well as of 'planting and building up' (v. 6; compare 1:10).

But those who thought to stave off this inevitable judgment by expedient military and political alliances with Egypt failed utterly to see the true depth of the nation's need. They were trying to staunch a fatal haemorrhage with sticking plasters. Further, they were placing their confidence in their own guile and sagacity, as well as in other human powers. For the prophet, there is only one object of true and sure confidence—and that is in God alone.

A PRAYER

O Thou, from whom to be turned is to fall,
To whom to be turned is to rise,
And in whom to stand is to abide for ever:
Grant us in all our duties thy help,
In all our perplexities thy guidance,
In all our dangers thy protection,
And in all our sorrows thy peace,
Through Jesus Christ our Lord. Amen

Augustine of Hippo (354–430)

REASONS *for* GOD'S JUDGMENT

This passage not only spells out the theology that lay behind the vision of the good and bad figs in chapter 24 (see comments on pp. 124–125), but also serves as a summary of Jeremiah's preaching and prophetic activity to the point where the threat from Babylon was beginning to become ominously obvious.

The date of this 'word' is 'the fourth year of king Jehoiakim' (v. 1), that is, 605/4BC. That is also the date given for the dictation of God's words by Jeremiah to Baruch, to be inscribed on to a scroll (36:1). The point is that it is not only the fourth year of Jehoiakim, but it is also the year that sees Nebuchadrezzar firmly established on the throne of Babylon (v. 1). That is why this is such a pivotal moment, when the warnings that Jeremiah had so persistently given, and which had been laughed out of court with equal persistence (17:15; 20:7–8), were all too likely to be fulfilled. The reference back to 'the thirteenth year of Josiah' in verse 3 is to the year given in 1:2 for the date of Jeremiah's call to be a prophet, 627BC. Thus this section acts as a kind of resumé of his ministry. Indeed, with its reference to 'this book' in verse 13, it may be intended to summarize all that was written there.

Jeremiah's message

Many of the main themes of Jeremiah's teaching that we have encountered in this first section of the book are to be found here. God has continuously spoken to his people through him and other 'true' prophets (vv. 3–4; 7:25). Those prophets have warned the people against religious apostasy (vv. 5–6; 2:23–28). They have called them to repentance, with the promise that, if only they would listen, God would avert judgment (v. 6; 4:1–2). But the people have refused to listen (v. 7; 6:16–17). The consequence is that judgment is coming from God at the hands of an alien power, a 'foe from the north' (vv. 8–9; 6:1, 22). The people will be exiled from the land and all signs of its joyful occupation will be extinguished (vv. 9–11; 15:5–9). Here the exile is said to be for 'seventy years' (v. 12; 29:10). This is not meant to be a literal calendrical calculation. It means that it will be no quick affair. There are therefore no grounds for shallow optimism. The exile will span at least two generations: that is the sense given to the number here and in 29:4–10.

Nebuchadrezzar, God's 'servant'

It is remarkable that the Babylonian king is referred to by God as 'my servant' (v. 9). This does not mean that he was a worshipper of Yahweh, or that he had any intention in his imperial expansion of furthering Yahweh's purposes. Yet the prophet who had been reminded at his call that his ministry was to 'the nations' (1:10, and see comments on pp. 18–19) is shown that God's sovereign power and redemptive purposes extend beyond the boundaries of Israel. God is not Israel's private property. The same point is made later, towards the end of the exile, by another prophet through whom God refers to the Persian king, Cyrus, as 'my shepherd' (Isaiah 44:28) and even as 'his Messiah' ('anointed', Isaiah 45:1), both royal titles given to Yahweh's king in Israel. This seems to have got the prophet into some bother from his stricter hearers, for in Isaiah 45:9–13 he portrays God refuting those who argue that he could not possibly use such a man. It is always tempting for the people of God to want to 'domesticate' him. God is not the God of the Church only but of all the world, and we should recognize thankfully that he often carries out his purposes of love and good through those who do not acknowledge him—or who do not use the words of faith or the forms of worship that we think essential.

FOR MEDITATION

The first great epoch in a Christian's life... is when there breaks into his mind some sense that Christ has a purpose for mankind, a purpose beyond him and his needs, beyond the churches and their creeds, beyond heaven and its saints—a purpose which embraces every man and woman born, every kindred and nation formed, which regards not their spiritual health alone, but their welfare in every part, their progress, their health, their work, their wages, their happiness in this present world.

Henry Drummond, *The Programme of Christianity*, 1882

The CUP *of* JUDGMENT

The oracles against the nations

This passage is most fittingly seen as an introduction to the oracles against the nations in chapters 46—51. Whatever the case with Jeremiah's other prophetic actions, the impracticality of this action means that it must be regarded as symbolic. The picture of God's judgment is often likened to his dispensing a 'cup' (Psalm 75:8). It is this concept of God as judging the wicked of the earth—typified all too often by oppressive nations and their rulers—which is to the fore here, rather than any crude nationalistic xenophobia. (For other examples of the image, see 51:7; Isaiah 51:17; Lamentations 4:21; Ezekiel 23:32; Habakkuk 2:16). The background to the picture may well be that of a host at a banquet, handing (usually) a special cup to favoured guests as a sign of honour, a picture here grotesquely reversed. Or it has been suggested that the background is the drinking of a cup in a trial by ordeal, in which it proves fatal only to the guilty (Numbers 5:23–28).

Judgment on 'the household of faith'

Another factor that delivers the 'oracles against the nations' in the book of Jeremiah from being mere xenophobic rantings against foreigners is that they come in the context of a book dedicated mainly to attacks on the wickedness God finds among his own people. And that is stressed here at the beginning of the tirade (v. 18) and the end (v. 29). It is like Amos, who, after his denunciation of other peoples, confronts his Israelite hearers with the fact that God will judge them also for the same sins (Amos 1:3—2:16, especially 2:6–16; see 1 Peter 4:17).

Judgment on the nations

The section from verse 19 to verse 26 begins and ends with Israel's powerful neighbours, Egypt and Babylon, at whose hands they suffered so much. But doubtless, their other neighbours mentioned here, some also traditional enemies, had at various times meted out to them treatment which would have lived long in bitter memories. Egypt was the land of oppression and bondage. Uz (v. 20), where Job lived (Job 1:1), is otherwise unknown to us. The Philistine cities are also mentioned (v. 21). These people, representatives of the advanced civilization of the Aegean islands (the use of their name as examples of inartistic vandals is one of the cruel ironies of history), arrived on the south-western shore of Palestine (today's Gaza Strip) at about the time that the Israelites were beginning to set up a united kingdom of their own. Naturally, warfare was common until David largely subdued them and incorporated them into his kingdom. The Phoenicians (Tyre and Sidon, v. 22) were powerful neighbours to the north-west, made wealthy by their commanding trading position on the Mediterranean coast. Wise Israelite kings kept them friendly by forging trade and political ties with them, sometimes cemented by royal marriages. Dedan, Tema and Buz (v. 23) were probably situated in north-western Arabia, from where Israel would have had contacts with them through the Bedouin tribes who roamed the desert areas (v. 24). Zimri (v. 25) is unknown to us, but Elam and Media were constituent parts of the powerful kingdoms to the north-east which played so significant a part in Israel's history. The climax comes with the reference to the king of Sheshach (v. 26), a cryptogram form of the name of the king of Babylon (51:41).

These are all examples of 'the kings of the north' (v. 26), that is, those nations whom God has used at one time or another to punish his own people in judgment, all thus symbolizing 'the foe from the north' (6:1). Yet, as verses 12–14 had predicted, the fact that God had used them for his purpose would in no way spare them from punishment for their neglect of him and contempt for his laws. A century earlier, Isaiah had made the same point about Assyria (Isaiah 10:5–19).

A PRAYER

Lord, I find it easy to see, and judge, the failings of others. Show me my own faults, and forgive them and help me to overcome them, so that I can continue to be an instrument you can use for your purposes of love in the world. Amen

GOD JUDGES *the* WHOLE WORLD

Drinking 'the cup of judgment'

These verses are closely linked with the preceding section on the 'cup' of Yahweh's judgment given to the nations, by their picture of judgment as the treading out of grapes (v. 30), God's legal dispute with the nations (v. 31), and the fate awaiting the kings ('shepherds', vv. 34–38). The final reference to the 'sword' (v. 38) also looks back to 25:16.

The passage draws on a number of traditional prophetic motifs. The picture of God roaring like a lion from his 'dwelling place' occurs in Amos 1:2 and Joel 3:16. For God's judgment being like the treading out of grapes, see Lamentations 1:15. It gains grim lifelikeness from the fact that wine-pressers became splashed and stained with the red juice of the grapes, as invaders become stained with the blood of their victims (Isaiah 63:1–3).

A further traditional prophetic feature is that of God bringing a lawsuit against those who have wronged him (v. 31; compare Hosea 4:1; Micah 6:2 and Jeremiah 2:9), in this case against Israel ('his fold', v. 30), and the nations.

In addition, a number of other themes and phrases common to Jeremiah are expressed. For verse 33, for example, see 8:2 and 16:4, while the section on 'the shepherds' (vv. 33–38) answers to passages such as 10:21 and 23:1–4.

What kind of God does this?

It is possible, then, that this whole passage draws on traditional cultic material, familiar from the worship of the Jerusalem temple, and that it has been put here, together with 25:15–29, as a kind of summary of Jeremiah's warnings to his own countrymen. It also serves as an introduction to the 'oracles against the nations' section which comes later in the Hebrew text (chs. 46—51), but occurs earlier in the book in the Septuagint.

Nevertheless, for all its echoes of Jeremiah's teaching, the passage by no means contains the whole of his message. While, as in 25: 15–29, it is made clear that God judges wickedness wherever he finds it, even among his own people (25:18; compare v. 30), there is nothing here of the intense agonizing of the prophet in his deep love and concern for his people, nor any of the thought that God's ultimate aim, the other side of judgment, is one of mercy and redemption. What are we, as modern readers, to make of such a picture of God?

First, it has to be said that God is a God of righteousness, and that there is such a thing as judgment. It would be intolerable if there were not, for then there would be no hope of an ultimate dealing with, and removal of, the large-scale injustice, inhumanity and oppression of some by others which continues to plague the human scene now, as in Jeremiah's day. If God did not care about evil, we would live in a hopeless universe. And, it must always be remembered, Jesus himself had some stern things to say on the theme of God's judgment.

But, for Christians, two of the pictures in verses 15–30 of this chapter of Jeremiah have acquired new overtones. One is the 'cup of judgment' in God's hand, which represents the true judgment that he, in his righteousness, must make on sin. But we recall Jesus praying on the eve of his death on the cross, 'My Father, if it is possible, let this cup pass from me; yet not what I want but what you want' (Matthew 26:39; Luke 22:42). The other picture is of the 'red blood' splattered when the grapes are crushed. The two pictures come together when Jesus hands the cup to his disciples and says, 'This cup that is poured out for you is the new covenant in my blood' (Luke 22:20; 1 Corinthians 11:25). The mystery is that God himself takes the cup in the suffering of Jesus and, because of that, the cup that is passed to us is 'the cup of salvation'. Such a truth about God is hinted at already in the book of Jeremiah. The awesome words of this passage must not be excised from the book, but neither must they be read apart from the context of that book or of the rest of the Bible as a whole.

FOR MEDITATION

Thine was the bitter price,
Ours is the free gift given;
Thine was the blood of sacrifice,
Ours is the wine of heaven.

Elizabeth Charles (1828–96)

The PROPHET'S WARNING & ITS RESPONSE

A new section of the book begins with chapter 26. Apart from 30:1 to 31:40, it consists mainly of prose accounts of Jeremiah's prophetic ministry and the response his message evoked. It has often been described as a 'prophetic biography' and its composition attributed to Baruch, Jeremiah's companion and amanuensis (32:12–16; 36:4–8). Others have suggested, however, that while such a narrative may have constituted the basis for these chapters, their present form owes much to Deuteronomistic editors in the time of the exile. Their aim was to show *why* disaster had befallen Jerusalem and its temple, king and people (that is, because they had refused to hear and obey God's word spoken through a 'true' prophet), and also to call for a response of penitence and faith from the exiles so that they might experience again the covenant mercies of God.

The temple sermon

Verse 2 seems to link this episode with the 'temple sermon' of chapter 7. However, verse 1 gives a more exact, although still general, historical context: 'At the beginning of the reign of King Jehoiakim' (who came to the throne in 609BC). The detailed contents of the original sermon, which specified just *which* commandments had been broken (7:5–6, 9), are summarized by the phrases 'to walk in my law' and 'heed the words of my servants the prophets' (vv. 4–5). The reference to the fate of Shiloh is repeated, however (v. 6; compare 7:12–14). Again, the originally more detailed description of the fate of Jerusalem if she remains disobedient (7:34) is summarized here by 'I will make this city a curse…' (v. 6).

Not surprisingly, representatives of the temple ('priests' and 'prophets', v. 7) and all the habitual worshippers who heard Jeremiah's words reacted angrily, on the 'shoot the messenger' principle. Hearing the rumpus, the 'civil' authorities, the 'princes' (vv. 10–11), representatives of the king under whose jurisdiction lay order in the temple precincts and the city at large, came to investigate. Lacking the authority to impose the death penalty themselves, the temple leaders accused Jeremiah of treason in prophesying 'against this city' (v. 11). (One is reminded of the trial of Jesus before Pilate at the instigation of the religious authorities of his day.) We have to remember that prophecy was seen not merely as 'announcing' something to come, but as actively setting powers in motion which would bring it about (see Numbers 22:6). The thrust of Jeremiah's words had been directed against the temple, but the fortunes of temple and city were so interwoven that the destruction of one implied the destruction of the other (v. 6), as indeed proved to be the case in 586BC.

Jeremiah, of course, said that the threat was conditional (vv. 3–4). The people had the opportunity to avoid the disaster by sincere repentance (compare Ezekiel 18:21–23). As Ezekiel said, God loves sinners and longs for them to be saved. In his grace he always offers a way of escaping judgment. Christians came to see that such a way of escape was provided in the life, death and resurrection of Jesus Christ—a 'way of escape' that people ignore at their peril (Hebrews 2:3).

Ambivalent judgment

The officials hold court by the 'New Gate' (v. 10). The only other mention of this gate is in 36:10 as the place where Baruch read the scroll of Jeremiah's words to the royal officials. The 'gate', which in this context means the open square inside it, is often mentioned as the place where judicial cases were heard (Amos 5:15). In this instance it is the priests and prophets, doubtless stung by the prophet's attacks on them, who pronounce Jeremiah guilty of treason and deserving of the death sentence. By their judgment of God's word and its messenger, they were in fact passing judgment on themselves. We need to be careful how and what we judge. Our preferences always show us for what we really are.

PRAYER

Lord, may I hear your voice, not only when you say what I want to hear, but also when you speak to challenge and rebuke me. Amen

The PROPHET'S—*and the* PEOPLE'S—LIFE *in the* BALANCE

The prophet's authority

No one could accuse Jeremiah of temporizing. Clearly on trial for his life, he unequivocally reaffirms his message. Perhaps the most important words are those with which he cites his authority: 'The Lord sent me to prophesy...' (v. 12). It is this conviction of acting under the divine compulsion that gives prophecy its authority and underlines the urgency of its message. It was the conviction of the first of the prophets whose words are recorded in a book: Amos says, 'The Lord God has spoken; who can but prophesy?' (Amos 3:8). Jeremiah has said that even when he tried to stop prophesying, an irresistible compulsion drew him on (20:9). He is full of scorn for the false prophets of whom God says, 'I did not send them, yet they ran. I did not speak to them, yet they prophesied' (23:21). A similar sort of compulsion led Martin Luther to say, 'Here stand I: I can do no other.' It has been the compulsion to mission for the people of God in every age.

Counsels of caution prevail

The civil leaders (the 'princes', v. 16) check the urge for revenge expressed by the outraged religious leaders whose proprietorial interests have been threatened by the prophet and his message. Again, it is similar to the trial of Jesus, where Pilate said to the priestly circles of his day, 'I find no crime in this man' (Luke 23:4).

Either 'the people' changed sides (v. 16; compare v. 8) or those mentioned here represent a wider cross-section of the population than those who were habitually concerned with the temple. The intervention of the princes does not necessarily mean that they accepted the truth of Jeremiah's preaching. In their view, it was politic to respect anyone who claimed to speak 'in the name of the Lord our God'.

In case there was any chance of their succumbing to pressure (as Pilate did), others recall the response of King Hezekiah a century earlier. Micah had brought a similar warning to the city of Jerusalem, but king and people had listened to what he said and repented, thus averting the threat, just as Jeremiah said it could happen now (26:3, 13). Interestingly, this is the only instance of one prophet being mentioned by name in another prophetic book in the Old Testament.

God's word rejected

There could be no starker contrast than the reactions of Hezekiah and Jehoiakim. Perhaps thwarted in his desire to have Jeremiah eliminated by the judicial fairness of the princes and the protection offered by powerful figures like Ahikam (v. 24), Jehoiakim vented his vindictiveness on another, perhaps less well-connected, prophet—Uriah. The mention of this otherwise unknown prophet reminds us that God had many of 'his servants the prophets' (26:5), and that there were those who were faithful to his word, of whose teaching and life no written record remains. Such was Jehoiakim's vindictiveness that, not content with silencing Uriah by causing him to escape to Egypt, he actively had him brought back and summarily executed. If Uriah was one of the early faithful prophetic 'martyrs', Jehoiakim was to illustrate all too clearly how wilful rejection of God's word always brings judgment, for the legacy he left his son and his kingdom was exile and destruction.

Those who serve God quietly

Uriah the prophet obviously lacked influential friends and evidently attracted none who recorded his words and passed them on, as Baruch and others did for Jeremiah. Ahikam was an official of some importance who exercised considerable influence in his time (2 Kings 22:12, 14). His son, Gedaliah, became governor after the fall of the monarchy (2 Kings 25:22). Yet both faithfully served God in their different ways. The purposes of God are carried forward in every age by the famous and the unknown. The important thing is faithfulness. The results can always be left to God.

PRAYER

O God, help me to be faithful and true to you in every part of my life today, knowing that my 'labour is not in vain in the Lord'
(1 Corinthians 15:58).

GOD—LORD *of the* NATIONS

An address to foreign envoys

The Hebrew of verse 1 reads, 'In the beginning of the reign of King Jehoiakim...'. Yet it is clear from what follows that the first deportation of 597BC has taken place and that Nebuchadrezzar has already plundered the city and the temple (27:16–22). Thus it seems that we must follow some Hebrew manuscripts and other ancient versions, as well as the opinion of most scholars, and read 'In the beginning of the reign of Zedekiah...' (so NRSV), particularly as chapter 28 links Hananiah's activity with that of Jeremiah here and places the events in Zedekiah's reign.

This reading is made the more likely by the statement in 51:59 that Zedekiah went to Babylon in the fourth year of his reign (28:1). The delegation of ambassadors from Edom, Moab, Ammon, Tyre and Sidon to see Zedekiah (v. 3) has all the appearance of a move to discuss concerted action against Babylon. This plan was fiercely denounced by Jeremiah and evidently came to nothing, but it may have led to Zedekiah's own mission to Babylon to assure his political overlords that he was planning no such revolt.

An act of prophetic symbolism

Jeremiah is instructed to perform an act of prophetic symbolism in which he constructs and wears the kind of yoke used to harness and drive oxen (v. 2). We have seen other examples of the use of prophetic symbolism (see 13:1–11 and comment on pp. 74–75). They were designed not merely as dramatic 'visual aids' but, as with the spoken prophetic word, as a means of bringing about the very thing symbolized. The Hebrew of verse 3 reads 'send *them*' to the kings of the various nations, but it is unlikely that Jeremiah sent replicas of his yoke, so we should probably read just 'send' (NRSV 'send word')— that is, send the message which the symbolic act proclaimed.

That message is uncompromising and wholly consistent with all that the prophet has said up to this point. Babylon has been appointed by God for his purpose of judgment. Nebuchadrezzar is even spoken of as 'my servant' (v. 6), not because he worshipped

Yahweh but because he was unwittingly fulfilling God's purpose. Any human attempt to thwart Nebuchadrezzar is therefore an attempt to thwart God's plans.

We might have expected such a message to be addressed to God's own people, but here it is addressed to surrounding nations, each of whom sees itself as under the protection of its own god(s). Yet Jeremiah has been commissioned to speak to the 'nations' (1:5, 9–10). Nor is this an isolated instance of such a ministry by a prophet in the Old Testament: Elijah is sent by God to Syria (1 Kings 19:15–16), and all the major prophetic collections have sections containing oracles concerning foreign nations.

God, Lord of creation and of history

This is no diluted word that is given to the foreign envoys. It is the God of Israel who has created the whole earth and placed human beings and animals in it, and it is he who controls events and orders the rise and fall of nations (vv. 5–6). The (temporary) rule of Babylon (v. 7) is part of his greater purpose. The reference to Nebuchadrezzar's 'son and grandson' in verse 7 is a general statement rather than being literally true. Nebuchadrezzar was succeeded by his son Amel Marduk, the 'Evil-merodach' of the Bible (2 Kings 25:27; Jeremiah 52:31), but he was followed not by his son, but by his brother-in-law, Neriglissar. However, the prediction that Babylon's rule was to be of limited duration (compare 29:10) proved correct.

Evidently Judah had no monopoly on nationalistic and chauvinistic prophets (vv. 9–10). Nor is this surprising. The basic function of prophecy was seen to be that of support for the ruling powers and the achievement of national prosperity and success. As the example of Uriah showed (26:20–23), it took great courage to stand out against popular expectation and bring the uncomfortable and discomfiting truth from God.

FOR MEDITATION

Just as it is easy to lag behind God's leading when he calls us to some duty we find uncongenial, so it is easy to run before his leading when we want to foist some enthusiasm of our own off on him and legitimate it as 'God's will'.

NO HOPE APART *from* GOD

The challenge of the symbol of the yoke

Verse 12 confirms the view that it was Zedekiah (not Jehoiakim) who was addressed in verse 1 (see comments on pp. 136–137). It also brings home the symbolism of the prophet's action in making a yoke and wearing it (v. 2). The word of God to the king, and through him to all the courtiers and statesmen (the 'you' of the address is plural in Hebrew), is that it is God's plan to bring them under Babylonian rule. Rebellion against Nebuchadrezzar's rule is not only military and political suicide (v. 13) but rebellion against God, whose agents for judgment the Babylonians are. Thus the nationalist prophets who are falsely preaching imminent victory over the Babylonians are prophesying not only strategic folly but theological deception. They have not been commissioned by God (one sure sign of the 'true' prophet, 1:7; 23:21) and their so-called 'prophecies', if acted on, would prove a short cut to disaster.

No hope in the temple

Jeremiah brings substantially the same message to a wider audience, 'the priests and all the people' (v. 16). Now, however, that message includes a new twist. At one time the people had placed their confidence in the safety provided by the mere existence of the temple (7:4). Since it was God's 'dwelling place', it was unthinkable that it could be destroyed or that those who worshipped there would ever know military defeat. That confidence had proved sadly misplaced in 597BC (see 2 Kings 24:10–17), when the Babylonians had carried off some of the temple's sacred vessels as plunder. Yet apparently, to some, the very existence of those vessels, even in Babylon, represented some kind of continuity with the past and guarantee of its renewal. They still believed that there would be an early victory over Babylon, brought about miraculously by God, and that these vessels would be returned. Indeed, some had been left in Jerusalem (vv. 19–20; see 2 Kings 25:13–17). The vessels left behind included the pillars, Jachin and Boaz (v. 19; see 1 Kings 7:15–22), which probably commemorated God's choice of the Davidic dynasty and the divine establishment of palace and temple; the 'sea' (v. 19; 1 Kings 7: 23–26), a vast bronze container holding more than 10,000 gallons of water, probably symbolizing God's subduing of the waters of chaos at creation; and other bronze vessels. All these the prophets and their willing hearers saw as grounds of hope that God had not abandoned them. They were surely guarantees of immunity from any further judgment. It was exactly the kind of false confidence their predecessors had placed in the mere physical presence of the temple among them.

A call—and a threat

Jeremiah is clear: if they were any kind of true prophets, then far from plying their hearers with groundless and false hopes, they would be exercising that other vital prophetic role of praying for the people (v. 18). How often Jeremiah himself had undertaken this ministry. True prophets see, and address, people's real needs. They do not peddle false and shallow palliatives to a people whose sin is mortal and whose situation is dire. One test of true prophecy, indeed, is how far it addresses the deepest and most real of human needs.

Jeremiah warns that even the remaining temple vessels in which prophets and people placed such hopes would be carried away (v. 22), as indeed they were (2 Kings 25:13–17). Zedekiah himself was to suffer a dreadful fate (2 Kings 25:1–7).

It is always important for the people of God of every age to place their hope in God alone. Human achievements, even the structures and life of the Church, are effective sources of hope and power only in so far as they point beyond themselves to the One for whom they exist and who alone has made them possible.

FOR MEDITATION

Pride of man and earthly glory,
Sword and crown betray his trust;
What with toil and care he buildeth,
Tower and temple, fall to dust.
But God's power,
Hour by hour,
Is my temple and my tower.

Robert Bridges (1844–1930)

A CONFLICT *between* PROPHETS

The events narrated in chapter 28 mark a sequel to chapter 27. Verse 1 picks up the reference in 27:1 to 'the beginning of the reign of Zedekiah' (see comments on pp. 136, 138) but adds a note that all these events took place in the fourth year of Zedekiah's reign. 'In the beginning of' must therefore be tantamount to 'in the early part of' the reign of Zedekiah, a reign that lasted altogether eleven years (2 Kings 25:1). It has been pointed out that it would have taken some time for Zedekiah to become sufficiently established on the throne to arrange for a delegation from all the surrounding countries, and thoughts of revolt are unlikely to have formed immediately after the disaster of 597BC (so Nicholson).

A challenge from Hananiah

To patriotic and nationalistic prophets like Hananiah, the words and powerful symbolic action of Jeremiah recorded in chapter 27 must have seemed an outrage, not only announcing disaster to come on the people of God but actively helping to bring it about. It would have seemed a denial of God's promises and of his power to protect his people. Thus Hananiah announces exactly the opposite message, that God proposes to break the power of Babylon, not to impose it on his people. Indeed, so certain is he of this, and of its imminent fulfilment, that he speaks as though God has already done it (v. 2). In common with other prophets, he uses what is often called 'the prophetic perfect', in which a certain future event is spoken of as already having happened, so strongly is it fixed in the purpose of God. For good measure he also, like Jeremiah, performs an act of prophetic symbolism, in this case breaking the yoke (vv. 10–11) with which Jeremiah had signified the coming subservience to Babylon.

'Tests' of a true prophet

There is much that is mysterious in the account of Jeremiah's response to Hananiah (vv. 6–9). It seems as if he really does entertain at least a suspicion that this might be a genuine word from God, for in verse 6 he expresses the hope that Hananiah might be right. After all he has said—that judgment must first come on the nation and that salvation can lie only the other side of that judgment—it seems extraordinary that he should entertain Hananiah's message even for a moment. Some have suggested that his reply is mockingly ironic, but there is no clear indication of this in the text. Perhaps it indicates that, even for the prophet who 'stands in the council of the Lord' and whom the Lord 'sends', discovering the will of God is always a complex and difficult affair. Perhaps, further, it shows how, in his yearning for the well-being of his people, Jeremiah really does hope he has been mistaken in announcing the judgment that he never really wanted to proclaim (17:16). His doubts show, however, in his conviction that, in contrast to Hananiah's message of shallow optimism, the overwhelming testimony of the prophets is that when people remain unrepentant, God always acts in judgment (vv. 7–9). The onus of proof is on the one who feels confidently that all will be well for such a people (v. 9).

Jeremiah rejects Hananiah's message

In time, Jeremiah became convinced that Hananiah's word was not God's word to the people at this time. The Hebrew of verse 13 reads, 'You have broken wooden bars but you will make in their place bars of iron.' This is usually emended to read '(God) will make bars of iron', but the Hebrew is perfectly intelligible as it stands. To try to evade God's judgment and fail to repent is to put oneself in far greater danger. Hananiah, whom God has not 'sent' (v. 15), has lulled God's people into a sense of false security. His own judgment follows speedily, symbolizing the judgment to come on the nation as a whole (v. 17).

FOR MEDITATION

'Whom the Lord loves he chastens' (Hebrews 12:6, NKJV). It is far better to accept the discipline of a loving Father than to deny that there is anything wrong with us.

JEREMIAH'S LETTER *to the* EXILES

Submit to God's judgment

Apparently, there were false, nationalistic prophets like Hananiah among the exiles in Babylon, who were urging the Jews there to revolt in the belief that this would precipitate God's intervention and lead to an early return home. So counter was this to all that Jeremiah understood to be the purpose of God, in both judgment and deliverance, that he took advantage of the journey of a diplomatic mission to the Babylonian court (v. 1) to send a letter by highly placed and well-disposed officials (v. 3; see 26:24; 36:25). In it he warned against the shallow optimism of such prophets (vv. 8–9).

Some differences between the Hebrew and Greek texts of the letter suggest that various editions of it existed. Perhaps Jeremiah's original letter was adapted by the Deuteronomistic editors in Babylon to make it continuingly relevant to the unfolding situation there.

Nevertheless, there is nothing in the text as it stands that is inconsistent with Jeremiah's teaching. The exile is God's judgment on his people for their sin and it will last for a considerable time (the 'seventy years' of verse 10 is probably intended as a round number suggesting several generations). The prophet therefore advises the exiles to settle down, build houses, grow food and maintain the line by marrying and rearing children (vv. 5–6). The evidence of the book of Ezekiel suggests that they did settle in groups (Ezekiel 1:1; 8:1), such settlements being granted considerable freedom by their captors. There is even archaeological evidence for some commercial activity among them.

One is reminded of Paul's advice to the Christians in Thessalonica. Some of them had evidently misinterpreted his references to the return of Jesus as an excuse for giving up work, living on hand-outs and avoiding responsibilities as they waited excitedly for the end of the world. Paul tells them to settle down and maintain themselves by their work (2 Thessalonians 3:6–13). The people of God always live as citizens of two worlds and are called to discharge their responsibilities to both.

Pray for the peace of Babylon

Verse 7 is remarkable by any standards. Jews were used to the idea of praying for the peace of Jerusalem (Psalm 122:6–7). One exile must have spoken for many when, in his bitterness, he could manage only a curse against Babylon (Psalm 137:8–9).

There is, of course, a measure of self-interest in praying for the 'well-being' (*shalom*) of Babylon. Only those who have never lived under the threat, nor endured the reality, of civil unrest and war could undervalue the importance of civil order and stability for citizens and people of God alike. Nevertheless, a positive attitude, even towards pagan society, is a responsibility for the people of God of all ages and in all circumstances. Paul said that all governing authorities are 'ordained by God' (Romans 13:1) and must be obeyed wherever possible. Indeed, active and positive citizenship is the only kind of discipleship that can find warrant from the Bible.

God's plans for the future

After this call to oppose the false and shallow optimism of their prophets by facing creatively and positively the responsibilities of the present and the future, Jeremiah nevertheless points forward to God's ultimate plans for his people's 'well-being'. Just as now they are called upon actively to promote the *shalom* of their captors, so God plans *shalom* for his people (v. 11). But this apparent *volte face* is based not on caprice but on the consistent purpose to which Jeremiah had testified all along. The people were being judged for their sin, and only on the other side of that judgment could salvation come. When it did, it would consist not merely in a change of fortunes, a return to all the circumstances of the old Davidic kingdom, but in a moral and spiritual regeneration of the people, made possible by the grace of God. It will be when, with a change of heart (17:9), they seek God in reality that they will find him. Salvation will consist not merely in a physical change of location but in a change of heart (v. 13).

FOR PRAYER

Lord, I often blame my circumstances for my unhappiness. Give me that inward change by which I may find your purpose for myself and others in those circumstances, and use them creatively. Amen

Reactions *to* God's Word

False prophets in Babylon

Jeremiah's letter continues in verses 15 and 21–23 (for vv. 16–20 see below), naming two of the ringleaders among the false prophets who have been inciting the whole exiled community to insurrection (29:8–9) and whom some believe to have been truly raised up by God (v. 15). They are identified as Ahab and Zedekiah (v. 21, otherwise unknown to us). Jeremiah takes the view that if their rash, hotheaded militarism were to be taken seriously, it could threaten the whole Jewish community. In fact, Babylonian special agents were evidently quick enough to spot potential trouble, for the two were executed by burning and their fate subsequently became a cautionary example of misfortune, the subject of spiteful curses thereafter (vv. 21–22). Apparently their ill-founded enthusiasm for revolt was compounded by a colourful personal lifestyle (v. 23). As we have seen, it was not always as easy to identify which were the 'true' and which the 'false' prophets.

Denunciation of Zedekiah

Verses 16–20 do not appear in the Septuagint. They interrupt verses 15 and 21 and consist of an attack on Zedekiah and those who remained behind with him in Judah. As we have seen, these people also finally rebelled against Babylon and suffered the fate broadly predicted for them here (2 Kings 24:18—25:7). The description of them as 'bad figs' (v. 17) reminds us of chapter 24. The book of Jeremiah as a whole takes a pro-Babylonian exile stance, believing that the purposes of God for the future redemption of his people lay through them and not through those who remained in Judah.

Perhaps this parallel passage to chapter 24 was inserted here to correct the impression given by chapter 29 as a whole that all the fault for such misinterpretation of the will of God lay with the exiles.

Further exchanges of letters

It seems that men such as Ahab and Zedekiah were not alone in regarding as treacherous Jeremiah's warning that the exile would be a long one and that the proper attitude was to settle down and collaborate with Babylonian rule. Extremists they may have been, but Shemaiah, an otherwise unknown but obviously influential figure among the exiles, wrote letters critical of Jeremiah to a number of prominent people in Judah, including the priest, Zephaniah (vv. 24–25). Zephaniah figured in a number of important exchanges between the royal court and the prophet (21:1; 37:3). Here he is reminded in no uncertain terms of his responsibility to keep order in the temple precincts, which includes checking the babblings of any 'madmen' who prophesy (v. 26; compare the verdict of Hosea's hearers, Hosea 9:7). Shemaiah obviously regards the words of Jeremiah's letter to have been an example of such madness (vv. 27–28).

Zephaniah is reminded that he has been called to his office by God for just this purpose and that he is following an illustrious predecessor—none other than Jehoiada who, by implication, made a much better job of the priestly office. Poor Zephaniah would not be the last servant of God to be threatened by the example of the great man he was following!

He was at least honest enough to read the letter in full to Jeremiah (v. 29). Just what his motives were in doing so, we are not told. It would be nice to think that he was the honest, balanced and fair leader (perhaps even one in sympathy with Jeremiah's views) that some scholars have believed him to be. Unfortunately he was not to survive the coming disaster in 587BC of the fall of Jerusalem (2 Kings 25:18–21; Jeremiah 52:24–27). His action prompts the prophet to send another letter denouncing Shemaiah and warning him that, because he failed to recognize the word of God, no successor of his would live to see the ultimate salvation that that word promised (vv. 30–32).

A PRAYER

Lord, keep me faithful to you, even when the answers I want to my prayers seem a long time in coming. Amen

The PROMISE of DELIVERANCE

'Write down all the oracles'

These opening words of a new section (vv. 1–3) link back with chapter 29 and Jeremiah's prediction that God *would* deliver his people, but only after a long and painful period of judgment for their sins (29:10–14). It is not clear just how much material is included in the written 'book' that God commands Jeremiah to make. Most agree that it includes at least chapters 30—31, while some believe that it encompasses all of chapters 30—33, a section of Jeremiah united by its common theme of future hope, which scholars have given the title the 'Booklet of Consolation'. Its purpose was to preserve a reminder of the promises as a record for the much later time when they would be fulfilled (as in Isaiah 30:8). They would be a reminder that 'all' the words of the prophet had come true, not only the threats of judgment which are the predominant theme of most of chapters 1—26, but also the promises of future salvation the other side of judgment. The promises concern not only the exiles from Judah in Babylon but all the descendants of those who had been exiled earlier, by Assyria, from the northern kingdom of Israel (v. 3; see 2 Kings 17:1–6).

The horror of the tribulation

Verses 4–7 stress the full terror of the present time of defeat, destruction and exile, and so reinforce Jeremiah's warning that deliverance would come only after judgment. Its vividness is highlighted by the graphic picture of men behaving as though they were experiencing the pains of childbirth (v. 6). In some sense, the present time of distress indeed is like labour pains, and so it has been pictured by other prophets (for example, Isaiah 26:17–18). But deliverance is promised (v. 7).

An end to 'chastening'

The material in this chapter, although united round the central theme of hope, is very varied and disparate. Verse 8 is a direct address by God to the Israelites, promising an end to their time of forced servitude to foreigners. The Hebrew has God addressing them directly:

'I will break the yoke from *your* neck.' Usually this is emended to 'their' in English versions, so as to fit with the third person 'and strangers shall not again make servants of *him*' (that is, Judah) and the word 'they' in verse 9. It all looks rather an editorial mix! In any event, the sudden reference to David is unexpected in this context. Whether these are the words of Jeremiah or subsequent editors, who have extended an original 'core' of general promises with other material as events unfolded, it is now impossible to say. It is also extremely hazardous to try to date the material by the events to which they are supposed to refer. The language is general enough to apply in many different situations. Yet, while the promises may be general, their tenor is clear. Verse 8 promises an end to the servitude of exile and verse 9 envisages a restoration of the old Davidic kingdom embracing both the former northern and southern kingdoms of Israel and Judah. The release of the Davidic Jehoiachin from prison in Babylon (2 Kings 25:27–30) may have triggered this particular hope, but it is impossible to be certain.

Verse 10 is remarkably similar to the promises to the Babylonian exiles made in Isaiah 41:10; 43:1 and 44:2. All dispersed exiles will be brought home and all Israel (Jacob was seen as the 'father' of Israel: see Isaiah 41:8–10; Jeremiah 2:4) will live in peace and security (v. 10). God himself will break the power of their oppressors. Their present suffering has been intended as 'chastening', aimed at bringing them back to himself. Total destruction of his own people has never been God's intention (v. 11).

The promise of God to his people, 'I will be with you to save you' (v. 11), even in troubles brought about by their own fault, received powerful fulfilment in the life and death of Jesus, called 'Emmanuel', 'God with us'. The promise assured the exiles then, and all the 'exiled people of God' of all times since, that there can be no circumstances in which he abandons us and there are no trials through which he cannot work his redemption for us.

FOR MEDITATION

When through fiery trials thy pathway shall lie,
His grace all-sufficient shall be thy supply;
The flame shall not hurt thee, his only design
Thy dross to consume and thy gold to refine.

Attributed to Robert Keane in *Rippon's Selection of Hymns*, 1787

The HEALING *of* GOD'S PEOPLE

No physician but God

Verses 12–15 probe the present wounds of the community in painful detail and realism. Perhaps the first stage in any process of healing is adequate diagnosis. So great is the community's wound that it is inoperable (v. 12). In any event, there is no one who cares enough to investigate and so no one to offer any cure, even supposing that any (human) medicine could be effective in such a case (v. 13). This is a melancholy echo of 8:22.

All her so-called 'lovers' have forsaken her—an allusion to nations such as Egypt with whom Judah had sought military and political alliance. But such nations had no concern as such for the Israelites, who were merely pawns in a political power game and, once defeated, of no further use or interest.

In fact, it was God who dealt the blow to his people because of their sins (v. 14). It was he who used these nations as pawns for his purposes (v. 15).

The word 'therefore' at the beginning of verse 16 reads strangely, and some have sought to emend it or give it an adversative rather than a causative force ('yet', NEB; 'but', NIV). Nevertheless, the meaning 'therefore' can stand. It is *because* the oppressor nations have acted with utter self-regard from start to finish that they themselves will know the same fate as they meted out. It is *because* there is no medicine sufficiently effective, or physician capable and caring enough to help Judah in her mortal illness, that the way is open for God to show the healing grace of which he alone is capable (v. 17). 'Zion' appears to have become an 'outcast', but no one is ever cast out beyond the reach of God's grace.

Restoration of joy

In verses 18–22, some specific details are painted into the general sketch of God's future plans for his people outlined earlier in the chapter. The ruined homesteads will be rebuilt and the returned people will live in them again. The 'city' will be rebuilt. The word translated in RSV as 'palace' more often means 'citadel' or 'stronghold' (v. 18, so NRSV)—perhaps the main defensive point of a town, rather like a castle 'keep'. These will be restored in their customary place of prominence, acting as effective deterrents against attackers.

Afforded such security, the inhabitants will again raise all the familiar sounds of festivity; their families, no longer depleted by the effects of war, will increase and they will achieve the kind of prosperity that will give them respect ('honour') in the eyes of others. Their description as a 'congregation' (v. 20) probably refers not only to their worship, but to their post-exilic life as a theocracy.

They will no longer be ruled by foreign overlords but by one of their own (v. 21). It is strange, especially in view of verse 9, that the word 'king' is avoided. Some have seen this as a deliberate repudiation of the old pre-exilic monarchy with all its corruption and failures (in which case this must be from a different hand than verse 9). Others have suggested that the reference here is to the high priests who achieved such influence after the exile. The words 'I will make him draw near to me' do recall the promise of Zechariah to the high priest Joshua: 'I will give you the right of access among those who are standing here' (Zechariah 3:7). Both king and priest exercised a mediatorial role between God and people and so either could be meant here. The real emphasis, however, is that the people are now ruled by their own leader. Further, it emphasizes the truth that just as God alone can 'heal', so only God can make people fit to approach him.

The real goal of the 'healing' is the renewal of the old covenant relationship between God and Israel (v. 22). With that relationship restored, everything else fits into its place in God's overall scheme of 'healing'.

Verses 23–24 occurred also at 23:19–20 in the attacks on false prophets. Recalled here, they promise that God will root out all evil from his people.

A PRAYER

Lord, in all our inner tensions and our divisions from other people, grant us the healing and renewal that only you can give. Amen

67

The JOY *of* GOD'S FUTURE

The nation reunited in God

Verse 1 takes up the theme of 30:22, renewing as it does the old covenant formula, the words God spoke when he first entered into the special covenant relationship with Israel (Exodus 6:7) by which they became 'his people' and he 'their God'. The renewal of the covenant will include 'all the families of Israel', and so the divided northern and southern kingdoms will again be united by their new relationship with God.

The 'covenant' theme is developed further in verses 2–3 with a reference to the deliverance from Egypt ('the people who survived the sword') and the wandering in the wilderness that followed when Israel was looking for 'rest', that is, a safe area in which to settle. The reference in the phrase 'the Lord will appear to him from afar' is to God's revelation of himself on Mount Sinai where the covenant ceremony was enacted (Exodus 19; 24). The tradition that God travelled 'from afar' to make this revelation of himself on Sinai is enshrined in some ancient songs in the Old Testament (Judges 5:4–5; Psalm 68:7–8; Habakkuk 3:3–4).

Verse 3 expresses the divine love on which the covenant was based and whose 'everlasting' nature will ensure its renewal. The last line mentions God's *hesed*, that great covenant term that spoke of love, loyalty and unswerving faithfulness. The English versions translate the accompanying verb as 'continued' (NRSV) or 'maintain' (NEB). But it also occurs in Hosea 11:4 where it speaks of God, in his love, 'drawing' Israel to himself as a parent does with a child. McKane, who notes this, translates, 'I love you with an everlasting love and *draw you to me* with constant kindness'.

The picture of the community as a 'virgin', one kept pure for her husband to claim, had been used of the northern kingdom of Israel in a context of judgment by Amos (Amos 5:2). That judgment will be reversed as God claims his people again and restores them to their former glory, joy (v. 4) and prosperity (v. 5). The 'watchmen', posted to look out for the first sign of an invading army, will now declare the country to be safe, so that all God's people will be able to renew their pilgrimage to Zion, there to be reconciled with God and with each other in their common worship of him (v. 6).

A people delivered

To some extent, verses 7–14 restate the promises of verses 1–6 in fuller detail and in language reminiscent of Isaiah 40—55, a fact that has led some scholars to posit a later, exilic date for it, although there are also clear links with other material in Jeremiah. The call to replace the mourning of the exile with the joyful shouts of those who have been delivered (v. 7) is echoed in Isaiah 49:13. The promise that God will bring back the exiles from the 'north country' (v. 8), however, reverses all the earlier threats in Jeremiah of judgment at the hand of a 'foe from the north' (for example, 6:1).

There is some splendid poetry in verses 8–9 describing God's tender and careful leading of even the weakest and least able of the community back home. Their 'weeping' as they journey no doubt springs from the memory of all the horrors they have suffered and sheer relief at their deliverance. We can compare these verses with Psalm 84:6, which describes pilgrims to Jerusalem passing through the valley of 'Baca', which also means 'weeping'. God leads them like a father (v. 9) but also like the 'good shepherd' (v. 10) of Psalm 23, Ezekiel 34:11–16 and Isaiah 40:11.

The joy described in verses 11–13 closely mirrors that described in verses 4–6, while the reference to their prosperity being such that there will be plenty of 'tithes' to maintain the priesthood (v. 14) again points to the resumption of temple worship at the centre of their life. Indeed, other post-exilic prophets reminded the restored community that their prosperity depended on this (Haggai 1:3–6; Malachi 3:6–12).

A PRAYER

Lord, give me not a shallow joy, indifferent to the suffering of others and to all the horrors in the world, but a joy that comes from a knowledge of your presence, and certainty in the ultimate promise of your love. Amen.

68 JEREMIAH 31:15–26

The LAST WORD—GOD'S LOVE

Weeping turned to joy

Rachel, one of Jacob's wives, was the mother of Joseph and Benjamin, two 'tribes' that comprised the northern kingdom of Israel. Ephraim (v. 18) was Joseph's son (Genesis 41:52) and his name came to denote the northern kingdom (Isaiah 7:17). Ramah was a town on the border between the north and south. Although situated only about five miles north of Jerusalem, it was just in Benjaminite territory. One tradition associated it with the place where Rachel was buried. 1 Samuel 10:2 places it in the same area, which, if true, would make the reference here to Rachel weeping for her exiled 'children' (v. 15) more meaningful. In both Genesis 35:19 and 1 Samuel 10:2, the name 'Ephrath' for her burial place led to a wrong identification with Ephrathah (= Bethlehem, see Micah 5:2), giving rise to Matthew's linking this verse with Herod's slaughter of the innocents in Bethlehem (Matthew 2:18).

It is strange that this weeping is described as 'work' which will be rewarded (v. 16), but it becomes clear that it expresses not merely grief for the suffering and deprivation imposed by the exile, but a frank recognition that all was just judgment for her waywardness (v. 18: she was an 'untrained calf'; compare Hosea 10:11). Indeed, all she has suffered has led to a new awareness of her sin (v. 19) and this in turn led to repentance and remorse, expressed by the strange phrase 'I beat my thigh', probably equivalent to 'I beat my breast'. Her longing is not just for a literal return to the land but a restoration to her old relationship with God (v. 18). She has become ashamed of her state of estrangement from God (v. 19).

This 'turning' leads to a turning in God's treatment of his wayward child whom he has loved all along in spite of her sin. The words of verse 20 are again reminiscent of Hosea, especially Hosea 11:8–9. The exiles are invited to return home along the very road by which they went into exile, marking out the way so that all will be able to follow it (v. 21). Again the wording echoes that of another prophet, Isaiah of the Babylonian exile (Isaiah 40:3). Here too the Israelites are called to set aside all doubts about whether God can accomplish this (v. 22; compare Isaiah 51:12–14). The strange phrase that ends verse 22, according to how we render the Hebrew, means either that God is going to miraculously overturn all the present order as much as if a woman were to change into a man, or that conditions of peace will be such that a woman will be able to protect a man. Warriors will belong to a past age.

Zion and Judah restored

Verses 15–22 offered hope to the exiles of the old northern kingdom of Israel. Yet all along, Jeremiah has insisted that God plans to reunite both kingdoms (31:1). Now the promise is extended to Judah. Their restoration also will mark a return of Jerusalem and Judah, symbolized by the temple 'hill' at the centre, to its true calling of 'righteousness' (v. 23; compare Isaiah 1:21–26). Both settled agriculturalists and nomadic shepherds will know security and plenty (v. 24). The weakness from which they now suffer will be turned to strength as God nourishes them with all the abundant fertility of the land (v. 25; compare Isaiah 40:28–31).

Dream or reality?

Verse 26 remains an enigma and is too brief to offer a platform on which to rear subtle interpretations. The prophet has not mentioned falling asleep, and the oracles of chapters 30—31 have been offered not as dreams, but as solid promises of God's future deliverance of his people. It is usually taken, therefore, to be a marginal comment by a copyist, perhaps speculating on the contrast between such hopes and present experience.

FOR MEDITATION

Whatever the original meaning of verse 26, the fact is that, for Christians, the conflict between present tears and future salvation finds some resolution in the present experience of the new life of the age to come in Christ (Romans 8:18–25).

The NEW COVENANT

God 'watching' over his people

In the context of hope for the future (the unifying theme of the 'Booklet of Consolation'), verses 27–28 look back to, and reverse, earlier threats of judgment. Passages like 5:17 and 12:12–13 saw the aridity of the land and failure of harvests as signs of God's judgment. Now God is going to make all fruitful so that the land will again sustain a large number of cattle and people (v. 27). Verse 28 looks back to the terms of Jeremiah's call (1:10), which was to announce that God intended first to 'pluck up' and 'break down' before he could 'build' and 'plant'. There, as here, Jeremiah is assured that God is 'watching' over his word to bring it about (1:12). Both passages make use of the double sense of the verb 'to watch' that we also know in English. We speak of 'watching over' someone in love and care but we also say, threateningly, 'I'm watching you.' Now God is still 'watching' over his word to bring about the promise it held out on the other side of judgment (v. 28).

All are free to turn back

The law had spoken of the consequences for future generations of the sins of their ancestors (Exodus 20:4–6). Sometimes a whole family was seen as involved in the guilt of its head, as with Achan (Joshua 7:24–25). This insight was evidently enshrined in the popular proverb quoted here in verse 29 (and also in Ezekiel 18:2). The apparent thoroughgoing individualism of verse 30 may raise as many questions for us as the more collective view of the old Ten Commandments. The fact is that other people *do* suffer the consequences of our sins. None of us lives in a hermetically sealed world of our own but in a complex network of relationships in which we affect, and are affected by, the good and evil of others. Perhaps, in context, this is meant more as a word of hope for the exilic generation. In spite of what the law said, they are not bound by their fathers' guilt (although they are suffering its consequences). Each generation is free to turn back to God, and that is true of each of us as individuals. We cannot shuffle off our own real responsibility entirely by claiming that we are bound by what we have inherited from others.

A new covenant

The book of Jeremiah has realized frankly that, without the grace and intervention of God, people cannot save themselves. The human heart is 'deceitful above all things' (17:9). The leopard cannot change its spots (13:23). Only God can renew the inner intentions and springs of motive, all that is meant by 'the heart' (24:7). This is something that the Deuteronomists had also recognized. Israelites were called not just to obey the letter of the law, but to respond to God with whole-hearted love and with their whole personality (Deuteronomy 6:5). But such a response needed the grace of God, a 'circumcision of the heart' which only God could achieve (Deuteronomy 30:6; Jeremiah 4:4). It is this that is being promised now (vv. 31–34) in a 'new covenant' whose demands are no longer written merely on (external) tablets of stone (Deuteronomy 4:13) but on their very hearts. Now, inward desires and human promptings will correspond in perfect harmony with the wishes of God as the covenant relationship is renewed because all past sins are forgiven. The law will not be dispensed with, but its demands will become a ruling disposition of the heart. The repeated injunction of Deuteronomy that the law be taught to each generation (Deuteronomy 11:19) will become superfluous.

This is one of the finest passages not only of the book of Jeremiah, but also of the whole Old Testament, and it was in the mind of Jesus at the Last Supper (Mark 14:23–24; Matthew 26:27–28; Luke 22:20). He saw the shedding of his blood on the cross as the means by which the forgiveness of sins would be achieved, the foundation of the new covenant relationship with God by which the hearts of sinful human beings would be renewed.

A PRAYER

Lord, so write your law on my heart that 'I will one will with you'.
Amen.

GOD'S FAITHFULNESS IS CERTAIN

The dependable God

The sense of verses 35–37 is clear and fits well with the general note of promise that has run through the 'Booklet of Consolation' (chs. 30—31). The utter dependability of the created world with its 'fixed order' (literally 'these statutes', v. 36), in which the sun gives light by day and the moon and stars by night, shows the durability of the word of God by which Israel has become a nation 'before me' for all generations. The 'before me' suggests that they are, and always will be, an object of his special care. Yet it also suggests that they will 'serve' God and do his will, since 'to stand before someone' has exactly this sense. In 1 Kings 12:6, for example, Rehoboam consults the elders who 'had stood before Solomon' but rejects their advice in favour of the younger counsellors who 'stood before him' (v. 8).

The form of words recalls other prophetic passages. Three 'doxologies' in Amos (4:13; 5:8; 9:5–6) all hymn God's work in creation in similar phrases and end with the refrain 'the Lord (of hosts) is his name'. Verse 35 here is almost exactly echoed in Isaiah 51:15, and there are similar appeals to God's creative work as the basis of his trustworthiness in Isaiah 40:26; 42:5; 44:24 and 45:18. The story of God's creation in Genesis 1, probably written by Priestly writers in the time of the Babylonian exile, emphasizes his power in subduing and containing the waters of chaos. Jeremiah 31:37, however, stresses that all remains subject to God. The reliability of nature is the basis of the covenant with Noah (Genesis 8:22). Perhaps, then, these verses are taken from the worship of Israel in the second temple period, assuring those of the post-exilic period of the reliability of God's earlier promises through the prophet Jeremiah.

Rebuilding and sanctifying Jerusalem

The temple, we know, was rebuilt under the leadership of Joshua and Zerubbabel, inspired by the promises of the prophets Haggai and Zechariah. It was completed and dedicated in 515BC (Ezra 6:13–15). Yet the ruined state and defencelessness of the city remained a cause of sorrow and anxiety for many years. It troubled Nehemiah, away in the Persian court, enough for him to seek and gain permission to return, to see to the rebuilding of the city wall in 445BC (Nehemiah 1:1–3; 2:1–8). The promise of the city's rebuilding is the theme of verses 38–40. It foresees the use of the builder's measuring line (Ezekiel 40:3, 5; Zechariah 2:1). Probably just a few sites are mentioned to suggest widespread rebuilding. The Tower of Hananel is mentioned in Nehemiah 3:1 and 12:39, and stood on the north side of the city. The Corner Gate was on the north-west of the city wall and was first built by Uzziah (2 Chronicles 26:9). Neither the Hill of Gareb nor Goah are mentioned elsewhere so we can only surmise that perhaps these few names are given to suggest a complete circuit of the city. (A similar passage occurs at Zechariah 14:10–11). The Kidron brook and the Horse Gate were on the east side of the city, which rather strengthens this impression.

The Hebrew adds a strange detail. 'The whole valley of the dead bodies and the ashes' (v. 40) rather suggests the Valley of Hinnom, a valley to the south of the city where the city's waste was disposed of. But it was also said to have been the site for child sacrifice (2 Kings 23:10; see Jeremiah 7:31–32 and comments on p. 52). The Septuagint lacks this phrase but its addition makes a bold claim. Not only a physical rebuilding of the city is being promised but a radical renewal based on a cleansing away of the kind of sins that brought about the judgment of the city's destruction in the first place. That would make these three verses a fitting addendum to the promises of the new covenant in verses 31–34, even if they also are later additions to the chapter.

A PRAYER

Lord, as we try to build a just society in a world where so much has gone wrong, may we always be encouraged by a vision of your perfect plans and your promises of renewal. Amen

JEREMIAH BUYS LAND

Jeremiah in prison

The situation for Jerusalem was certainly desperate in 'the tenth year of Zedekiah' (v. 1). In 597BC Nebuchadrezzar had captured the city and taken prisoner the king, Jehoiachin, removing him and many of the leaders of the community to Babylon in exile (2 Kings 24:10–16). Then he took Jehoiachin's uncle, Mattaniah, changing his name to Zedekiah to show that he was the puppet-king of the Babylonians (2 Kings 24:17). Zedekiah's reign was to last for eleven years but, towards the end of that time, he foolishly allowed himself to be persuaded to rebel against the Babylonians, whose revenge was swift and deadly. They arrived again at the gates of the city and besieged it until there was no food left and thus little strength for the defenders to withstand the enemy's battering rams.

For Jeremiah to have been predicting the downfall of the city in such a time was to incur the greatest hostility. Not only might he be 'lowering morale in time of war', as we might say, but there was a real belief that the prophetic word had power to bring about the very thing it declared (see Isaiah 55:10–11; Ezekiel 12:28). The account of Jeremiah's imprisonment in 37:15–21 is slightly more sympathetic to Zedekiah. That suggests that he was thrown into prison because of the hostility of 'the princes' and that Zedekiah was more favourably disposed towards him, although he saw that the prophet's own safety made his detention prudent.

Nevertheless, the message is uncompromising enough (vv. 3–6). No escape is possible either for the city or Zedekiah himself. Indeed, there is a special poignancy about the phrase that Zedekiah will see Nebuchadrezzar 'eye to eye' (v. 4) in the light of the terrible punishment meted out to Zedekiah, by which he was blinded after having witnessed the execution of his own sons (2 Kings 25:7). The Babylonians are God's appointed means of judgment, as Jeremiah has made clear all along. That is why it is not only futile to try to resist them, but an act of rebellion against God himself, an action destined to incur judgment (v. 5).

A symbol of hope

Nevertheless, this chapter fits into the theme of hope sounded in chapters 30—31. For, beyond judgment, God has his plans for the redemption of his people and the renewal of the land. This is brought home by a further act of prophetic symbolism (vv. 6–15). Jeremiah's cousin, Hanamel, offers land to Jeremiah for sale. It is an extraordinary time to be thinking of purchasing land, on the eve of military disaster and foreign occupation. Hanamel appeals to the 'law of redemption' spelled out in Leviticus 25:25–28. This stresses that if someone falls into poverty and has to sell up, then the nearest relative (the Hebrew word is *goel*) has the first obligation to purchase it. This practice helped to keep property 'within the family', a very important concept for the Hebrews, as the story of Naboth's reluctance to sell his land outside the family, even to the king, shows (1 Kings 21:3). For Jeremiah, however, this is more than an act of family duty: it is a statement of faith that God has a future for his people back in their own land after the judgment of military defeat and exile (v. 15).

The concept of the *goel*, often translated 'redeemer', is a very important one in the Old Testament, for it leads to one of the great descriptions of God as Israel's 'Redeemer' (for example, Isaiah 41:14). He acts as his people's 'nearest relative', paying the price to 'redeem' them from slavery (Exodus 6:6) or from servitude in exile (Isaiah 52:9).

The transaction by which Jeremiah purchases the land is effected by Baruch, mentioned here for the first time but destined to play an important part in the prophet's later ministry. It consists of the payment of seventeen shekels of silver (a 'shekel' originally indicated a weight, of about 11 grammes or half an ounce), and then burying the two title deeds, one sealed, the other open to show the contents without breaking the seal of the original (vv. 11–14), as a witness of the promise for the future.

FOR MEDITATION

After all the promises of chapters 30—31, we are plunged back into the grim reality of life in the imperilled city. It is important for us, in all our dark times, to see them against the promises of God.

NATION'S PAST & GOD'S FUTURE

Jeremiah's prayer

Jeremiah is concerned about the wisdom of the command to buy land at the very moment when the Chaldeans are at the door (v. 25). He acknowledges the power of God in creation, accomplished by his 'outstretched arm' (v. 17), a term often used of God's redemptive act in delivering his people from slavery in Egypt (for example, Deuteronomy 26:8). But, as Isaiah of Babylon was to show, it is because Yahweh is the creator God that he has the power and 'control' of the world's history to overcome his people's oppressors and 'redeem' them (Isaiah 40:12–17, 25–31).

Yet, from the human side, this story has been marred by the continuing disobedience of God's own people, a truth expressed again in sharply Deuteronomistic terms (v. 23; Deuteronomy 13:4), and it is this thwarting of God's purpose that has led to the present state of crisis, the imminent destruction of city and land at the hand of the Babylonians (v. 24). All that has happened illustrates two further Deuteronomistic assertions, apparently contradictory, but in fact complementary. One is that those who come after us suffer the fall-out and consequences of our sins (v. 18; see Deuteronomy 5:9–10). The other is that each of us is responsible for our own sins (v. 19; see Deuteronomy 24:16).

Nevertheless, the present generation is suffering the consequences of the cumulative sin and guilt of past generations. Thus the question for Jeremiah remains. In spite of God's power as creator and redeemer, what is the point of the action God has commanded his prophet to fulfil? (v. 25).

The reasons for God's judgment

God replies by taking up Jeremiah's words in verse 17 ('Nothing is too hard for you') and reasserting their immutable truth (v. 27). The prophet would not be the first of us for whom there is a gap between the soundness of our theological affirmations and our expectation of what can reasonably be expected of God in our present, impossible situation!

What follows is an account of the repeated sins of the Israelites, in language strongly reminiscent of that of the Deuteronomists in the books of Deuteronomy and Kings (compare v. 32 with 2 Kings 17: 11–13, and v. 33 with 1 Kings 14:9) as well as of earlier oracles in the book of Jeremiah (2:4–8, 23–24; 7:31).

Strictly speaking, verses 28–35 are not necessary to the logical structure of the whole chapter, which has to do with God's command to the prophet to buy land as a sign that there is to be, by God's grace and power, a future for the whole territory. But, as throughout the book, it is made clear that such a future can lie only the other side of judgment, a judgment meted out not by caprice but because of the cumulative effects of Israel's sin in every generation.

God's glorious future

The prophet's misgivings about his purchase are misplaced. God intends to bring the exiles home (v. 37). The promises of the new covenant (31:31–34) are renewed (vv. 38–40), and God will follow the 'plucking up' with a 'planting'. Indeed, the basis of the life of the restored community will be nothing less than the 'faithfulness' of God, as opposed to the faithlessness of the people in earlier times, and the fact that they will be the object of a divine love that perfectly exemplifies the love for which God called from his people—'with all my heart and soul' (v. 41; see Deuteronomy 6:5).

Verses 42–44 specify that land will again be bought and sold as normal life is resumed under safe and prosperous circumstances. All the environs of Jerusalem, Benjamin to the north, the Shephelah to the west and the Negeb to the south, will become again a hive of agricultural and economic activity (v. 44). The prophet and, through him, the people are called to view the present state of distress with the eye of faith, an eye focused on the power of God to act. If this passage owes something to the Deuteronomistic editors of the exile, then it is a reminder that the call to see present suffering with the eye of faith extended to them, as it does to the people of God in every generation.

FOR MEDITATION

We see in vision fair a time
When evil shall have passed away;
And thus we dedicate our lives
To hasten on that blessed day.

M.J. Savage (1841–1918)

HOPE *in a* TIME *of* DARKNESS

Restoration of Jerusalem

Verse 1 links this final chapter of the 'Booklet of Consolation' with the previous one, where Jeremiah was in prison. It is a desperate situation, for Jeremiah himself certainly, but even more so for the city and people as a whole. Yet it is at just this moment that God comes again to his prophet and reminds him of his great power as creator of the whole earth. (The Hebrew of verse 2 actually says 'who made *it*' but the feminine pronoun shows the reference to be to the world.) Isaiah 40—55 makes the same point. God is able to redeem because, as creator of the world, he controls the affairs of all its nations (Isaiah 40:12–17). God invites Jeremiah to seek him for a revelation of the wonderful mysteries of his ways (v. 3) and thus to show that relationship of dependence on God and quiet waiting for his word which has been shown to be the mark of the true, as opposed to the false, prophet (23:21–22).

There is some difficulty with the Hebrew of verses 4–5. NRSV probably has as good sense as may be achieved. The allusion to the destruction of some houses to create defensive works points to the desperate attempts of king and citizens to stave off inevitable defeat at the hands of the Babylonians, inevitable because God has appointed them as his agents for judgment on his people for their sin. Frenzied human activity undertaken independently of God is, therefore, contrasted with the prophet's quiet waiting on God.

Where some might see only danger and hopelessness, the one who is in direct touch with God can see hope with the eye of faith. God assures his prophet that, after judgment, he will restore city and people (vv. 6–9). His purpose includes not merely a change of outward fortunes, but real 'healing' for their spiritual condition of blindness and rebellion (vv. 6–8; 30:17). Yet God's purpose includes not only his own people. He intends so to restore his people that their life, character and fortunes will be a witness to God's grace and power before all the nations of the earth (v. 9). The second half of Isaiah also makes a similar point in predicting God's restoration of his people (Isaiah 51:4–5). God always says of the people whom he redeems, 'You are my witnesses' (Isaiah 43:9–10).

Restoration of joy

Several times the terrible and devastating fate which is to overtake the community has been vividly portrayed by picturing the desolate silence that will mark it. Typical will be the absence of wedding banquets, symbolizing as they do a community's hope for the future (7:34; 16:9; 25:10). Now all this will be reversed (vv. 10–11). But at the heart of their joy will be their renewed praise of God in a restored temple, for the words of the hymn they will sing closely echo some Psalms (for example, Psalm 106:1), while the 'thank offerings' they bring will be carried into 'the house of the Lord' (v. 11).

Sheep may safely graze

Not only in Jerusalem, but throughout the whole region (see 32:44), shepherds will again pasture their flocks in safety (v. 12). Indeed, in view of what is to follow, there may just be a *double entendre* here. We have seen how kings and other leaders were often spoken of as 'shepherds' who could, and often did, betray their trust (23:1–2). The interesting phrase here that the shepherds will 'count' the sheep under their care ('hand') may suggest a real care for every one of their people by those 'shepherds' God has promised to raise up (v. 13; 23:3–4).

A PRAYER

Lord, in times of darkness and distress, when it is so easy to lose faith, keep me close to you so that I may see events and experiences with the eye of faith, illumined by your wonderful, but sometimes mysterious, purposes. Make me the kind of person whose life is an attractive testimony to your love and grace, holding out hope for all who are in trouble. Amen

GOD *as* SURE *as* DAY & NIGHT

A new Davidic king

It is not hard to imagine how devastated many in the community must have felt during and after the exile, especially with the institutions of monarchy and temple, at which a regular priesthood served the God who dwelled there, both gone.

Expectations of the restoration of a king and priesthood have not played a prominent part in the book as a whole until now. But the issue is firmly addressed in this passage. Strangely, verses 14–26 do not appear in the Septuagint text of the book of Jeremiah and this, together with the uniqueness of their contents, has led many to believe that they were a later addition to the book. In their present form they may well be, reflecting hopes expressed elsewhere in the post-exilic literature. Nevertheless, Jeremiah, in attacking the false 'shepherds', had expressed the hope that one day God would set up those who would discharge their office faithfully (23:1–4). That last passage also led on to a promise of a righteous 'branch' of the Davidic line (23:5–6; compare 30:9). Further, it is not quite true to say, as some commentators have done, that verses 14–26 have *no* links with what has gone before. We saw the reference to 'shepherds' in 33:13 and, earlier in the same passage, the restoration of temple worship was promised (33:11), implying a restored priesthood. Verses 14–26 may, therefore, be the work of those who tried to meet the disappointments of their contemporaries by filling out general promises of Jeremiah in greater detail.

One difference between verses 14–16 and 23:5–6 is that, whereas there the righteous king was to be called by the name 'The Lord is our righteousness', here that name is to be given to Jerusalem (v. 16). Doubtless, a righteous king will bring about a righteous community.

Kings and priests together

The promise to David made by Nathan when God established his covenant with him (2 Samuel 7:16; 1 Kings 2:4–5; 8:25) is reaffirmed (v. 17). To it is now added the concept of a similar promise made to the levitical priesthood. The Hebrew of verse 18 reads 'the priests, the Levites'. That is the normal title given to the priesthood in the book of Deuteronomy and does not yet suggest the (later) distinction between the full Zadokite or Aaronic priests and the Levites, who were reduced to a subservient role (Ezekiel 44:10–27). Nevertheless, since the sacrifice of burnt offerings could be offered only by the duly ordained priesthood and could take place only in the consecrated temple, this implies the rebuilding of the temple after the exile. The books of Haggai and Zechariah also reveal hopes of a joint rule by priest and (royal) governor immediately after the exile (Haggai 1:12; Zechariah 6:12–14).

The renewal of the covenants

Again, to the mention of the covenant with David is added the thought of a covenant between God and the priesthood (vv. 21–22). This is referred to only in later texts. It is found in a late strand of the Pentateuch (Numbers 25:12) and is referred to in Nehemiah 13:29 and Malachi 2:4–9. Verses 19–22, therefore, probably reflect the growing influence of the priesthood after the exile. The 'covenant with the day and the night' (v. 20) may be an allusion to the covenant made with Noah after the flood (Genesis 8:22), while the promise of innumerable offspring to royal and priestly lines recalls the covenant with Abraham (Genesis 15:5). God is going to fulfil all his ancient promises for his people after the exile.

Confirmation of God's promise

Some express their scepticism about God's promises to his people (the 'two families' in verse 24 probably allude to the kingdoms of Israel and Judah and so include the *whole* community). We may compare the doubts of 'these people' with those that Malachi cites in 3:13–15, showing how widespread such attitudes must have been. But God's compassion and regard for '*my* people' (as opposed to 'these people' who doubt) is sure. His mercy was not only for the great heroes of the faith in times past. It remains secure for all now.

FOR MEDITATION

Many men and women believe that God is All-Mighty and may do all; and that He is All-Wisdom and can do all; but that He is All-love and will do all—there they stop short.

Lady Julian of Norwich (?1342–c.1413)

MORE WARNINGS *to* ZEDEKIAH

This short passage consists of two distinct words of Jeremiah to Zedekiah. Their apparently contradictory nature presents some difficulties for interpretation.

Jerusalem is doomed

The timing given for Jeremiah's approach to the king at God's command is during the siege of Jerusalem by the Babylonian forces, which were supplemented with troops drawn from the people they had conquered elsewhere (v. 1). This was common practice, followed later by the Romans. Zedekiah had been placed on the throne by the Babylonians themselves after the failure of Jehoiachin's resistance (2 Kings 24:17). However, he also allowed himself to be led into rebellion by the pro-Egypt party in the Judean court, and it was in response to this that Nebuchadrezzar arrived with his mixed forces to lay siege to Jerusalem (2 Kings 25:1–3). Perhaps at an early stage in the siege, Jeremiah is sent by God with this assurance that, however hard they try and however courageous their resistance, the city is doomed (v. 2). The closeness of the message contained in verses 2–3 to that recorded in 32:3–5 suggests that these two passages are parallel accounts of the same encounter. Both predict that Zedekiah himself will not escape but will be taken prisoner. Both mention his speaking with Nebuchadrezzar 'face to face' and seeing him 'eye to eye', an ironic phrase in view of his ultimate fate in being blinded (see comments on 32:3–5, pp. 158).

Some mitigation for Zedekiah?

In view of what the prophet has just said (and the eventual fate that befell Zedekiah), the promise that follows in verses 4–5 is very strange. Being blinded after seeing one's sons killed can hardly be seen as a fulfilment of the promise to 'die in peace'. Further, the sign of divine favour and public honour in the carrying out of the proper burial rites can hardly have taken place in Babylon, and if a return to Jerusalem was envisaged, they are no more likely in that ravaged city. For the burning of spices as a sign of public honour and lament over the death of a loved monarch, see 2 Chronicles 16:13–14, where such rituals were performed over King Asa; and 2 Chronicles 21:19, where they were withheld from the dishonoured Jehoram.

The only possible reconciliation between these two oracles can be that the second was conditional upon Zedekiah's obedience to God in desisting from his rebellion and surrendering voluntarily in the light of the warning he had just been given of the fate of the city. In fact, he persisted, trying to escape when the consequences of his folly caught up with him and his people (2 Kings 25:1–7).

The evident signs of defeat

Perhaps the brief conclusion in verses 6–7 underlines such an interpretation, for it shows that Zedekiah's position was hopeless. Outside Jerusalem, trapped in a ring of besieging forces, only Lachish and Azekah of the fortified towns remained unconquered. Strangely, both are mentioned in one of the few examples of classical Hebrew literature outside the Old Testament, the *Lachish Ostraca*. These manuscripts were found hidden in the base of the tower of ancient Lachish, soon to be reduced to ashes by the Babylonians. The captain of some military outpost reports to the commander of Lachish that he is waiting for a signal (perhaps a beacon fire, as in Jeremiah 6:1, correctly translated by NEB as 'fire the beacon') from him, since he no longer sees any from Azekah. All this should have been warning enough to Zedekiah of the truth of the prophet's assessment of the situation. But even then, Zedekiah remained obdurate.

A PRAYER

Lord, I know how easy it is when I have really set my mind on something to be blind to your warning promptings that it is neither your will nor in my best interests. Keep me open and sensitive to all the leading of your Spirit, even when your way seems different from my wishes. Amen

A FAILURE *to* HONOUR VOWS

Forgetting inconvenient promises

In general, Zedekiah does not get a very good press in the Old Testament. Yet this passage reveals that he did make a strenuous effort to avert God's judgment by bringing the community into obedience to the law, the very kind of 'justice' that was the king's responsibility to establish (22:3). The covenant law stated that Hebrew slaves should be freed after six years' servitude (Deuteronomy 15:12–18), even where it did not disapprove of the enslavement of such anyway (Leviticus 25:39–46). Apparently, this law had long been in practical abeyance in Judah and that was why the king led the people in a solemn covenant ceremony, entered into before God in the temple (v. 15). Perhaps this particular reform is singled out as sign of a more general intention of being obedient to God in the face of the terrible danger they were facing.

Failure to learn from history

The word of God through the prophet reminds the people that the original law had been brought in because, ironically, all his people had been slaves in Egypt and he had delivered them (v. 13). It was only fitting, therefore, that they who had been freed should be generous in their treatment of each other, especially of the poor, the weak and defenceless in their society. But their ancestors had conveniently forgotten that law (as well as many others). Their history showed again and again how judgment had followed that disobedience. Yet they were now repeating the same mistakes as their fathers had made (vv. 11, 16). Presumably, the original vow had been occasioned by the danger they were in. Yet verse 21 suggests that the danger appeared to have been lifted, as the besieging Babylonian army had withdrawn. Chapter 37:5–11 tells us that this withdrawal was to meet the threat of an advancing Egyptian army, the very source of hope on which Zedekiah was basing his policy of resistance. Zedekiah and his wealthier subjects would not be the last to make promises to God in times of crisis and then conveniently forget them when the danger passed! Indeed, by emphasizing that this promise to their fellows was also a solemn pledge undertaken before God, this passage reminds readers of all ages that all our promises, whether to other people or to God, are binding on those who acknowledge God's lordship over their lives.

Announcement of judgment

There is an ironic play on the Hebrew word for 'freedom' used in this passage—the freedom they promised to their Hebrew slaves (v. 8), and the 'freedom' God is going to grant to the means of their judgment (v. 17). Verse 18 contains another 'covenant' allusion, this time to the kind of ancient covenant ceremony described in Genesis 15:9–10, 17. An animal was killed and cut in two and the two parties to the agreement passed between the pieces. The exact significance of the symbolism is obscure. Possibly it signified that two people were bound by the common life of a third. Almost certainly it signified the fate to which either party laid themselves open if they broke the terms of the agreement (Judges 19:29; 1 Samuel 11:5–11). Similarly, this act of disobedience (v. 16), proving as it did that the community had not had a real change of heart at all (13:23), is presented as removing any last chance they might have had of deliverance. The Babylonians soon dealt with the threat from the Egyptians (so much for Zedekiah's hopes) and returned to their siege of the city—this time not to withdraw until they had captured it (39:1–10).

The language of this whole passage is strongly Deuteronomistic, which suggests that this lesson of the importance of keeping the spirit and the letter of the law, especially towards the weakest members of society, was not lost on the exilic and post-exilic communities (compare Nehemiah 5:1–13). It remains relevant for its readers in every age. Any community is strong just in so far as the word and promises its members make to each other are seen as binding and trustworthy.

A PRAYER

Lord, you have given me grace to make my promises to you. Grant me strength and love so that I may keep them when they are hard as well as easy, costly as well as pleasant, inconvenient as well as joyful. And keep me true to all the promises I have made to others. Amen

An EXAMPLE *of* FAITHFULNESS

Jeremiah's test of the Rechabites

The juxtaposition of chapters 34 and 35 shows that, for the final compilers of the book, thematic and theological considerations mattered more than history for its own sake. The account of the broken covenant in chapter 34 is dated in the reign of Zedekiah (34:8). The incident involving the Rechabites is placed in the reign of the king before Zedekiah (and before the brief reign of Jehoiachin), namely Jehoiakim (v. 1). The whole point of the arrangement is to highlight the contrast between the faithfulness of the Rechabites and the faithlessness of the Israelites in general, and to show how obedience or disobedience affects the outcome of judgment or deliverance (34:21–22; compare 35:18–19).

We have very little information about the Rechabites other than that given in this chapter. 1 Chronicles 2:55 links them with the Kenites. Jonadab (= Jehonadab, vv. 6 and 8) was one of Jehu's supporters in his coup against the royal house of Ahab in the name of loyal and exclusive worship of Yahweh (2 Kings 10:15–28). So it seems that they were a tribe of nomadic people who never adapted themselves to settled urban and agricultural life in Canaan, refusing to drink wine because it was the fruit of the vines of the land (v. 9). They saw this as a call to keep the pure flame of the faith alive, uncontaminated by any contact with the Canaanites and their way of life.

We have to see the strange episode of Jeremiah's test (v. 5) as a kind of act of prophetic symbolism. It takes place in the temple, in the chamber of a group of (presumably temple) prophets under their leader Hanan, with the blessing of other named officials with various custodial responsibilities in the temple. The point of the story is not, however, to be found in the circumstantial details but in the test of the loyalty of those who were bound by a vow, just as those in chapter 34 had bound themselves (34:10).

The obedience of the Rechabites

The Rechabites respond with a strong declaration of their principles (vv. 6–10). The passage cannot really be used as a biblical basis for teetotalism as such, since their vows also included not living in houses or engaging in any kind of agriculture, neither of which may be seen as inherently evil in themselves. The whole passage does, however, raise interesting questions about how far obedience to God involves withdrawal from the surrounding culture. Other Old Testament passages suggest that the land was God's gift to his people and that their settling in it and enjoying its produce was all in his purpose (Deuteronomy 28:1–12; Amos 2:9–10). Nevertheless, the Deuteronomy passage shows how those gifts were conditional upon obedience, and the Deuteronomists saw all too clearly what a fatal temptation Canaanite religion and ways of life often proved, while the Amos passage urges respect for those who keep a sterner discipline alive (2:11–12).

A necessary compromise

The threat from the invading Babylonians had forced the Rechabites to seek the shelter of the city (v. 11), although they strongly disapproved of building cities and living in them! It was not, however, seen by them, or by the final editors of this chapter, as an abandonment of principle, but a necessary accommodation to the realities of their situation forced on them by circumstances.

This whole passage highlights the tensions always involved for the people of God as they make their pilgrimage through the world as those who are really citizens of another. Total denial of our surrounding culture may be a tempting option, but is sometimes easier than trying to work out how we obey God while living in the real world. Furthermore, opting out also reduces any influence we may exercise from within that culture. On the other hand, it is easy to be swamped by the standards and values of our environment and forget our true calling.

A PRAYER

Lord, help your people in all the day-to-day decisions of principle that they have to make as your subjects in this world. May they be involved in all the concerns of the world as those whose first love is to you. Amen

FAITHFULNESS & UNFAITHFULNESS

The fidelity of the Rechabites

The painful contrast between the complete fidelity of the Rechabites, underlined by their refusal to compromise when confronted by Jeremiah's 'sign-test', and the repeated fickleness of the Israelites as a whole, is driven home in the prophet's words that follow (vv. 12–17).

The inverted parallels are drawn out with every word. The 'sign' had been intended as a warning rebuke to Israel as a whole. The word the prophet uses of it in verse 13, variously translated as 'instruction' (RSV), 'lesson' (NRSV, NIV) and 'correction' (NEB, REB), certainly contains the idea of 'disciplinary correction' or a 'stern warning aimed at a change of life'. The Rechabites had demonstrated their faithfulness in the temple (35:4), the very place where so often the Israelites had indulged in shallow and hypocritical religious exercises (7:4). The 'command' that Jonadab had given the Rechabites (v. 14) is the same word used again and again for the 'statutes' that God had given Israel. The same verse shows how they 'obeyed' his 'command', the word used this time making up the usual pairing that refers to the 'statutes and commandments' with which God had bound Israel (Deuteronomy 6:1).

Interestingly, the Hebrew phrase that tells of God's word 'to the *men* of Judah and the inhabitants of Jerusalem' has 'man' in the singular (v. 13). The use of the word as a collective singular is quite common in Hebrew but sometimes carries the idea of the solidarity of the community, as in Judges 20:11 where it is expanded with the phrase 'as one man' ('united as one', NRSV). The sin, and the terrible judgment it brings in its wake, is communal. But each individual makes his or her own contribution and each is individually responsible for the state of their society as a whole. This is a truth of which we, with our greater Western stress on individuality, can easily lose sight. Its significance for the book of Jeremiah is shown by the address of the word of God to 'every one of you' (v. 15, where the same singular word for 'man' is used again).

The contrast between the Rechabites and the Israelites as a whole is still further emphasized. The Rechabites were commanded once by their ancestor, and kept his command. But the Israelites persisted in their disobedience to God's commands in spite of the fact that he constantly sent prophets to them throughout their history (vv. 14–15). The wording of these two verses closely echoes a Deutero-nomistic editorial comment on the reason for the fall of the northern kingdom of Israel in 2 Kings 17:13–15. This close parallel suggests that the lessons were seen by the editors of the book of Jeremiah as perpetually relevant for the people of God in all ages, not least for those who had survived the exile and needed to be exhorted to learn its warnings for themselves.

The promise to the Rechabites

A striking promise is made to the Rechabites for the continuing sur-vival of their community under the watchful care of God (vv. 18–19). Yet even here they are serving as a warning for Israel, for the terms of the promise could not but recall the very similar promise that had once been made to David (2 Samuel 7:13, 16). In fact, when the dying David gives charge over the kingdom to his son, Solomon, his words are almost exactly those that occur in verse 19: 'If your heirs take heed to their way, to walk before me in faithfulness with all their heart and with all their soul, *there shall not fail you a successor on the throne of Israel*' (1 Kings 2:4).

The real lesson of the Rechabites, then, is that the very similar promise made to David had failed because David's successors had for-gotten the condition of faithfulness on which its fulfilment depended. And this is the lesson that not only Jeremiah's audience, but also those who heard and read his words during and after the exile, had to assimilate. The disaster had struck kingdom and people because of faithlessness. Let them learn the lesson of the Rechabites and remain firm if they are to know the wonderful future God has promised them.

FOR MEDITATION

When we as individuals also feel helpless to influence society, it is worth recalling the words, 'The only thing necessary for the triumph of evil is for good men to do nothing' (Edmund Burke, 1729–97).

79 JEREMIAH 36:1-10

JEREMIAH'S WORDS *on a* SCROLL

The command to write

Chapter 36 marks the end of the section of the book that began with chapter 26 (see Introduction, p. 14). The section opened with an account of the hostility Jeremiah encountered, especially from King Jehoiakim, and it ends on the same note. Taken as a whole, it shows that the reason for the disaster that befell the nation at the hand of the Babylonians was the stubborn refusal to hear and obey God's word on the part of people, officials and, above all, kings.

The date given in verse 1 may well be significant. The fourth year of King Jehoiakim was 605BC and that was the fateful year when the Babylonians defeated Egypt at the battle of Carchemish, thus opening up the whole of the ancient Near East to their imperial thrust and the march of their armies. Now it must have been evident to Jeremiah that the Babylonians were 'the foe from the north' and that the writing of God's judgment for the nation was on the wall (36:29).

The command to write down the substance of all his preaching from his call in 626BC until the present (v. 2) is interesting because it is one of the very few mentions we have of prophets committing their words to writing. Isaiah was told to write the ominous name of one of his children (Isaiah 8:1) and, later, to write his warnings in a book (30:8). There the suggestion is that it will be a written record of the warnings God had given through his prophet. That may be part of the reason here too, although the implication of verse 3 is that it might lead to second thoughts and repentance.

Chapter 36, with its record of the committing of the prophetic word to writing, is thus a reminder of the very process by which the words of God, originally given to specific people at particular times, continue to prove their relevance and authority for later generations. It points towards the formation of our Bible and the way we read it and respond to it. Robert Carroll (p. 668) put it memorably: 'Committed to writing, the word has a permanence beyond the exigencies of human existence and can survive even the absence of its original bearer.'

Jeremiah instructs Baruch

We have already encountered Baruch in chapter 32, where he played a vital part in Jeremiah's purchase of land. Here, in verses 4–10, he serves as the recorder of the prophet's teaching and his close supporter.

Just why Jeremiah was restrained from going into the temple himself is not clear. It may have been because of his earlier clashes with some of its officials (20:1–6) although, later, he was able to take the Rechabites into the temple with the help of influential friends there (35:4). His instruction that Baruch was to read the book 'on a fast day' suggests that what he had in mind was not one of the statutory fast days but one called in the face of some national threat. Baruch had, indeed, to wait for the following year for such an occasion (v. 9). No doubt the prophet hoped (against hope?) that, face to face with destiny, the people might be in a suitable frame of mind to hear and obey the call to repent (vv. 3, 7). Gemariah, who supplied the room in which the public reading took place, may well have been sympathetic to the prophet and his message (36:25). It seems strange that, for a public reading, a chamber in the temple should have been selected, but perhaps it had a window or balcony from which the reading could be heard by 'all the people' in the 'upper court' (vv. 9–10). Had they known it, this was their last chance. Their response to what they heard was, literally, momentous. Whenever God speaks it is always a case of '*Today* if you will hear his voice...' (Psalm 95:7).

A PRAYER

Lord, we thank you for the Bible: for all to whom you spoke across the ages; for all who preserved their words and have faithfully passed them on; for all who sacrificed everything to bring it to us in our own language; and for all who have helped us to understand it. May we always treasure it, walk in its light and pass on its message to others. Amen

The KING BURNS *the* SCROLL

The scroll is read to the officials

To grasp fully the significance of the events recorded here, it is necessary to have other chapters in mind: chapter 26, which tells of another encounter of Jeremiah with the court and temple officials and of the reaction of King Jehoiakim; and 2 Kings 22, which relates the response of Jehoiakim's father, Josiah, when a scroll containing the law was read to him.

In chapter 26, the furore caused by Jeremiah's 'temple sermon' led to an appeal being made to those officials responsible for the good order of temple and state (26:10–11). On that occasion, the officials stood between Jeremiah and the priests and prophets who were calling for his death (26:16). Now, Micaiah (grandson of Shaphan, king's secretary in the reign of Josiah, who had played a vital part in bringing the book of the law to the king's attention) decides that the explosive words of Jeremiah's scroll must be brought to the attention of the temple and state officials (vv. 11–13). They instruct Baruch to come with the scroll and read it to them, treating him with some courtesy and respect (vv. 14–15).

The response of the officials is one of 'fear' (v. 16). Was that fear compounded by horror at the sinful state of affairs that Jeremiah's prophesying had attacked? Was it due to the fearful judgments with which the prophet had threatened the state? Was it based on fear of the reaction they expected from the king? We are not told, although their reaction is strongly contrasted with that of the king and his entourage, none of whom, when 'they heard all these words, was afraid' (v. 24). That the officials' fear was at least in part due to the reaction they expected from the king is shown by their counsel to the prophet and his companion to hide themselves, once they had determined that the words were indeed those of Jeremiah (vv. 17–19). One of them, at least, had good cause to know what might well happen to them when King Jehoiakim heard, for Elnathan, son of Achbor (v. 12), had been despatched to bring Uriah back to his fate (26:22–23).

The king's response

The graphic description that follows in verses 20–26 tells its own story. But, at every point, the contrast with Jehoiakim's father, Josiah, is painfully obvious. Then Shaphan, father to one of those present now, Gemariah, had also brought a scroll containing the divine word to the king and read it to him (2 Kings 22:10). When Josiah heard God's words he was deeply convicted and 'tore his clothes' as a sign of penitence and determination to act in obedience to what he had heard (2 Kings 22:11–13). The result was his great reform, in which he sought to base national life on the words of the law (2 Kings 23:1–25). Jehoiakim, far from tearing his clothes, tears up the scroll and burns the fragments, presumably to nullify the force of the threatened judgments it contained (v. 23), and the contrast with Josiah is still more forcefully drawn out as we are told that he and his courtiers were not 'alarmed, nor did they tear their garments' (v. 24).

It is interesting that among those who had the courage to advise the king to take a different course were Gemariah, son of Shaphan (v. 25). Another of Shaphan's sons, Ahikam, had been instrumental in saving Jeremiah's life (26:24), while a third, Elasah, had been one of those who conveyed the prophet's letter to the exiles in Babylon (29:3). It seems that there was a strong pro-reform party in the court. Theirs was a courageous stand while Jehoiakim was on the throne. Another, Elnathan (v. 25), possibly had a change of heart because of disquiet over the fate of Uriah.

These councillors, well-placed as they were and brave as they were, could not successfully save the prophet and his companion. However, we read that 'the Lord hid them' (v. 26). Powerful as Jehoiakim and all tyrants like him may be, they cannot ultimately defeat God's purposes.

FOR MEDITATION

In heavenly love abiding,
No change my heart shall fear.
And safe is such confiding,
For nothing changes here.
The storm may roar without me,
My heart may low be laid,
But God is round about me,
And can I be dismayed?

Anna Laetitia Waring (1823–1910)

The SCROLL REWRITTEN

The command to rewrite the scroll

If the king's intention in burning the scroll was to destroy its power and escape the judgment it predicted, then it was futile. Jeremiah himself had likened God's word to a 'hammer that breaks a rock in pieces' (23:29), and neither a deaf ear nor a stubborn heart has ever been enough to escape its challenge and its effects. The words are committed to writing again and God remains a force in the affairs of state and nation with which the king, for all his arbitrary power, cannot dispense.

Judgment against Jehoiakim

We learn in verses 29–31 just why the king was so outraged by Jeremiah's written oracles. Not only had they served as a merciless exposé of the social abuses that flourished during his reign, but they had clearly and repeatedly threatened judgment at the hand of the 'foe from the north', now identified with Babylon, if king and nation did not repent and change their ways (v. 29).

The announcement of judgment here again echoes the strong contrast afforded by the faithful Rechabites and the promise that their ancestor Jonadab would 'never lack a descendant to stand before me for all time' (35:19). Jehoiakim would have no one to succeed him (v. 30). In fact, his son Jehoiachin did follow him to the throne, but his reign was so short (three months) and ended in such humiliating defeat in exile that the spirit of this prediction might be said to have been fulfilled, if not its exact letter (2 Kings 24:6–16).

More puzzling is the prediction that Jehoiakim would die in disgrace and be denied a proper and honoured burial, substantially a repetition of the threat of 22:18–19. There was no greater disgrace for a member of the royal family than to be denied some kind of memorial (see Elijah's prediction of the dishonourable death that would befall Ahab's descendants, including his wife Jezebel, in 1 Kings 21:23–24). On the other hand, the prophet Ahijah, in announcing a similar threat to Jeroboam, promises an exception in the case of one son 'because in him there is found something pleasing to the Lord'

(1 Kings 14:11, 13). In fact, however, in spite of its negative evaluation of Jehoiakim, the book of Kings appears to know nothing of such a fate for him, his end being described in such a way as to suggest a perfectly normal death and burial (2 Kings 24:6).

How can this be explained? It should be noted, for one thing, that this difficulty does not suggest that the whole book of Jeremiah is the result of a radical rewriting, or even new invention, during and after the time of the exile, as some have come near suggesting. There can be no doubt that it contains much exilic and post-exilic application of the prophet's words and ministry to those of later times. But the fact that this prophecy has not been tailored to suit events suggests considerable respect for the original words of Jeremiah.

We have to recognize that prophecy is more a matter of the spirit of truth than a pedantic, literalistic prediction of events down to the last detail. That is the way New Testament writers understand Old Testament 'predictions' of the birth, ministry, death and resurrection of Jesus Christ. Jehoiakim's defiance of God's word proved totally ineffective, as Jeremiah predicted it would. The ridicule and opprobrium with which posterity viewed his reign (see 2 Kings 23:36—24:4) was exactly as great as that for one who suffered a dishonoured death and burial. Jeremiah was essentially right in predicting the futility of Jehoiakim's defiance of the word of God.

The triumph of God's word

The rewriting of the scroll (v. 32), with the addition 'of many similar words' (probably a reference to the rest of the book), proved beyond doubt that human attempts to muzzle the word of God are laughably ineffective. However we oppose, or even fail to promote, God's self-revelation by his 'word', history shows that God never leaves himself without witness.

FOR PRAISE

Lord, thy word abideth,
And our footsteps guideth;
Who its truth believeth,
Light and joy receiveth.

H.W. Baker (1821–77)

FRESH WARNING *of* IMPENDING DANGER

This chapter begins a new section of the book which extends to chapter 45 (see Introduction, p. 14). It recounts the last years of Judah from events during the reign of Zedekiah to the fall of Jerusalem in 586BC and the flight to Egypt of the group that took Jeremiah with them. The preceding section has recounted how the word of God, delivered through his prophet, was rejected by leaders and people alike. Now the tragic story of the inevitable judgment that Jeremiah had predicted unfolds.

The rejection of God's word

Verse 1 gives a brief resumé of the accession of Zedekiah to the throne, placed there by the Babylonians after they had deposed Jehoiachin for his father's rebellion (2 Kings 24:17). The fact that they changed his name (from Mattaniah to Zedekiah) shows that they regarded him as their puppet-king, appointed to carry out their policies. But 2 Kings goes on to say how he too rebelled, following a statement that 'he did what was evil in the sight of the Lord', which may well have referred to his rejection of Jeremiah's counsel to submit to the Babylonians because they were God's appointed instrument of judgment. This is drawn out in Jeremiah by the statement in verse 2 which affords a kind of summary of all that has been recorded in the preceding section of the book and acts as a link to what is to follow now in the story of defeat and disaster.

The king's embassy to the prophet

King Zedekiah sends delegates to Jeremiah asking him to intercede with God for the deliverance of the community (v. 3). The incident affords an interesting parallel to a similar request recorded in 21:1–7. It could even be a different version of the same event, for while the name of the chief delegate is different (Pashhur in 21:1, Jehucal here), the priest Zephaniah is mentioned in both. However, whether it is the same or a different incident, the fact mentioned in verse 5 that it occurred during the temporary lifting of the Babylonian siege when the Egyptians marched out to intervene is significant. For we have earlier read that it was during this time that the Judeans reneged on their pledges to release their slaves, made during the crisis when the siege was at its height (34:8–22; see especially v. 21). So this request for prayer for national safety was not matched by proper repentance and obedience to the word of God. It was 'skin deep' in the almost literal sense that their only concern was for the safety of their skins, and not for a deeper renewal of their life as the people of God.

The message of judgment

The utter futility of their prayer is matched only by the ineffectiveness of the Egyptians against the Babylonian might. It did not take the army of Nebuchadrezzar long to despatch the Egyptians back to their own borders, and very soon the siege was resumed, as Jeremiah here announced it surely would be (vv. 8–9). Indeed, so inevitable is the Babylonians' victory against Jerusalem that they could effect it even if all their men were walking wounded! (v. 10). But this 'inevitability' is not only due to the Babylonians' superior military skill and might; it is because they are carrying out a task appointed them by Yahweh. The 'inevitability' is due to the rejection by king and people of God's word, the sorry consequences of which are to be the theme of the chapters that follow.

A PRAYER
Lord, amid all the duties and tasks of my life today, its joys and sorrows, its successes and failures, its hopes and its doubts, keep me alert to your voice and confident that you are with me in everything, working for good. Amen

JEREMIAH ARRESTED

The prophet charged with desertion

Verse 12 tells how, during the lull in the Babylonian siege, Jeremiah sets out to go to his home district of Anathoth to see to some (unspecified) piece of family business. Since Anathoth was in the district of Benjamin (1:1), the 'Benjamin Gate', mentioned by this name only in the book of Jeremiah, presumably lay on the north side of the city leading to Benjaminite territory. Anathoth, identified with modern Ras el-Kharrubbeh, lay only about two and a half miles to the north-east of Jerusalem.

Considering that Jeremiah is recorded as having counselled desertion to the Babylonians (21:9) and that some were acting on the advice (38:19; 52:15), the sentry's suspicions (v. 13) were not altogether unreasonable.

Coming on top of the prophet's repeated warnings of defeat at the hands of the Babylonians, the anger of the officials is also understandable, particularly as they were responsible for maintaining public morale in a situation which, for all the hopes aroused by the departure of the besieging army to confront the Egyptians, was still clearly fraught with danger and uncertainty. They react harshly, with a flogging and imprisonment in a vault in a secure place. The fact that it had been specially created beneath the official residence of the royal secretary (v. 15) meant that it was under the closest possible supervision. Jeremiah was incarcerated there for 'a long time' (v. 16), possibly even until the time when the Babylonians returned to the siege, for it did not take them long to deal with the so-called 'threat' from Egypt.

The prophet and the king

King Zedekiah's attitude towards and relations with Jeremiah are presented in a very mixed way, ranging from downright hostility, through cautious respect, to kind consideration. Perhaps he was a weak and vacillating man. Perhaps his moods swung between despair and optimism as events took first this turn and then that. Certainly it seems strange that, after Jeremiah's blunt reply to an earlier approach

(37:3–10), Zedekiah should approach him again with a similar request for 'a word from the Lord' (v. 17). Possibly, as hinted above, the crisis had deepened again as the Babylonians returned to the siege, and perhaps we all sometimes hope that when God says what we do not want to hear, that is not his final word! Whatever the reason, the answer is as blunt and uncompromising as before (v. 17).

But now the prophet adds a new and almost personal note (vv. 18–19). He seeks to detach his message of the implacable judgment of God from his own personal animosity towards the king. Indeed, he argues that it is he, rather than the false prophets who assured the king that there was nothing to fear, who has been a true friend to king and people. The false prophets of comfort and 'peace' had sought only their own popularity and profit. He had sought the true welfare of his people at whatever cost to himself. Sometimes, a person's or a society's best friends are those who have the courage to speak the truth, even when that truth can be hurtful to others and injurious to the friends' own comfort.

Perhaps the king realizes this in his softer response to Jeremiah's request for a more tolerant treatment (vv. 20–21). Perhaps, deep down, he realizes that the prophet may well be a true representative of God and that, at the very least, it would be imprudent to emerge as his bitterest and most implacable enemy. Probably, he was just unsure whether Jeremiah or his own more amenable court prophets were speaking the truth. He must have hoped it was the latter, but he could not blind himself to the truth that Jeremiah had just spoken. The Babylonians were at the door again. Zedekiah would not be the last to try to 'play it both ways' when confronted by God's word. The trouble is that God's word does not offer two ways, only one—the way of obedience, even when that obedience may prove costly and call for courage.

FOR MEDITATION

The love of our neighbour is the only door out of the dungeon of self, where we mope and mow, striking sparks, and rubbing phosphorescence out of the walls, and blowing our own breath in our own nostrils, instead of issuing to the fair sunlight of God, the sweet winds of the universe.

George Macdonald, *Unspoken Sermons*

JEREMIAH'S LIFE *in* DANGER

The prophet cast into 'the pit'

The story of Jeremiah's arrest, interview with King Zedekiah and partial deliverance as told in chapter 38 shows several differences from that in chapter 37. Nevertheless, it seems best to regard them as accounts of the same episode which have come to us from two different traditions. The question arises, then: are there any particular theological emphases to be found in this account in chapter 38?

Again we read how the public preaching of Jeremiah aroused the hostility of some of the officials (vv. 1–4). By predicting the fall of the city to the Babylonians and the death of those citizens who stayed in it (v. 2; 21:8–9), the prophet was not only lowering public morale but, by the prophetic word, helping to bring about the very event predicted. The phrase 'this man is weakening the hands of the soldiers who are left in this city, and the hands of all the people' interestingly echoes exactly a phrase from one of the *Lachish Ostraca* (see comments on 34:7, p. 167), which says, 'The words of the princes are not good but… weaken our hands' (*Ostrakon 6*).

Again, the king gives way to his counsellors (v. 6; as in 37:15). But an interesting note appears in this account. The prophet was cast into a 'cistern' (Hebrew: *bor*) in which, we are told, 'there was no water' (v. 6). This cannot but recall the story of Joseph's being cast into a 'cistern' in which 'there was no water' (Genesis 37:24). The point is, of course, that Joseph was delivered from the pit, taken to Egypt and prospered there under the hand of God, thus, in a real way, symbolizing the story of Israel itself being preserved in Egypt and subsequently delivered by God. This same theme is echoed in a late, post-exilic prophecy, where God promises his subject people that 'I will set your prisoners free from the waterless pit' (Zechariah 9:11). The emphasis on the 'waterless pit' in this account of Jeremiah's imprisonment, then, may well be also to stress that he symbolizes the story of God's faithful people. If they submit to his judgment and remain faithful (see the prophet's words to the king in 38:17–20), they also will eventually be delivered by God from their own experience of 'bondage in Egypt'—that is, Babylonian exile.

Ebed-melech rescues Jeremiah

Verses 7–13 tell in graphic detail of the intervention of Ebed-melech (the name means 'servant of the king') on the prophet's behalf. The account in chapter 37 tells simply how the king 'sent for' Jeremiah (37:17), which does not, of course, preclude the possibility of a response to mediation. The king was sitting at the Benjamin Gate, possibly hearing legal cases there, when Ebed-melech, whose status as a 'eunuch' (v. 7) suggests a prominent place in the royal palace, put Jeremiah's case. His intervention is ostensibly purely on humanitarian grounds, that the prophet will be neglected and die in such a place (v. 9). Yet it is possible that he shared the prophet's view that his message was in fact the only one that could ultimately save the kingdom, and that he was therefore the king's friend. In any event, Ebed-Melech's plea is successful and, with the king's permission, he goes to raise the prophet from the cistern and have him placed in 'the court of the guard'. In chapter 37 it is said merely that this happened on the king's own initiative (37:21), but the two accounts are not incompatible, of course.

Yet the detail in the narrative of the prophet's rescue (vv. 10–13) here does suggest that this account finds particular significance in it. The prophet himself embodies the message that God will deliver those who are faithful to him. The account also highlights the influence that otherwise unknown people can have in the working out of God's purposes. The decision was the king's, as chapter 37 shows. But it came about because of the faithful humanity of one of the king's, and God's, servants. Ebed-melech lived up to his name as servant of both the earthly and the heavenly king.

A PRAYER

Lord, King of all, in the limited circumstances of my life,
may I faithfully play a part as your servant today in your
greater purposes for all people. Amen

JEREMIAH ADVISES SURRENDER

The king sends for Jeremiah

In all the strange twists and turns of the accounts of Zedekiah's relations with Jeremiah and his apparently endless vacillations, we have to remember the difficult and delicate situation he was in. He was a puppet of the Babylonians, put there as 'their man' after they had deposed and deported Jehoiachin, whom many Judeans still regarded as their legitimate king. If Zedekiah failed to toe the Babylonians' line, he could expect little mercy from them, as events were indeed to prove. Yet, if he displayed submission to the invaders, he would arouse the wrath of his still fiercely patriotic and anti-Babylonian court. This is why he tiptoes between the two and, in the end, as so often in such cases, succeeds only in arousing the wrath and hostility of both groups.

Small wonder, then, that he anxiously desires a word from God through Jeremiah, but that he sends for him secretly, trying to keep any account of their meeting from the officials (vv. 16, 24–25). Jeremiah has been here before, however, and seeks first an assurance that, if his 'word' again appears unpopular, his life will not be in danger. What he fears, of course, is not so much the king as the implacable opposition of the patriotic party at court (38:4). The king is equally anxious to avoid their wrath (vv. 24–26)! But, after long experience, Jeremiah is also resigned to the fact that the king is unlikely to follow his advice (v. 15).

The king's stark choice

Jeremiah counsels surrender as the only practical policy (vv. 17–23). He might have in mind the comparatively lenient treatment meted out to Jehoiachin who did surrender to the Babylonians (2 Kings 24: 10–15). He might well have seen that there was simply no realistic alternative but surrender, for, in spite of the hot-headed rhetoric of the patriotic officials, Judah stood no military chance against the vastly superior might of the Babylonians. At a deeper level, however, Jeremiah knew that the city would fall since he firmly believed that the Babylonians were God's instrument of judgment against his people for their sin.

What a choice for a king, however, who is responsible for his people's safety! Well might he fear the wrath of those of his own entourage who would see his capitulation as cowardly treason (v. 19). The prophet can bring him no comfort. Only in surrender is there any hope. In a vision he has seen the consequences as the women of the royal harem are led away into captivity, chanting a poetic lament bewailing the desertion of all friends and allies (vv. 21–22). Capture of the harem was always a sign of the transfer of power, which is why Absalom entered his father David's harem as a sign of his revolt (2 Samuel 16:21–22). Possibly, the words of the women are indeed from a psalm which speaks of the feet of the sufferer being sunk in the mire (Psalm 69:2), in which case there is an ironic contrast between the fate of the king and the prophet's deliverance from 'the pit' (compare Psalm 69:15, and see comments on 38:6–13, pp. 184–185). In the account in this chapter, the two men symbolize the different fortunes awaiting the obedient and the disobedient in the community.

Jeremiah's life spared

The king's fear of offending his powerful officials lies behind the ruse he suggests (vv. 24–26). If it were known that he had been consulting a prophet whose message was so deeply suspect, he would have had a powerful faction up in arms against him. That he was merely agreeing to the prophet's request for a more comfortable and less threatening place of confinement gave a cover for their meeting together. So Jeremiah remained in 'the court of the guard' for the remainder of the siege.

FOR MEDITATION

Zedekiah thought that he wanted a word from the Lord which would miraculously transform his situation, as we often do. What we more often need is a word from the Lord which will transform us, so that we can face our situation creatively with God.

JERUSALEM FALLS *to* BABYLON

The city is taken

A slightly fuller account of the Babylonian siege and fall of Jerusalem is to be found at 52:4–11 and also in 2 Kings 25:1–7. The placing of an account here may be because the editors saw it as theologically pivotal to the story they are telling in the book. The king and people have rejected God's word (chs. 26—36) and his messenger (chs. 37—38). Now comes the disaster that has been the subject of so much of the prophet's preaching and of anxious enquiries from the king. His fate, which epitomizes that of the city, is also highlighted. It is possible that this has led to some dislocation of the original text. For example, the court held by the Babylonian officials and described in verse 3 is not mentioned in chapter 52 and seems a little early in the proceedings. Perhaps originally it was connected with the decisions they made concerning Jeremiah (39:11–14). However, the editors are more interested in theological lessons than in exact chronological reconstruction of events. For some reason, at which we can only guess, verses 4–13 do not appear in the Septuagint version of the book.

The siege, which lasted eighteen months (v. 2), came to its inevitable end in the eleventh year of Zedekiah (either 587 or 586BC). Even if the account of the court held by Babylonian officials is out of place in verse 3, it portrays in a dramatic and stark way the transfer of power, effective, with all its innumerable consequences, from that day on. In some English versions the names and titles of the officials have been muddled. In the light of Babylonian inscriptions and the list in 39:13 we should probably read them as Nergal-sharezer of Shimmagir (a region of Babylon)—probably the same individual named again later in the verse and described as the 'commander of the army' (Rab-mag)—and Nebu-shazban the Rab-saris (the title of a court official).

Zedekiah's flight and fate

The terrible incident in verses 6–7 is reported in all three accounts of the capture of the city. It is ironic that Zedekiah, like Jeremiah before him (37:12–15), attempts to leave the city, in this case by stealth in flight; and that he is chased and stopped by Babylonian soldiers and brought before Nebuchadrezzar, just as the prophet had been stopped by a sentry and brought before officials. Nebuchadrezzar, who had entrusted the conduct of the siege to his generals, was camped at Riblah, a strategic place to the north, situated where the roads to Egypt and Mesopotamia intersected (v. 6).

The king who stubbornly refused to 'see' the truth of God's word brought to him by the prophet is blinded after witnessing the terrible sight of his sons' execution. While the prophet was spared, Zedekiah was taken prisoner to Babylon, where he died (see 52:11).

A second deportation

In the manner of those days (although events in our own time show that the ancients had no monopoly on cruelty in war), a terrible punishment was meted out to the city and its inhabitants. Many officials were killed (v. 6); the royal palace (which, of course, included the temple) was burnt, and so were many of the houses of the people. The text in verse 8 speaks of the '*house* of the people' but as no such building is known and 2 Kings 25:9 has the plural, that should probably be read here. The exact number of those deported to Babylon is differently estimated in the Old Testament and was probably not known. The picture given here of only a handful of the poorest and lowest being left behind probably exaggerates. Such exaggeration would be due partly to the belief shown in the book that the purpose of God lay with the 'real Israel' in Babylon rather than with those who remained in Judah or who went to Egypt (compare the vision of the 'good' and the 'bad' figs in ch. 24). It may also be due partly to the very human reaction in times of real disaster to imagine that *everything* has been lost and the situation is utterly hopeless. But the prophet who had warned of the disaster had also assured anyone who would listen that God had plans beyond the exile. All is not lost while God is still around.

A PRAYER

Lord, we pray for all in our day who have been driven from their homes by war, by political, racial or religious persecution, or by natural disaster. May they not lack the help of those individuals and organizations which seek to show your care for the needy, and may we, who dwell securely, genuinely welcome those who seek to start a new life among us. Amen

Trust In God Vindicated

Jeremiah receives protection

It may seem strange that the great Nebuchadrezzar should take a personal interest in the welfare of the prophet, Jeremiah (v. 11). No doubt the instructions were given in his name and with his authority from someone further down the chain of command. But the incident shows that the Babylonians knew that Jeremiah had counselled surrender and that they therefore regarded him as a friend worthy of support, especially as they would have known the danger he was in from having antagonized the powerful nationalist faction. They may well also have thought that his influence would be a help to them now in settling the conquered territory. Some of the same Babylonian officials mentioned in verse 3 saw to his release from the 'court of the guard' (vv. 13–14; see 37:21; 38:28).

It is interesting that they put him for safety in the care of Gedaliah whom they intended to appoint as governor (40:5, 7; 2 Kings 25:22). Gedaliah's father, Ahikam, had been one of Jeremiah's protectors (26:24) and his son was probably of the same party that supported the prophet's counsel of surrender to the Babylonians. This was certainly his advice to all and sundry on his appointment (40:9), in words very reminiscent of the prophet's advice to the Jews who had been deported in 597BC (29:5–7).

But, again, the main thrust of these verses is to contrast the faithful prophet's fortunes with those of the faithless Zedekiah and the many who refused to accept the word of God that the prophet had ceaselessly and faithfully proclaimed.

Deliverance for Ebed-melech

It is clear from the command to the prophet to 'Go, and say to Ebed-melech…' that events in verses 15–18 are out of chronological order, especially as the message he is to take is to announce the capture of the city as an event still in the future (v. 16). We have already seen some evidence of parallel accounts of what is probably the same event in chapters 37 and 38 and, again, in chapter 39 (see comments on 39:3, pp. 188–189). But this account of the promise of God to the faithful Ebed-melech is another example of the editors wishing to draw a particular theological lesson from the events. We have seen the detailed way they have contrasted the fates of Zedekiah, his officials and the mass of the people with that of Jeremiah. We have seen some evidence to suggest that the picture of Jeremiah's being shown leniency by the king was to portray Jeremiah as a 'type' of the true and faithful Israel, delivered from danger in the same way that Joseph had been in Egypt—a picture seen as symbolic of the future promise to Israel in Zechariah 9:11 (see comments on Jeremiah 38:6, p. 185). Now, again, a contrast is drawn between the fate of the disobedient majority and such a faithful and obedient servant as Ebed-melech. Indeed, the promise of deliverance is explicitly made to him '"because you have put your trust in me", says the Lord' (v. 18).

All of this means that we should read the accounts of events in those confused last days of Judah with an eye and an ear open to the theological truths drawn from the prophet's words and ministry, rather than getting bogged down in trying to sort out a consistent and fully coherent reconstruction of those events down to the last detail.

FOR MEDITATION

It is those who put down the sheet-anchor of faith in God who have a better chance of riding out life's roughest storms and of being a help to those who are drifting.

GOD'S CARE *for* THOSE *who* TRUST HIM

God speaks through events

It is interesting that this short section of narrative begins with an opening usually associated with a prophetic oracle: 'The word that came to Jeremiah from the Lord…' (v. 1). There are two significant points about this. The narrative tells of Jeremiah's release by the Babylonians following the capture of Jerusalem. Thus an *event* is being described as 'a word from the Lord'. It reminds us that God's word in the Old Testament is seen not only as declaratory, but as a matter of deeds and action. He created the world by his 'word' ('God *said*, "Let there be…" and there was…', Genesis 1:3 and so on). When he speaks through a prophet, forces are released by which he brings about the results that are predicted (Isaiah 55:10–11: 'my word… shall *accomplish* that which I purpose'). In this connection it is interesting that the Hebrew for 'word' (*dabar*) means both a 'word' and an 'event'.

God works through the events of history, whether those events seem good or bad to us, or merely everyday and ordinary. There is no situation in which he is not present in what is happening and able to work out his purpose through it for those who trust him (Romans 8:28). His care of his faithful servant Jeremiah, even in these tumultuous times, is a declaration of his power and love, and is included by the editors as an object lesson for all the people similarly to trust God and remain faithful to him. Then they too will know a similar deliverance.

God speaks in unexpected ways

The second remarkable thing about this 'word from the Lord' is that it is spoken through the mouth of a Babylonian army officer (v. 2). It seems strange that such a person should utter the same theological truth that the prophet has proclaimed consistently—and in very much the same words. Of course, we know that the report of Jeremiah's advice to king and people to surrender had reached the

Babylonians, leading to their decision to treat him leniently (39:11–14). Further, there are other instances in the Old Testament of a foreign general quoting the Israelites' own faith back at them (Isaiah 36:7). But, if we allow that the editors have at least polished Nebuzaradan's words, the point remains that to their eyes of faith the Babylonians are, however unwittingly, fulfilling God's purposes, just as Isaiah long before had said that the Assyrians were 'the axe in God's hands' (Isaiah 10:5–19). Jeremiah had said persistently that the Babylonians were the agents by whom God was going to judge his people for their sins. If his people would submit, however, and turn to him in faith and obedience, then God would not forsake them and, eventually, they would know deliverance. As we have seen in these chapters, Jeremiah embodies in his own person a powerful demonstration of God's power to act to deliver his people. The prophet is a prototype of God's people as a whole if only they would listen and obey.

These are the important things about the record here. As we have seen, some of the details are obscure, and it is difficult to reconcile exactly what happened to Jeremiah once the city fell when we compare 38:28b, 39:11–14 and 40:1–6. Probably they are parallel, independent accounts, although this one may give more details of what is described more generally elsewhere. The important thing is that they teach the power of God to guard his people in all situations, however strong their human enemies may seem.

In the light of the book's insistence that the purpose of God lay with those who went into exile in Babylon (see the vision of the good and bad figs in ch. 24), it is strange that Jeremiah elected to stay with those left back in the land. While it is possible that the final editors of the book wanted to stress that the returning exiles were a legitimate part of the people of God, the 'true Israel', it is also possible that the prophet, as a good 'pastor' ('shepherd', see 23:1–4), decided to stay with those whose need was greatest.

PRAYER

Lord, when the circumstances of my life frighten and depress me,
help me to look to you and be ready to work with you,
in faith that you can bring your purposes out of them
for my good and the good of others. Amen

The PROMISE *of a* NEW BEGINNING

Gedaliah acts on Jeremiah's teaching

After all the horror and carnage of the Babylonian attack and capture of Jerusalem, this passage carries an almost idyllic note of hope and serenity. Jeremiah is not mentioned, but his influence and teachings are very strong, nevertheless.

We have already heard of Gedaliah's appointment by Nebuchad-rezzar (40:5). When news that the destruction and forced exile of the native population were not so total as to prevent some kind of life continuing in Judah, with hopes of order and good government, many who had escaped or survived the fighting began to return. A list of some of the most prominent in verse 8 almost exactly corresponds to the historical notice recorded in 2 Kings 25:23.

In Gedaliah's counsel to them in verse 9, we hear the strong influence of Jeremiah. Indeed, the counsel to settle down, accept Babylonian overlordship and 'dwell in the land' is very reminiscent of his advice to the Jewish exiles in Babylon (29:5–9). Gedaliah and Jeremiah may well have been very close. The new governor's father, Ahikam, had once been instrumental in saving the prophet's life (26:24). Gedaliah himself seems to have accepted Jeremiah's advice that the best policy lay in submission to the Babylonians. Indeed, it may well have been his known espousal of this line of action that led to his appointment by them.

Gedaliah's following of this policy of quiet submission may have been, for him, primarily a matter of practical politics. Resistance was recklessly foolish and doomed to failure, as events had shown all too clearly. Yet, in echoing the words of the prophet, he voices the theological conviction of Jeremiah that, since the Babylonians were God's appointed instrument of judgment on his people for their sin, submission to them expressed deeper submission to God. And the prophet had shown again and again that only through this door of penitence, faith and obedience lay the way to future salvation.

The possibilities of life with God

This point is certainly not lost on the editors of the book. The almost idyllic picture painted here is a poignant indication of what might have been, had this lesson continued to be taken to heart. Even amid all the ruins of land, temple and homes, a good life was possible for a community who lived in obedience to God.

Gedaliah promises to act as mediator between them and the Babylonians (v. 10), thus representing the good and strong government that any community needs, especially in such critical and dangerous times. With Jerusalem in ruins, he moves the seat of government to Mizpah, a town on the border between Judah and Benjamin some five miles north of the capital. But the very name has theological significance for the editors. It is related to the Hebrew verb 'to watch' and this form of it can mean 'a watchtower'. That is how it can also carry overtones of God's 'watching' over his people (Genesis 31:49).

Further, the promise is of fruitful harvests being known again and of community life gradually being rebuilt in the towns that had been deserted (v. 10). Again, a promise of Jeremiah for the future seems to be beginning to be fulfilled (31:5).

And when news of this hopeful development, suggesting signs of hope and of God's blessing on the community, begins to seep through, others begin to return 'from all the places to which they had been scattered' (vv. 11–12) to join in the security and prosperity, a small foretaste of the promised return of all 'exiles' in the future (31:8). Indeed, to drive the point home, even the word 'remnant' is used of this little community under Gedaliah (v. 11; 31:7).

The passage thus reinforces Jeremiah's message at every point. It indicates what could have happened had those left in the land remained faithful to God. Alas, it was not to be. The message of the book is that hope for the future lay not with them, but with the exiles in Babylon.

FOR MEDITATION AND PRAYER

For all sad words of tongue or pen,
The saddest are these: 'It might have been'.

J.G. Whittier (1807–92)

Lord, help us, your people, not to miss your purposes for us and
with us through neglect, lack of vision or fickleness of faith. Amen

ISHMAEL'S REVOLT & TREACHERY

The idyll of Gedaliah's short rule is rudely and violently shattered. Hopes that the little community might form the basis of a true 'remnant' (40:11), enjoying all the promises of God's blessing, are broken on the reality of the sheer evil of the human heart. In one way, the Genesis story of Paradise is tragically re-enacted. For all the further details given here in comparison with 2 Kings 25:25–26, many questions remain unanswered, chief among them being the reasons for Ishmael's assassination of Gedaliah and apparently senseless and wanton orgy of killing. We can only guess at the answers to problems which have perplexed all commentators. Perhaps, in the end, it is all too real a statement of the fact that much evil is irrational and pointless.

Gedaliah is warned

Johanan, with Ishmael, had been one of the early leaders to rally to Gedaliah (40:8) but, unlike Ishmael, he remained loyal and, learning of his colleague's plot, warned the governor. Ishmael's motives are never made clear. Perhaps he represented the 'anti-Babylonian' policy of some in Zedekiah's court who resented Gedaliah's policy of passive submission. Not is it clear why Baalis, the Ammonite king, had suborned Ishmael and supported him in his enterprise (v. 14). Perhaps he also wanted partners in a drive against Babylonian rule or, possibly, he did not want too strong a resurgent Judah on his own doorstep. We are not told.

Gedaliah comes across as a good, trusting man who wanted 'a new style of politics' as we say now, a society not based on intrigue, counter-intrigue and ruthless jostling for position. He refuses to doubt an old ally and declines to let Johanan take matters into his own hands. Johanan, however, uses an ominous phrase in verse 15. If Ishmael were to succeed, 'the *remnant* of Judah' would perish. In the bloodbath which is to follow, all hope that Gedaliah's community might form the basis of a 'new Israel' will be the first victim.

Ishmael assassinates Gedaliah

Gedaliah's trust and gentleness proved tragically misplaced. Ishmael, breaking all the Middle Eastern laws of trust between host and guest, takes advantage of their utter unpreparedness and assassinates Gedaliah and his entourage (vv. 1–2). For good measure, they even put some Babylonian soldiers to death. This might indicate either Ishmael's 'anti-Babylonian' intentions or his desire to eliminate any unwanted witnesses. It might, however, just have happened, unplanned, in the heat of the moment, which would explain why Ishmael flees, any ulterior motive unfulfilled, to escape Babylonian vengeance (41:10, 15).

The massacre of the innocents

If it is hard to fathom Ishmael's motives in assassinating Gedaliah and his followers, the massacre of pilgrims to Jerusalem from the north (vv. 4–8) appears nothing but wanton violence for its own sake. The site of the ruined temple evidently attracted pilgrims coming to lament its fall (note the traditional signs of mourning, vv. 5–6). Evidence of the persistence of the custom is found in Zechariah 7:2–3. Possibly, the book of Lamentations contains some of the laments used on such occasions. Ishmael employs further treachery to lure them to their death, although a few show the kind of sagacity that would appeal to so ruthless a man: 'If you spare us, we'll make it worth your while' (v. 8). Ironically, a defensive trench, symbol of the old divisions and hostility within Israel (v. 9; see 1 Kings 15:22), now being so sadly renewed, becomes their mass grave, a war crime for which there have been plenty of recent parallels. After such an orgy of bloodletting, Ishmael decides to make for the shelter afforded by his backers, the Ammonites (v. 10).

Commentators often wonder why such a story has been included in the book, since Jeremiah apparently plays no part in it. Yet, as with 40:7–12, it illustrates some profound truths of his teaching. A new community needs more than renewed circumstances. It needs renewed hearts (17:9–10; 31:31–34).

FOR THOUGHT

This passage shows two ways of trying to deal with evil. Johanan's is to meet it with its own kind of violence. Gedaliah's is to deny its reality in the weakness of naïve trust. Archbishop Tutu said that black South Africans chose the way of 'truth'—recognizing the reality of evil, and then paying the price of its forgiveness. In his words, 'They chose the middle way of individual amnesty for truth—the essence of being human.'

JOHANAN DEFEATS ISHMAEL

Ishmael is routed

Tragically, because of Johanan's loyalty to Gedaliah, it is only after his leader's death that he can attack Ishmael—having been forbidden by Gedaliah to do so (40:15–16). He gathers a force large enough to despatch the ringleader and save all the hostages, although the canny Ishmael manages to escape back to his friend, the king of the Ammonites, with a depleted handful of followers (v. 15).

Two place names are singled out by the narrator which help to give a certain theological interpretation to events. Johanan and his force come upon Ishmael at 'the great pool that is in Gibeon' (v. 12). That very site played a significant part in the account of Abner's revolt against David when he supported Saul's son, Ishbaal (2 Samuel 2:12–16). It was there that the revolt against the legitimate king (as David was regarded) was broken. Similarly it is described here as the place where Ishmael's challenge to God's chosen ruler was defeated.

Then, after their victory, Johanan's men wisely decide that Judah is not likely to be a very safe place once the Babylonians hear of the murder of their appointed governor and some of their own troops (41:2–3). When troops come in force seeking vengeance, they are not likely to be too precise in legal enquiries as to who was actually responsible. Vengeance aimed at 'encouraging the others' tends to be vehement and indiscriminate. So, they begin to muster at a convenient place for escape to Egypt, near Bethlehem (v. 17). But, again, a place name is significant. 'Geruth Chimham' means the 'holding of Chimham'. Chimham was a close associate (son, according to the Septuagint) of Barzillai, who also played an important, loyal role in another revolt against David, that of Absalom his son (2 Samuel 19:31–40). Barzillai sent him to accompany David on his return to ultimate victory in Jerusalem. No wonder David charged Solomon with the responsibility of looking after the sons of Barzillai (1 Kings 2:7). It seems possible, then, that this land near Bethlehem was remembered as the 'land granted to Chimham'.

Thus, the mention of these two places seems to be aimed at demonstrating that, like David, Gedaliah had been a ruler chosen by

God (even though appointed by the Babylonians). Ishmael's revolt therefore represented a revolt against God and his purposes for the little 'remnant' in Judah who are, in fact, so described in 42:2 (and see 40:11, 15).

The 'remnant' consult Jeremiah

Jeremiah reappears in the narrative at 42:1–2, although, as we have seen, he has never really been absent, the influence of his teaching and ministry apparent everywhere in the way the events have been recounted.

Emigration to Egypt with their families, leaving behind their houses, land and livelihood, was obviously a grave and major step to take, and we can imagine that a good deal of debate went on among Johanan and his forces. They decided to consult Jeremiah and ask him to act in his prophetic role as intermediary between God and people, bringing them the mind of God in this matter. In this way they showed the same kind of model of trust in God, and, we must assume, sincere desire to obey his word, that Gedaliah had done. Such response would show them to be a true 'remnant', genuine inheritors of the role of the 'true Israel' (40:11).

There can be no real communion with God unless there is openness to whatever it is he wants to say. Nothing could be more open than the prophet's promise to relay to them *whatever* God says (v. 4) and their undertaking to be obedient to *whatever* it is they hear (vv. 5–6). Indeed, they voice the theology of the prophet and the editors of the book when they piously say, 'It may go well with us when we obey the voice of the Lord our God' (v. 6).

FOR MEDITATION AND PRAYER

'Stand at the crossroads… and ask where the good way lies; and walk in it, and find rest for your souls' (6:16).

Lord, may I be attentive enough to hear your voice today, and loving enough to obey it. Amen

'REMAIN *in* JUDAH!'

God's promise to his 'remnant'

It is striking that, with the people awaiting so momentous a decision, Jeremiah takes ten days before he feels confident of bringing them God's word (v. 7). It reminds us that a prophet's communication with God is not an 'instant' affair, as though knowledge of the mind of God comes with the flick of a switch. We have seen an earlier example of this in the prophet's confrontation with Hananiah (28: 12–14). We do not know how prophets became convinced of what God was saying, but the process clearly involved a great deal of prayer and meditation.

Jeremiah brings them a promise from God, although a conditional one, the opening word being 'If' (v. 10). And in his assurance of what God wants to say at this juncture, his own experience clearly plays a part. In the account of his commissioning, Jeremiah was told that his mission would be 'to build and to plant' as well as 'to pluck up and throw down' (1:10), so he is able to be confident in announcing that God's desire for them is 'to plant you' (v. 10). Further, he is able to meet their very natural fear of the Babylonians with the assurance that God himself will protect them (v. 11), exactly the promise God had made to him at the start of his ministry (1:19).

It sounds strange to hear that God 'repents' of his former judgment on his people (v. 10; NRSV 'I am sorry for'). However, this does not imply fickleness or inconstancy on God's part. On the contrary, when his people respond to his will for them, the way to all his good purposes is opened up. Choosing their own plans for themselves switches the points on to another line, leading to a different destination.

The results of disobedience

If verses 15–22 seem a harsh denunciation of any intention of going down to Egypt, it has to be remembered from what the prophet has already said that this would be to show lack of trust in the very promises that have been made to them in God's name. There is also the very realistic note sounded that if they are looking for safety from the Babylonians, Egypt is an improbable place to find it. Egypt would be no match for the vastly greater power. In 568BC Nebuchadrezzar was to invade Egypt, demonstrating this all too clearly.

Warning of the fate in Egypt

The severe warning extended in these verses about the fate that would await them if they still insisted on going to Egypt probably suggests that, by now, Jeremiah suspected which faction was going to gain the upper hand among the 'remnant of Judah', so-called twice in a desperate attempt to recall them to their true calling and real destiny (vv. 15, 19). The enormity of such an action is underlined by a third reason. Not only would it show lack of trust in God's promise and be a futile act in itself, but it would be to disobey a specific command that God gave their fathers when he brought them out of Egypt. They were 'never to return that way again' (Deuteronomy 17:16), words explicitly recalled in verse 19. God had delivered them from the place of slavery. To go back would be to deny their status as God's redeemed people, a people to whom he can give more than ever they may hope to receive from the Egyptians. It would be to deny their status as 'a remnant'.

Indeed, Jeremiah even echoes the solemn words of Moses when he gave the covenant people the law, that 'this day I have set before you life and death' (v. 21; Deuteronomy 30:19–20).

FOR MEDITATION

Speaking of the phrase that 'God repents' (v. 10), Carroll says, 'It is one means of expressing the view that the past need not be overdeterminative of the future. It is the language of possibility and renewal…' (p. 718). God's word to us is always of possibility and renewal. Only our failure to hear closes down the horizon.

JEREMIAH'S WARNING UNHEEDED

The 'remnant's' rejection of God

There is no doubt for the narrator of this passage that what Jeremiah has said expresses the 'words of the Lord their God' (v. 1; see 42:7, 9, 18). In spite of the pledge the leaders had given that they would obey that word, whatever it turned out to be (42:5), now that it seems to threaten what they see as their own best interests, they reject it as 'false' (a 'lie', v. 2). It is ironic that they use the same term with which Jeremiah himself has rejected the words of the 'false' prophets (8:8; 14:14).

Possibly it is suggestive that the order of the leaders' names has changed (v. 2; see 42:1), implying that Azariah has taken charge. Yet Johanan seems content to go along with his counsel. Those agreeing with this ringleader are described as 'insolent' men (v. 2). The word can also mean 'scornful' or 'presumptuous'. Nothing more deafens people to God's true word than an arrogant assumption that it is we who know best. From their perspective, their action seems reasonable enough. The coming of Babylonian troops to avenge Gedaliah's death would mean danger (v. 3). The trouble comes when human beings imagine that their limited perspectives enable them to see more than God with his far longer vision.

The fateful decision to emigrate to Egypt is taken (vv. 5–7). The impression given that there was no one left in Judah cannot be right, but, again, the highly significant word 'remnant' is used (v. 5). This supreme act of disobedience to God meant that there was no community left behind who could prove to be the nucleus of God's new, true 'Israel'. Hope would lie with those in Babylon.

It is interesting that Baruch is thought to be a possible pernicious influence on Jeremiah (v. 3). We hear little about Baruch, but he was clearly a very close confidant of the prophet's, employed by him to record important deeds (32:12–16) and to take down a record of all his teaching (36:4, 32). We meet him again in a similar role in chapter 45. Both he and Jeremiah are taken to Egypt—we must assume against their will, in view of all that the prophet has said on the matter (42:15–17). From the human point of view, the prophet's life therefore ends in failure. He must have felt indeed like the 'suffering servant' of Isaiah 49:4. But God's plans were not thwarted by human intransigence and the prophet's words were to have lasting effect beyond anything he could have dreamed of.

God's rejection of the 'remnant'

Once in Egypt, Jeremiah is commanded to perform one more act of prophetic symbolism (vv. 8–13). Tahpanhes is usually identified with Tell Def-neh in the extreme north-east of Egyptian territory. The act of placing large stones in the paving in front of 'Pharaoh's palace' (v. 9: a large administrative building must be meant, since the 'palace' would have been in the capital) is intended to symbolize the fact that, one day, Nebuchadrezzar would rear his own throne there. Again the prophecy is of more symbolic than literal significance. Nebuchadrezzar is recorded as invading Egypt in 568BC, but a complete subjugation of the country is not reported. His punitive raid was enough to demonstrate that there was no secure hiding place there, however, and the point is clearly made that no community that had chosen to undo God's redemptive work by going back to Egypt would ever form the nucleus of the true 'remnant'. God had rejected Egypt and he now rejects those who have gone there in defiance of his word. Verse 13 shows that it is the idolatrous religious life of Egypt which is the reason for God's rejection, a matter to be brought out more fully in the following chapter.

FOR MEDITATION

Jesus went to the heart of the problem raised by this passage when he said, 'Anyone who resolves to do the will of God will know whether the teaching is from God or whether I am speaking on my own' (John 7:17). To be 'resolved to do the will of God' is to go a long way down the road of discerning what that will is.

The PROPHET WARNS the JUDEANS in EGYPT

The solemn warning of their history

Chapter 44 develops at length and in detail Jeremiah's warnings to those who chose to go to Egypt. The fact that the language and style are very much those of the prose sections of the book and strongly echo the Deuteronomistic writings suggests that we have here an expansion of the prophet's words by the editors who wished to apply his teachings to later generations. However, there is little here that has not been the theme of earlier poetic oracles.

Eventually there was a large Jewish population in Egypt. From the fourth century BC there was a Jewish colony forming a military garrison at Elephantine, an island on the Nile; and, later, those in Alexandria were numerous enough to warrant a Greek translation of their scriptures and to produce the Septuagint there. Yet perhaps the names of the places mentioned in verse 1 have theological as well as geographical and historical significance. Migdol was the name of a place where the Israelites encamped while leaving Egypt at the time of the Exodus (Exodus 14:2). Now some of them are back there, ignoring the command God gave their ancestors that 'they were never to return that way again' (Deuteronomy 17:16). Further, Tahpanhes is mentioned by Jeremiah in an attack on the sins of the people, which will surely lead to a judgment suffered at the hands of the Egyptians (Jeremiah 2:16–20). By returning there, they have turned their back on God whose loving care for them led him to deliver them from Egypt, and are seeking the protection of those who care for them not at all.

In verses 3–6 the reasons for their judgment are spelled out yet again. Jerusalem and Judah were defeated and devastated because of their religious apostasy and unfaithfulness, a theme of many of the poetic oracles (3:1–5). This was in spite of repeated warnings from the (true) prophets whom God kept sending to warn them (v. 4; see 7:25; 2 Kings 17:13). Yet still they are failing to learn the glaring lessons of history.

The 'remnant' reject their status

Yet again, the word 'remnant' is used in its theological sense of a community of those whom God has chosen as his own and through whom all his future plans of salvation are to be effected (v. 7). By their wilful acts they have deliberately rejected that status. It is not, in the first place, because God has rejected them. They have 'cut themselves off' from their true destiny by their choices, an evil committed mainly 'against yourselves' (v. 7). It is more than once suggested in the Bible that 'judgment', far from being the act of a capricious and wrathful God, is the fate that human beings choose for themselves when they cut themselves off from him (Romans 1:18–25).

Another reason for God's rejection of their plans to migrate to Egypt now appears. The temptation offered by the (false) religious practices of those among whom they have chosen to live is bound to lead them astray, as formerly they were led astray by the gods of Canaan (v. 8). Indeed, far from feeling any shame at their practices, they have not even thought of 'humbling' themselves and returning to the old laws that God gave their ancestors for their true well-being (v. 10; see 6:16). It is the complacent, self-satisfied, almost brazen attitude shown by those described as 'insolent men' in 43:2.

God rejects the Judeans

The truth of what they have done in cutting themselves off from their 'remnant' status is solemnly underlined by God's own formal rejection of them. This 'remnant' will know only defeat, suffering and rejection (v. 12), and not one of them will ever return to their homeland to form a community through whom God can build anew, except for a pathetic handful of refugees (v. 14).

A PRAYER

Lord, may I never wilfully or by neglect cut myself off from you and all for which you have destined me. Amen

TWO DIAGNOSES *of* JUDAH'S MISFORTUNES

The people's diagnosis

In this passage we are offered two completely contradictory explanations for the ills that have befallen the community in Egypt. The
people trace everything back to the fact that they abandoned the
worship of the 'queen of heaven'. Earlier the prophet had attacked
those who indulged in this pagan cult (7:16–20). Although this deity
is unnamed, it is usually assumed to be the Canaanite fertility goddess, Ashtarte.

The reason the cult was generally abandoned may well go back to
the time of King Josiah who, in his policy of religious reform in Judah
(2 Kings 22:11—23:25), 'deposed... those who made offerings to
Baal, to the sun, the moon, the constellations, and all the host of the
heavens' (2 Kings 23:5). We do not know how effective his reform
was 'on the ground', but his early death in battle (2 Kings 23:29–30)
must have been a severe blow to the reform party. The fact is that his
death began the slide of Judah towards defeat and exile, a fact that
the editors of the books of Kings put down to the continuing effects
of Manasseh's evil reign (2 Kings 23:26).

Nevertheless, there is a totally unrealistic element of 'the grass is
greener on the other side of the fence' in their attitude to their past
life in Judah (v. 17), similar to that of the people who complained to
Moses that they had been better off in Egypt (Exodus 16:3; Numbers
11:4–5). Although women appear to have taken the most active role
in the cult, it is made clear that all have been involved (v. 19), just as
it was in 7:16–20.

The prophet's diagnosis

Jeremiah turns the people's argument completely on its head (vv.
20–23). What has happened has been God's judgment on them for
just the kind of idolatry they are now practising, and which those
before them had practised in Judah. Such apostasy showed their
complete lack of trust in God for his help in their time of need and

their foolish substitute of an alien deity, to whom they turn in a virtually superstitious hope for a change of luck. The familiar phrase to describe this comes in verse 23: 'You did not obey the voice of the Lord or walk in his law.'

Judgment is announced

Again, just as it was the people who had 'cut themselves off' from God and his loving care (44:7), so now God allows them their own way (v. 25). That fateful phrase 'By all means, keep your vows and make your libations!' expresses the disturbing truth that human beings need to be careful over what they pray for. They are likely to get it!

Again, God's rejection of this community in Egypt is emphatically stated (vv. 27–29). There will be no more prayer heard by him from those who have chosen to direct their trust elsewhere. Those who refuse to pray lose the capacity for prayer, just as another prophet, Amos, said that the refusal to hear God's word leads to the silencing of that word (Amos 8:11–12). Apparently, as with physical attributes, so with spiritual ones, it is a case of 'Use it or lose it'.

The folly of going to Egypt for security is again underlined by a threat, this time more specific, against Egypt (vv. 29–30). Indeed, it will be the evident weakness of Egypt and its inability to provide sanctuary which will be the 'sign' that Jeremiah's word is the true one from God. Pharaoh Hophra ruled from 589 to 570BC. He had offered to help Zedekiah against Babylon, but his 'help' turned out to have no more than fleeting effect (37:5). Later he was deposed and assassinated, to be followed by Amasis, in whose reign Nebuchadrezzar made his punitive raid against Egypt. Such are those in whom this handful of Judeans are putting their trust!

FOR MEDITATION

Substituting the worship of Ashtarte for the worship of God is familiar to us moderns, except that the names of our gods are Fame, Wealth, Sex, Power and Happiness, among others. These things, good in themselves, when worshipped as gods exact a high price from their devotees.

GOD'S WORD *to* BARUCH

Baruch's complaint

This short account of a word from God to Baruch through Jeremiah is surprising in several ways. Up until now, Baruch has been a somewhat shadowy figure. Jeremiah committed the title deeds of the purchase of his uncle's tract of land to him (32:9–16). More importantly, the prophet dictated to him all his oracles delivered until the 'fourth year of Jehoiakim' (605BC), which Baruch then read publicly (36:1–10). When the king burned them, Baruch took down the prophet's words again, together with 'many similar words' (36:32). That might just indicate the role of 'amenuensis', but the fact that Baruch was suspected of influencing Jeremiah's warning against going to Egypt (43:3) suggests that he was recognized as a very close confidant and adviser of the prophet indeed. Yet this chapter marks the first break in his 'cover' as companion to the prophet, even if a very influential one, and his emergence as an individual. Some scholars have suggested that Baruch was Jeremiah's biographer, responsible for the prose narratives in the book. There is no evidence for this and it is more likely that, for all Baruch's importance as a source of knowledge of the prophet's life and teaching, the book as we have it is the work of editors in the time of the exile.

The other strange thing is that the date of this oracle is the same as that of the original dictation of the prophet's words cited in 36:1, and yet it comes after the accounts of all the events in Judah and Jerusalem that followed the fall of Jerusalem, recorded in chapters 39—44. Perhaps it has been placed at this point because Baruch's bitter sadness over the message he had to bring, and over the fate of the country and its people, was seen to fit even more poignantly at a time when Jeremiah's ministry appears to have ended in failure and he shares his master's exile to Egypt.

Now he utters a 'complaint' of his own (v. 3), just as Jeremiah had done so often (for example, 12:1–6). The 'objective' amanuensis breaks out in a bitter expression of his own sorrow.

God's reply to Baruch

Just as an 'answer' from God to Jeremiah's complaints is several times recorded (12:5–6), so God now responds to Baruch through the prophet (vv. 4–5). As to Jeremiah, the response is a fairly robust one, wasting little time on sympathy or superficial comfort. The terms of the call to Jeremiah (1:10) are repeated (v. 4). God had always intended that the people's sins, if unrepented, would bring judgment. The old order would be torn down so that a new one might be planted and built up. What Jeremiah and Baruch are now enduring is the essential negative aspect of that divine purpose—another confirmation that true prophets do not just deliver a message, like postmen, but are themselves fully involved in it and in the lives of those to whom they are sent.

The remainder of the message is perplexing. There has been no indication that Baruch has been seeking 'great things for himself' (v. 5). But perhaps it means that when we are called to God's service, our whole purpose is to be utterly dedicated to the work and to those among whom we are called. That does not mean that God always intends his service to be horrible. It means that our feelings and happiness are not our first priority.

But, perhaps, there is a hint of hope in the final word to Baruch, which substantially repeats the word given to Ebed-melech (39: 15–18). There, the promise that his life would be spared through all the disasters to come, 'as a prize of war', is based on his faithfulness to God through all ordeals, 'because you have trusted in me, says the Lord'. Perhaps the suffering but faithful Baruch was also a sign that, the other side of judgment, there were those through whom God's purposes for redemption would be realized.

FOR PRAYER

My gracious Lord, I own Thy right
To every service I can pay...
I would not breathe for worldly joy,
Or to increase my worldly good:
Nor future days or powers employ
To spread a sounding name abroad.

Philip Doddridge (1702–51)

An ORACLE *against* EGYPT

Oracles concerning the nations

A new section of the book begins here and continues to 51:64. It consists of a series of oracles against foreign nations. Similar collections are found in Isaiah 13—23, Ezekiel 25—32 and, to some extent, in Amos 1—2, while the short books of Nahum and Obadiah are individual examples of the genre.

It may be that this type of prophetic oracle had its origins in war. Curses against one's enemies were seen as a powerful means of enlisting supernatural forces in one's cause, as Balak hired Balaam to curse Israel (Numbers 22:1–6). That leaves the question of what they are doing in the major prophetic collections. Certainly, for most people, they are the least attractive (and least often read) part of such a book as Jeremiah.

We must remember that Jeremiah was called to be a prophet 'to the nations' (1:10), and many of his oracles deal with the way God uses foreign peoples and his purposes for them. They are therefore testimony to the belief that God is Sovereign Lord of the whole world and not just the domestic deity of Israel. As with oracles and prose sermons in other parts of the book, there is therefore no reason why Jeremiah should not have uttered some of them, even if, as elsewhere, his words have been expanded and used later on.

Another factor, however, suggests that in course of time the oracles against the nations came to have far deeper significance than merely to serve a spirit of nationalistic chauvinism. In Amos 1—2, the denunciation of the sins of Israel's neighbours serves only to lead to a denunciation of the same evils shown by Israel herself. We shall see how certain attitudes of pride and rebellion against God are highlighted in these oracles. They serve therefore as a warning to God's people for all time as well.

Egypt's advance—and defeat

The poem of verses 3–12 is a fine one, full of literary skill and forceful imagery which bring the battle vividly to the reader's eye. In 609BC, Necho, the Egyptian king, advanced north to help Assyria against the invading Babylonians. Josiah, fearing Egyptian control in the area, went to meet him in battle at Megiddo, but was killed there (2 Kings 23:28–30). Judah thus passed temporarily under Egyptian control. But in 605 Necho advanced against the Babylonians once more and met them at Carchemish on the Euphrates. There he was soundly defeated and lost control over the area of Judah (as 2 Kings 24:7 makes clear).

This poem vividly describes the proud advance (vv. 3–4). But the bustle and ostentation of the advance are only the prelude to ignominious defeat and rout (vv. 5–6). To drive home the theme of the 'pride' of Egypt, his advance is likened to the swelling floods caused each year by his own river, the Nile, typified by his proud boast that 'I will cover the earth' (vv. 7–8). Ironically the poet encourages the Egyptian army to advance with all their weapons and skilled mercenaries from various parts of Africa (v. 9).

God is in control

Neither the Egyptians nor any other great world empire have any power which is not granted them by God. He is in sovereign control of all the forces of the world and all the events of its history. That is the message of verse 10, which says that God has destined Egypt for defeat. The graphic picture of a bloody military defeat as a sacrifice is found elsewhere (for example, Zephaniah 1:7). There is no self-cure that Egypt can administer for her ills (v. 11), an ironic echo of Jeremiah's earlier threat against Judah herself (8:22). Only Egypt's cry of despair will 'fill the earth' (v. 12), not the glory of her military prowess as she boasted (v. 8).

FOR MEDITATION

Nothing hinders our real reliance on God more than complacent satisfaction with our own abilities and gifts. It is sometimes good to ponder Paul's paradox, 'Whenever I am weak, then I am strong' (2 Corinthians 12:10).

JUDGMENT & SALVATION *for* ISRAEL

The retreat back to Egypt

This poem vividly continues the theme of that in 46:3–12, which depicted the rout of the Egyptian army at the battle of Carchemish (605BC). Here the headlong retreat of the defeated army before the victorious Babylonians is either predicted or described. Underlying the poem are a number of strongly theological motifs to be found throughout Jeremiah and the other prophets. Those themes are the futility of trusting politically in other human powers and of turning to gods other than Yahweh for help and, above all, the supreme power and sovereignty of Yahweh over all other powers and other gods. These, rather than the literal details of any particular battle or campaign, are meant to engage the attention of the reader.

The announcement of imminent invasion is made in verse 14, especially to the northern parts of Egypt (see 44:1). The threat that Jeremiah had issued against Egypt when trying to dissuade the Judeans from going there (43:8–13) is about to be fulfilled. Apis (v. 15) was the sacred bull worshipped in Memphis, but it is powerless to stand before Yahweh at whose behest the Babylonians are advancing. Only panic-stricken retreat remains for the defeated army (v. 16), who serve a king who promises great things but achieves little (v. 17). What a contrast with Yahweh, the true sovereign King (8:19; 10:7, 10)!

The King of Israel, unlike the Pharaoh, speaks and brings about that which he predicts (vv. 18–19). The army marching against Egypt (at God's direction) is a very mountain of a power contrasted with Egypt (v. 18).

A number of striking poetical metaphors follow to describe Egypt's discomfiture. She is like fine cattle driven to distraction by biting insects (v. 20). Certainly all her expensively hired and famed mercenaries are unable to compete with a power sent by Yahweh (v. 21). Egypt is like a serpent gliding away for cover when the forest is felled (v. 22), an ironic simile since the serpent was an important religious icon in Egyptian religion. And a final echo from Jeremiah's preaching sounds ominously in verse 24. Egypt will be delivered into the hands of an enemy 'from the north', the very direction from which the prophet had seen the power sent by God against his own people (6:1). Again, it is stressed that all this is God's doing and no human power or false god can deliver those who resist him.

A false support removed

A short prose addition in verse 25 drives home the theological lessons of the poem. God announces explicitly that it is he who is bringing Nebuchadrezzar against Egypt. Yet he is attacking not only her political and military targets, her citadels and her kings, but her false gods, as he shows how vastly superior his power is to theirs. But this sweeps away the false sources of support to which 'those who trust in him' have turned—a prominent theme in Jeremiah (2:18–19).

This perhaps helps us to see one reason why the oracles against the nations have been preserved in the major prophetic books. They are there to serve as theological warnings and guidance for all future generations, not merely to whip up a mood of nationalistic revenge and xenophobia. 'Fear the evils they demonstrated rather than hating foreigners for their own sakes' seems to be the message. For their history shows that God judges such sins *wherever* he meets them, and so his own people are not immune if they commit the same sins.

Verse 26 does not appear in the Septuagint and may have been an addition to show that Nebuchadrezzar, having invaded and punished Egypt, did not stay to subjugate her entirely. He had effectively removed her as a threat from the international scene.

Future salvation for Israel

Verses 27–28 appeared at 30:10–11 (see comment on p. 147). In the Septuagint they come immediately before the oracles against Babylon. No doubt they were seen as promising the eventual return of the exiles from Babylon, another constant theme of the prophet's hope.

A PRAYER

Lord, we are often tempted to trust sources of help that appear closer, more attractive and more effective than you. At such times, keep us always in remembrance of your unfailing love, of all you have done for us and of your promise to keep us to the end. Amen

An ORACLE *against* PHILISTIA

The Philistines

This short oracle, while its main thrust is perfectly clear, presents several problems. The first is that no explicit reason is given for God's decision to wield his sword of judgment against Philistia, whereas in most of the other oracles against the nations, some sinful attitude of pride or contempt towards God or his people is said to lead to their fate. The passage also poses several difficulties of interpretation.

Philistia is the name given to the region in the south-west of the land of Canaan which today is called the Gaza Strip, comprising then the cities of Ashkelon, Gaza, Ashdod, Gath and Ekron. It was settled, at about the same time that Israel were settling in the land, by highly civilized people, originally from the Aegean islands, who had been driven from their homelands by invaders. The reputation of such a highly cultured people as 'uncivilized' is ironic and stems from the early rivalry between them and the Israelites as they had to accommodate to each other as neighbours in the land—the theme of many stories in the books of Judges and Samuel. Their power was eventually contained by David, although hostility always continued, a hostility reflected in other prophetic oracles (for example, Amos 1:6–8; Zephaniah 2:1–7).

The advancing army

Like the Egyptians (46:10), the Philistines are threatened with the same judgment as Israel, at the hand of a 'foe from the north' (v. 2). This suggests that the invading army is that of Babylon (if it is taken literally rather than symbolically) and so the reference to the Egyptian Pharaoh in verse 1 is strange. Some believe it may refer to an attack by Necho after his defeat of Josiah at Megiddo, an event hinted at by the historian Herodotus. Others suggest that it refers to the drive south by Nebuchadrezzar after the victory at Carchemish. The words do not appear in the Septuagint and we can only guess at their significance.

Again the invading army is likened to an advancing flood (v. 2; see 46:7–8; Isaiah 8:6–8). The terror of it is forcefully driven home by the impotence of parents to save even their own children (v. 3). The reference to Tyre and Sidon (v. 4) is strange since they are in Phoenicia, further north up the coast. The phrase 'to cut off... every helper that remains' may suggest some alliance between them and Philistia. Such alliances would be useless, since it is God himself who is destroying them (v. 4). Caphtor (Crete) was regarded as the home of the Philistines (Amos 9:7). Shaving off hair and cutting oneself with knives were traditional signs of mourning (officially forbidden to Israelites by the law, Deuteronomy 14:1).

In verse 5, RSV follows the Septuagint with its reference to the Anakim. Interestingly, Anakim are said to have sought refuge in Philistia after being defeated by Joshua (Joshua 11:21–22). But the Hebrew 'remnant in their valley', meaning probably 'in their strength', is better. No human might or defences can avail against God.

The unsheathed sword of God

Probably ironically, verse 6 makes a plea for God's sword to be sheathed and leave such work undone (see 46:10). Just as Jeremiah was told not to pray for a people whom God had destined for judgment (7:16), so now, it is made clear, nothing can stop the purpose of God from being fulfilled (v. 7).

This presents a grim and cruel picture. Perhaps the themes of attempts to thwart God's purposes by military might and by expedient political alliance are heard here as they are in the oracle against Egypt. It remains, however, a forceful, if strident, demonstration of the sovereign power of God over all nations and in all the world. It is futile to attempt to neutralize that power. People may work with God—and find all his blessings. Or they may oppose him and turn from his light into the darkness of judgment. The oracle remains in the book to serve as a warning to God's people as well as to 'Philistines'.

A PRAYER

*Lord, we pray for the Arabs who live in the Gaza Strip today.
Prosper the efforts of all who try to bring peace between them
and Israel, so that both peoples may learn to live together,
with justice for all. Amen*

MOAB *to* BE DESTROYED

The Moabites

This whole long chapter is devoted to oracles against Moab. It is not clear why the Moabites merit such extended treatment compared to the Philistines or the nations mentioned in the following chapter. Some of the material closely parallels Isaiah 15—16 and so must represent 'stock' prophetic material, even if there was a core of Jeremiah's own preaching here. Moab was situated east of the Dead Sea, and relations with Israel had shown many of the tensions and rivalries that inevitably characterized close neighbours. David subdued the Moabites (2 Samuel 8:2), although his harsh treatment of them was guaranteed to ensure the hostility that continued. The Moabite Stone of King Mesha (c. 830BC) narrates hostilities in which Israelite victory is attributed to the anger of the Moabite god, Chemosh, who has given his aid to Israel. Jeremiah warned against joining an anti-Babylonian coalition in which Moab played a part (27:1–11). But later the Moabites seem to have accepted Babylonian rule, for they joined in hostile action against Judah (2 Kings 24:1–2). After the Babylonian conquest, Moab, unlike Judah, never re-emerged as a kingdom. To that extent the prophecies here were fulfilled.

The attack on Moab depicted

Whether as a description of what has happened or a prediction of what is to come, the attack on Moab is pictured in vivid poetry. Some of the cities mentioned are known from other sources as Moabite or at least trans-Jordanian sites. Nebo, Kiriathaim and Heshbon are mentioned elsewhere in the Old Testament, and some appear on the Moabite Stone. Yet the places are mentioned for their poetic force rather than any attempt to trace a specific military campaign on the map. The name 'Heshbon' and the verb 'planned evil' are closely related in sound; 'Madmen' (a place otherwise unknown to us) is related to the Hebrew word for 'silence'. The cries of distress in defeat are forcefully portrayed.

Two reasons for the defeat are hinted at. Moab trusted in their own 'works' (as the Hebrew text has it) and their vast financial resources (v. 7). Further, as the Moabite Stone reveals, they trusted in their god 'Chemosh'. But a false god is as powerless to save as are vaunted human resources when 'the Lord has spoken' (v. 8). Only destruction awaits the kingdom and its strongholds. The text of verse 9 is obscure. One rendering gives the sense 'Set aside salt for Moab' (so NRSV). The practice of 'salting' a city laid under an interdiction is attested in such a passage as Judges 9:45. Such is to be Moab's fate.

No mercy to be shown

In a striking phrase, reminiscent of 47:6 where a plea for God's sword against the Philistines to be sheathed is voiced, a plea brusquely rejected (47:7), anyone who allows lack of zeal or even compassion to mitigate God's work is roundly condemned (v. 10).

Moab's complacency

A dramatic illustration from the process of wine-making is given in verses 11–13. Wine allowed to settle too long on its lees, without being agitated and poured from one vessel to another from time to time, loses its flavour and pungency (compare Zephaniah 1:12). Moab, untroubled for too long by any challenging dangers or need for strenuous action, has settled into an entirely ineffective complacency (v. 11). Now God is going to send one who will 'decant' them, that is, shatter their quiet ease with violent judgment.

Again, a 'theological' motif enters in. The Moabites will find which is the false and which the true God when their trust in Chemosh proves utterly ineffective. Yet there is also a word for later Israelites. They too in their history had needed to be shown that other gods, such as 'Bethel' (the name of a god here in verse 13, not the name of the town in northern Israel), were no substitute for the one, true and living God. Again, an oracle against the nations carries its warning for God's own people.

FOR MEDITATION

We often want God to send us a quiet life, perhaps misunderstanding the nature of his 'peace'. But is it more in times of challenge and disturbance that we are driven to greater depths, learn more of him and develop greater powers of character?

MOAB'S PRIDE *to* BE HUMBLED

Moab brought low

This passage contains a number of independent, short pieces united on the theme of the humiliation of Moab. It is not always easy to tell where one ends and another begins, and they are marked by a strong dependence on other biblical material, notably Isaiah 15—16, which also contains oracles against Moab.

Verse 14 echoes the proud boasting that characterized the fighting men of Moab. But all their boasting has proved vain because their real opponent has been not the forces of Babylon, but 'the King, whose name is the Lord of hosts' (v. 15). Ironically, all those who are familiar with Moab's 'name'—that is, his fearsome reputation—are invited to mourn the tragic reversal of his fate (v. 17). Dibon (v. 18) is of interest since it was the site at which the Moabite Stone was discovered and, like several of the places named here, is mentioned on the Stone. The Arnon (v. 20) is a river that runs into the east of the Dead Sea and formed the northern border of Moab. All nations beyond her boundaries will witness her humiliation.

Moabite strongholds captured

The place names in verses 21–24, although they mostly refer to real towns, seem to be piled up for literary effect, suggesting that there was no part of Moab that could escape the general judgment. In many instances they are mentioned in Isaiah 15—16, which seems to have been a major quarry for the material here. For these reasons, their exact geographical location is unimportant. The name 'Bozrah' signifies the fate of them all. The name means 'stronghold', although it is usually identified with Bezer, a town mentioned in Deuteronomy 4:43, rebuilt by the Moabite king, Mesha (a fact recorded on the Moabite Stone). However many mighty cities and strong defensive positions Moab could boast, they all suffer the same fate, for Moab's 'horn' (a symbol of national power, especially royal power: see Micah 4:13) is cut off, while the 'broken arm' signifies the utter defeat of her army (v. 25).

Moab suffers the fate she dealt out

The unattractive but vivid image of verses 26–27 recalls 25:15–29, which described an act of prophetic symbolism signifying God's intention to give the 'cup of judgment' to various nations. They would be drunk to the point of vomiting, indeed to 'rise no more, because of the sword that I am sending among you' (25:27). Moab used to mock Israel (v. 27). Now they would themselves become an object of derision, utterly powerless to act. This is one of the few occasions where the note of retaliation for injuries suffered by Israel is sounded in these oracles. Mostly they announce judgment because of the nations' sins against God.

Moab's glory departs

Again an ironic call is made to the Moabites to leave their proud cities and find shelter in the ravines in the desert where the birds find protection (v. 28). Here, once more, all the emphasis is on the pride, arrogance, self-sufficiency and 'insolence' of Moab (vv. 29–30). The 'insolence' is doubtless primarily seen to be against God for assuming they could overcome his people in the name of their god, Chemosh.

A lament for Moab

A kind of lament, drawn mainly from Isaiah 16:9–10, concludes this section of the series of oracles against Moab in the chapter.

It has to be acknowledged, once again, that they do not form the most appealing part of the book. Yet, for the most part, the sins of pride, rebellion and general 'insolence' towards God are being targeted, rather than mere feelings of national revenge bring expressed. The oracles therefore continued to serve as a warning to future generations that such sins, whether shown by Jews or foreigners, put people beyond the reach of God's grace and mercy.

A PRAYER

Lord, I acknowledge how often I am censorious about the sins in others which, all too often, I commit myself. Keep me humble enough always to see myself as you see me, and trusting enough to depend on you for your grace and strength by which alone I can become different. Amen

MOURNING *for* MOAB

Lamenting Moab's fate

Verse 37 describes all the traditional signs of mourning at the death of someone close that were widely practised in the ancient Near East. There was reference to them in the oracle against Philistia in 47:5. Strictly speaking, such practices were forbidden by the law to Israelites (Deuteronomy 14:1). Here the reference is to the Moabites, but the numerous allusions to such funeral rites in the Old Testament suggest that it may have been one of those laws on which it was difficult to achieve 'zero tolerance', as we say nowadays. Anyway, nothing is left but mourning now for the nation which once was the proud kingdom of Moab, for it is God who has rejected them. He discards them like a broken earthenware vessel, just as, in his sovereign power, he could discard a king of his own people, Jehoiachin (22:24-28). The once-proud kingdom, so arrogant and overbearing towards its neighbours, now can only hide its face in its national disgrace (v. 39).

No escape from the avenger

The vivid poetic imagery continues in this picture of the relentless and irresistible advance of the enemy who is God's agent appointed to bring about Moab's downfall (vv. 40-44). The attacker is like an eagle, able to soar to the most remote mountain crags. No defence, however strong or apparently inaccessible, is safe from his reach (v. 40). As a result, the Moabite warriors share the anguish of a woman as she experiences birth pangs (v. 41). All this is because the real sin of Moab was her great pride 'against the Lord' (v. 42) in her assumption that he had no real power compared with Chemosh, their god.

The forceful poetry continues with striking alliteration in the Hebrew of verse 43, which has the three words *pahad*, *pahath*, and *pah* for the three misfortunes awaiting Moab, an alliteration that NRSV tries partially to capture with its 'terror, pit and trap'. The relief of anyone who congratulates himself on escaping from one will be short-lived as he falls into another, a description of the inescapable consequences of the judgment of God on his 'Day' that occurs elsewhere (see Amos 5:18-20).

Help from Chemosh or the Lord?

Verses 45–47 do not occur in the Septuagint. Verses 45–46 are mainly citations from Numbers 21:28–29. There they are part of an ironic poem addressed by the Israelites to Sihon, king of the Amorites, who had refused them leave to pass through his territory on their way to the land of Canaan, and whom they then defeated. He had captured Heshbon from the Moabites, but his pride and boasting in the feat is mocked by those who have now defeated him. We have noticed that a good deal of the material about Moab in this chapter is drawn from other scripture, confirming the impression that any original words of Jeremiah have been augmented by traditional and familiar oracles on the same theme. The mention of Chemosh in verse 46 again underlines the utter ineffectiveness of this false god to deliver them from the action of the one, true God.

Verse 47 reads strangely with its note of hope for Moab 'in the latter days', after such bitter threats and diatribes against them in this long chapter. The significant thing, however, is that if there were to be any renewal, it would only be as the work of God himself. It is only he who can say, 'I will restore their fortunes.' But this is true of *any* people, including his own. The promise of the new covenant with Israel (31:31–34) shows that it is only the gracious, saving work of God that can renew them and make them truly 'his people'. The oracles against the nations are not claiming that there is some particular virtue about his own people which makes them intrinsically superior over other nations. It is only the grace of God that makes any people 'special'. It is a lesson that not only the Jews after the exile but the people of God of all times have firmly to learn and constantly to remember.

A PRAYER

Not what I am, O Lord, but what Thou art,
That, that alone can be my soul's true rest:
Thy love, not mine, bids fear and doubt depart,
And stills the tempest of my throbbing breast.

Horatius Bonar (1808–89)

An ORACLE CONCERNING AMMON

The Ammonites

The Ammonites were another neighbouring kingdom, closer to the northern kingdom of Israel than to Judah. Their territory stretched northwards from the river Arnon, bordering the northern boundary of Moab, and was situated mainly east of the river Jabbok, more or less the territory of the modern kingdom of Jordan. Their western boundary was not, however, the river Jordan, the strip between that and their land, Gilead, being often occupied by northern Israelites (Joshua 13:25). As with the Moabites, there was the inevitable history of warfare and rivalry between them and Israel. Tradition had it that their King Sihon refused Israel permission to go through their land on the way to Canaan, which led the Israelites to attack and conquer them (Numbers 21:21–30). David subdued them, as he did most of the surrounding countries (2 Samuel 12:26–31), but, as with others, his harsh treatment did nothing to quench continuing resentment and hostilities. Ammonites are linked with Moabites as those who allied themselves to Babylon against Judah (2 Kings 24:2) and yet, later, sought to make common cause against Nebuchadrezzar (27:3). Their lack of love for Judah, however, was apparent in the support and backing that their king, Baalis, gave to Ishmael in his assassination of Gedaliah (40:13–14; 41:10). The exact details of their later history are not clear but, like Moab, their land was eventually occupied by invading Arab tribes and the kingdom came to an end.

Ammon's fate

Verse 1 cites some act of aggression against Israel. It might be a continuing memory of the fall of the kingdom of Israel to the invading Assyrian forces under Tiglath-pileser in 732BC (2 Kings 15:29). It would have been very natural at such a time for the Ammonites to move in to territory denuded of many of its Israelite inhabitants. That, or a similar action on some other occasion, prompts the indignant questions asserting the rights of successive generations of Israelites to the territory.

Because of such aggression, the Ammonites themselves will hear the battle cry of an attacking Israelite army (v. 2), coming to avenge their own dispossession. 'Rabbah' was the name of the capital city, known as Amman today.

Verse 3 suggests that the Ammonites had themselves been engaged on a campaign of military aggrandisement, since they appear to have occupied the Moabite town of Heshbon (see 48:2, 34, 45). 'Ai', a name which in Hebrew means 'ruins', must have been another Ammonite city, otherwise unknown (unless it is a scribal error). Tradition knew of a place of that name also in Israelite territory, captured in Joshua's campaigns (Joshua 8:18–23). It is just possible that the mention of the name here is meant to recall past victories to which God had led his people. Nothing is left to the Ammonites but the self-inflicted wounds of funerary rites (v. 3: the word rendered in some English versions, such as RSV, as 'hedges', or its equivalent, almost certainly refers to the act of 'gashing oneself').

Milcom was the name of the Ammonite national god (1 Kings 11:5, 33; 2 Kings 23:13), for allowing whose worship Solomon himself was judged (1 Kings 11:5). Again, then, the assertion of Yahweh's sole and supreme power over all false gods is made. Milcom is powerless to deliver his people from Yahweh's acts of judgment.

Verse 4 sounds another theme already familiar from these oracles against the nations, that of the overweening pride and self-confidence of these people. The word translated 'valleys' (RSV) occurred also in 47:5. Some have linked it to a similar word in a related language meaning 'strength'. In any event, it is clear that the Ammonites thought that their military might and their great financial resources rendered them immune from any danger. Verse 5 announces how wrong they were.

Hope for Ammon?

Verse 6, which does not appear in the Septuagint, again sounds rather odd after the apparently total threats of verses 1–5. Perhaps it holds out hope for some, at least, of the Ammonite population. Again it is made clear, however, that any restoration will be fully and solely the work of Yahweh—certainly not of their god, Milcom.

A PRAYER

Lord, we pray for all the peoples of the Middle East today, heirs to centuries of enmity, distrust and cruelty. Raise up those with the vision to break out of the endless chain of retaliation and seek what is just and beneficial for all. Amen

ORACLES CONCERNING EDOM

The Edomites

The Edomites occupied territory to the south of the Dead Sea, stretching from the river Zered (making Moab a northern neighbour) to the Gulf of Akaba. Tradition had it that there were close relations between Israel and Edom since their ancestors, Jacob and Esau, were brothers (Genesis 25:23–26). It is quite possible that this truly reflects common national stock, for there are ancient traditions in the Old Testament that Yahweh came from the region of Edom (Judges 5:4; Deuteronomy 33:2). This did not prevent the usual outbreaks of hostility between two neighbouring peoples in the course of their history. It is clear from later, exilic and post-exilic texts that special resentment was felt among Judeans for what they saw as the treacherous actions of Edom at the time of the fateful Babylonian invasion which led to the fall of Jerusalem in 586BC (see Lamentations 4:22; Psalm 137:7). They must have seized their opportunity to invade and take advantage of Judah's defeat, although, strangely, they are one people not mentioned among those who collaborated with the Babylonians (2 Kings 24:1–2).

Edom's wisdom cannot save her

There are several mentions of Edom's special 'wisdom' in the Old Testament (for example, Obadiah 8). All courts had their 'wise men', those learned in reading and writing, well acquainted with their country's traditions, knowledgeable in matters of state, who acted as advisers to kings. The prophets can sometimes attack reliance on such human 'wisdom' instead of seeking direction from God (Isaiah 5:21; Jeremiah 8:8–9). Thus 'wisdom' is another human resource on which the Edomites rely in vain when God purposes to judge them.

'Teman and Dedan' (vv. 7–8) must refer to regions within Edom's territory whose exact location is unknown. Nothing is left for their inhabitants but flight. Verses 9–10 also occur in Obadiah 5–6, the numerous parallels in these oracles showing that much in them is drawn from a common stock of such material. The point is that even harvesters leave some gleanings and thieves seldom strip a house bare. Yet God is going to destroy Edom utterly. The exact force of verse 11 is obscure. It may be an ironic address to the fleeing Edomites. They will not be able even to defend their own children but will have to abandon them to God's care (compare 47:3).

Drinking the 'cup'

In verse 12, yet again the picture of judgment as receiving a 'cup' from God's hand is used as it was in 25:15–27 (see especially vv. 21–24) and 48:26. Bozrah (v. 13), a different place from that mentioned as belonging to Moab (48:24), has the same meaning in Hebrew, 'stronghold'. Neither Edom's wisdom nor her military strength can save her.

King and people will perish in Edom

Again, verses 14–16 occur as part of Obadiah 1–4. Graphically the prophet hears the divine messenger summoning the nations to battle against Edom. She who inspired terror will experience terror, and none of her military strongholds in apparently impregnable mountain positions will avail her.

Sodom and Gomorrah (v. 18), whose destruction by God is described in Genesis 19:24–25, became almost legendary symbols of sin and its inevitable judgment (see Isaiah 1:10). The fact that Isaiah could apply that description to Judah's own leaders shows that the nations in these oracles came to stand as symbols of certain types of sin that bring God's judgment on *whoever* commits them.

Verses 19–21 occur also in 50:44–46, applied to Babylon, showing again the 'stock' nature of some of this material. The 'shepherd' (v. 19) is a common Near Eastern picture for the king. He will be utterly unable to save his people, who will be torn away from the shelter of the 'sheepfold' (for a similar picture see Zechariah 13:7). Ironically, trying to escape the vengeance of their attacker, some of their warriors will fall at the 'Red Sea' (v. 21), the very place where God delivered his own people. The passage ends with a menacing picture of the approach of the invader (v. 22; compare 48:40–41).

A PRAYER

'Trust in the Lord with all your heart, and do not rely on your own insight' (Proverbs 3:5). Lord, give me the wisdom neither to despise nor neglect the intellect you have given me, nor to forget that only with your light can I use it aright. Amen

ORACLES CONCERNING DAMASCUS, KEDAR & ELAM

Damascus

Damascus was the capital of the Syrian state to the north of Israel with whom Israel had such a turbulent relationship over the years. Hamath and Arpad were major cities of regions of that state, and all fell to the same Assyrian invasion that led to the capture and fall of Samaria (in 722BC). Isaiah records the Assyrians boasting of these exploits in Isaiah 10:8–11. Syria did not again become an independent threat after being assumed into the Assyrian empire, and it is interesting that this oracle ends with a near quotation of Amos' (eighth-century) oracle against Damascus (Amos 1:4). Elsewhere, for all its vivid imagery of the fear and panic of the Syrians being like a heaving sea (v. 23), it employs some fairly conventional language, such as that describing the pain of a woman in childbirth which appears elsewhere in Jeremiah (6:24; 22:23) and other prophets (Isaiah 13:8).

Ben-hadad (v. 27) was the name of several Syrian kings. It means 'son of Hadad', Hadad being the storm god that the Syrians worshipped—hence the appropriateness of the heaving seas imagery in verse 23. He was the same god as Baal, whom the Canaanites worshipped, so once more these oracles attest the superior power of Yahweh over all other gods.

Kedar

Kedar (v. 28) was the name of an important Arab tribe living far to the east of Israel, in the desert to the east of modern Jordan. They are mentioned several times in the Old Testament (see Psalm 120:5) as a nomadic people, hence the mention of their open, defenceless lifestyle (v. 31) and the reference to their tents and flocks (vv. 29, 32). Hazor, here, is possibly a place name in the desert otherwise unknown to us. But a plural form of the word, meaning 'unfortified villages' occurs in connection with Kedar at Isaiah 42:11.

We know from Babylonian records that Nebuchadrezzar launched a campaign against the Arabs in this region early in the sixth century

BC, and this may well be the allusion in verse 30. A familiar Jeremian phrase occurs in verse 29—'Terror on every side'—to describe the horror and panic of judgment (6:25; 20:3, 10; 46:5). Utterly defence-less against so well-armed and mighty an enemy (v. 31), these people, marked by their shaven heads (v. 32; see 25:23–24), can only scatter, leaving their former dwellings to the wild animals (v. 33). No reason for their judgment is given or even hinted at. It suggests that these short oracles have been included to stress the completeness of God's sovereign rule over all peoples.

Elam

Elam (v. 34) was situated to the east of Babylon in the region we now call Iran. It fell to the Assyrians in 645. So this is another region, like Syria, which can hardly have played a lively part in events contemporary with Jeremiah, although it is true that we know little about its later history. The reference to their 'bow' (v. 35) suggests that they were famous for their archers and is, perhaps, a reference to their pride in their own military prowess. The reference to 'the four winds from the four quarters of heaven' (v. 36) occurs also at Zechariah 2:6; 6:5 and Daniel 7:2. Kings used to refer to themselves in the record of their mighty deeds as 'Lord of the four quarters of the earth'. This is, then, a statement of the universal Lordship of Yahweh, who can command all earthly powers to do his bidding. The same point is made by his assertion that 'I will set my throne in Elam' (v. 38). Presumably this means that he will set up the king of his choice in Elam in place of those who had ruled there. It is the same statement of faith in the universal sovereignty of God as that expressed during the Babylonian exile when Cyrus (the Persian who conquered Babylon) is called 'his anointed', that is, God's Messiah (Isaiah 45:1).

A statement about the eventual restoration of at least some Elamites is made (v. 39), similar to those found in 46:26; 49:6 and elsewhere.

FOR PRAISE

The Lord is king! Who then shall dare
Resist His will, distrust His care,
Or murmur at His wise decrees,
Or doubt His royal promises?

Josiah Conder (1789–1855)

BABYLON'S DOWNFALL FORETOLD

Babylon's gods helpless

This oracle introduces a long section in chapters 50—51 dealing with Babylon. It is not surprising that this whole section is almost as long as all those dealing with other nations, since Babylon, after the capture and destruction of Jerusalem and exile of so many of its people, was always regarded as the foe, symbolizing all that was most evil. Some have denied any part in these oracles to Jeremiah because their sentiments sit uneasily with those of the prophet who regarded Babylon as God's appointed 'servant' to punish his people (25:9; 27:6) and who encouraged the exiles to accept their fate and even to pray for Babylon's welfare (29:6-7). Yet acknowledging that God intended to use Babylon did not imply any special virtue on their part, and Jeremiah always taught that if only God's own people would learn the lessons of judgment and return to him, then they would know full deliverance, while those who refused to acknowledge him would be judged. These two themes of judgment for Babylon and ultimate salvation for Israel alternate through chapters 50—51. That is not to say, however, that the oracles as we have them have not been added to in course of time: many 'stock' parallels to other prophetic material suggest that this has been the case.

Verse 2 makes clear that it is Babylon's idolatry that brings about her judgment. Bel and Merodach are different names for the same god and the Babylonians believed that his triumph over the waters of chaos in the creation of the earth made him the 'king' of the gods. Such pretensions will be shown for what they are by the one and true 'King' of earth and heaven. Ironically, the Babylonians will fall to a 'foe from the north' (v. 3), they who had themselves been the 'foe from the north' used by God to judge Israel.

Israel reunited and repentant

The other theme, that of salvation for Israel, is proclaimed in verses 4-5. Their repentance, shown by their weeping for their sins, will be a sign of their inner renewal, and the old northern and southern kingdoms will rediscover their true unity in shared worship at Jerusalem.

That worship will be the outward expression of their new relationship with God, which will be at the heart of the new 'eternal' covenant (see 32:40).

A betrayed and wandering flock

God's people had been betrayed by their 'false' shepherds, kings and leaders who had been false to their God-given role (vv. 6–7; 23:9–11). Without leaders to keep them in a right relationship with the 'true' Shepherd, they have been prey to 'shepherds' intent only on despoiling and enslaving them (25:34–38). The excuse of such predators, that they are only doing the work of Israel's God and are therefore guiltless, is exposed at 2:3.

Defeat for Babylon

The announcement of coming disaster by the literary device of calling on inhabitants to 'flee' (v. 8) is a fairly stock one (48:6). Babylon's invaders are again described as a 'foe from the north', that is, one sent by God, while the military skill and efficiency of the warriors ironically recalls the way in which Babylonian soldiers were themselves described (v. 9; 6:22–23). The irony is further underlined with the statement that the 'plunderer' is to be utterly 'plundered' (v. 10). Again, these oracles against the nations stress the utter and sole sovereignty of the one, true God over all powers in heaven and all peoples on earth.

The proud conqueror humiliated

Babylon's joy and pride in her military achievements will be short-lived, as verses 11–16 show, since her actions were against Yahweh's own 'heritage'. The descriptions of her disgrace and public humiliation are again fairly stock ones (5:17; 15:8; 16:3–4; 25:18). Verses 14–16 adopt the literary device of a summons to Babylon's attackers to press their assault, also encountered elsewhere (46:3–4; 49:14).

AN AFFIRMATION OF FAITH

No strength of our own or goodness we claim;
Yet, since we have known the Saviour's great name,
In this our strong tower for safety we hide,
The Lord is our power, the Lord will provide.

John Newton (1725–1807)

The BATTLE *against* BABYLON

The restoration of Israel

Twice in her history Israel proved as helpless as sheep hunted down by lions—in 721BC when Assyria defeated the northern kingdom of Israel and in 586BC when Babylon destroyed conquered Judah. But judgment from God awaits this second 'devouring lion' as surely as it befell the first (v. 18). The names chosen to symbolize the whole of Israel (v. 19) indicate both fertility and reversal of fortunes. 'Carmel' means 'a fruitful place', while Bashan was a region noted for its lush pasturage and fat cattle (Amos 4:1). Yet Bashan had also been mentioned earlier by Jeremiah as a place where his people would know judgment (22:20). The promise here, therefore, is of a complete reversal of that earlier judgment to an experience of salvation. The name 'Ephraim' also means 'fruitful', and so is another symbol of renewal. The territory of Gilead stretched to the east of the river Jordan, and the reoccupation of that area again suggests military security and prosperity and a complete reversal of the people's futile earlier attempts to find 'balm' (that is, comfort) in Gilead (8:22).

That this will be the fulfilment of the promise of the 'new covenant' is shown by verse 20. The salvation of God's people is not only a matter of material prosperity but of the complete forgiveness of and deliverance from sin (31:34). Thus renewed, they live indeed as the true 'remnant' united with God and with each other, something God had promised that he would one day bring about (23:3; 31:7). We have seen how those left behind in Judah after the exile, and those who went to Egypt, had proved themselves by their actions not to be that remnant (see comment on chs. 40—44, p. 202). This saved remnant, therefore, will come from those who had been in Babylon.

God summons his agents

Symbolic names are also used to refer to Babylon as God calls upon the invading armies he has summoned to work his judgment upon her (v. 21). 'Merathaim' relates to the name of a region in the south of Babylon but also means 'doubly rebellious'. 'Pekod' relates to a tribe living in the east of Babylon, but the word also means 'punishment'.

The graphic poem describing the assault by which Babylon is utterly defeated and destroyed needs no prosaic comment. The reference to her 'bulls' in verse 27 says it all. The bull was a symbol of strength, as the psalmist lamented as he complained of the strength of the adversaries pitted against him (Psalm 22:12). The powerful scourge of the whole earth is to be reduced to impotence.

Some commentators, noting that eventually Babylon fell to Cyrus the Persian in 539BC without a struggle, have suggested that these oracles must predate that, since they speak so graphically of a titanic battle. That is possible, but it need not be so. The Persians had gained many military victories on the way to gaining a position where they could so easily subdue Babylon. But these symbolic names also suggest a truth we have had cause to note before. The evil powers that Babylon embodied are in fact the target of God's judgment. And that is why these oracles could go on speaking to generations long after the historical kingdoms had ceased to have any relevance. An example of this is found in the description of Rome as 'Babylon' in Revelation 14:8. Rome, to John, epitomized the sins of ancient Babylon.

Captives return and Babylon is attacked

This promise of the escape of the captives from Babylon to announce the good news of its fall back in Jerusalem (v. 28), so closely parallel to the promises of Isaiah 40—55 (for example, 40:9–11), once more firmly identifies the saved 'remnant' with those who had been exiled there.

Verses 29–32 clearly state the true nature of what is happening when the invaders defeat and destroy Babylon. Babylon's actions were, essentially, rebellion against God (v. 29). The actions of the invading army summoned by God are essentially *his* action against Babylon (v. 31). Again the note of reversal of judgment is sounded in verse 32 by the repetition of 21:14—there directed against the house of David, now directed against Babylon.

A PRAYER

Lord, we believe it is your purpose to champion the cause of the weak of the earth who are so often the victims of the powerful. May we show that faith by championing their cause ourselves whenever we can. Amen

GOD WILL REDEEM HIS PEOPLE

Israel's Redeemer

It is noteworthy that again the future unity of Israel is stressed in verse 33, just as it was in verse 4. God is going to deliver both oppressed and exiled former kingdoms, Israel and Judah. The nations who captured them proved far too strong for any hope of self-deliverance by way of rebellion or armed resistance. But 'their Redeemer is strong' (v. 34). The word used for 'redeemer' (*goel*) means 'kinsman'. The law of the *goel* is detailed in Leviticus 25:25–28, 47–54. If someone became poor, so as to be forced to sell some of his property, then it was the duty of his nearest kinsman to buy it back for him, thus 'redeeming' it. In this way it was not lost to the wider family. Even more, if someone had to sell himself into slavery because of his poverty, then the nearest kinsman might buy him back. The picture of God as *goel* therefore stresses God's kinship with his people, his love for them, and his determination to 'redeem' them from their bondage among foreigners.

God's curse upon the Chaldeans

In a series of vivid and poetic phrases God calls for a 'sword' to judge all sections of the Babylonians (vv. 35–37). The sword is, of course, his, even though he is summoning human agents to wield it. 'Chaldeans' (v. 35) was the name of a people who inhabited a southern region in Babylon and who gave their name not only to the region, but to the last ruling dynasty of Babylon. The name therefore became a symbol for the whole people. All ranks are to feel the 'sword'. The 'diviners' who gave Babylon her reputation for wisdom, and the warriors, cavalry and mercenary troops who gave her the reputation for her fearsome power, will all alike fall to it, and the fabulous wealth she amassed from her great empire will also be taken away. The change to 'a drought upon her waters' (v. 38) is strange after the series of invocations of the sword, but the same consonants spell both the word for 'sword' and for 'drought' in Hebrew. It is either therefore a play on words or has been changed by someone who thought it inappropriate to attack 'waters' with a sword! Either way it foretells that all the fertility of her land will cease as it becomes unproductively arid.

The 'sword' of God used in judgment is mentioned elsewhere in the book (see 9:16; 12:12; 14:12). In all those instances, however, it is to be used in judgment against his own people, so that here, once more, we have the theme of a reversal of judgment. Israel will know 'redemption', as the agent of her earlier judgment will experience it herself.

Like Sodom and Gomorrah

The fate of Sodom and Gomorrah (v. 40), cities so utterly destroyed that no trace of them was left (Genesis 19:24–25), has served as a picture of judgment before in the book. In 23:14 it is said that Samaria's prophets have become exactly like those two cities in God's eyes, and are destined therefore to share their judgment. In 49:18 the same words used here are directed against Edom. So, again, there is to be a reversal of judgment.

God rules over all

Verses 41–43 echo very closely a threat of judgment earlier uttered against Israel herself (6:22–24). Again this makes the reversal of judgment theme very clear. Verses 44–45 are a direct application to Babylon of the threat against Edom in 49:19–22.

The utter sovereign power by which God directs the affairs of all nations and appoints as their leaders those whom he chooses is stressed in verse 44. Perhaps there were those later in Judah with a rather narrower viewpoint, who found it hard to accept that God could choose heathen foreigners. Isaiah 40—55 challenges the same attitude, for the chapters record God disputing with those who could not accept that the Persian Cyrus was actually God's 'anointed', destined to play a vital part in his purposes (Isaiah 45:1, 9–13).

FOR MEDITATION

The trouble with many people today is that they have not found a God big enough for modern needs… they are cherishing a hot-house God who could only exist between the pages of the Bible or inside the four walls of a church.

J.B. Phillips, *Your God Is Too Small*, Epworth Press, 1952, p. vii

FLEE *from* BABYLON!

God has not abandoned his people

In Hebrew the same word, *ruah*, means both 'wind' and 'spirit'. In verse 1 the threat to Babylon could therefore come from 'a destructive wind' that God sends, or from an invading destroyer whose spirit God incites. But since a 'wind' here must be a metaphor for an army, it comes to much the same thing. There is a strange reference at the end of the verse. The Hebrew reads 'against the inhabitants of those who rise against me'. However, this appears to be a code for the Chaldeans, consonants a certain number from the beginning of the alphabet being replaced by those the same number from the end. Why it should be used here is itself a mystery.

The threat to Babylon is pictured as a 'winnowing'—that is, a threshing (v. 2)—from a number of foes who come at her from every side, against which any attempt at defence is useless (v. 3). Indeed the invaders are commanded 'utterly to destroy' her. The Hebrew term is to 'put her to the ban' (*herem*). This was a term from the holy war waged in Yahweh's name in which the Israelites were to destroy every captured city (Numbers 21:2), along with their inhabitants (Deuteronomy 7:2). God is waging his own 'holy war' against Babylon. All this culminates in the assertion in verse 5 that it is because God has 'not left Israel and Judah [note again the emphasis on the reunited nation] widowed'. This takes up the picture of Israel's early love for God as his 'bride' (2:2). She became shamelessly faithless (2:33). Still, however, God does not finally turn from her.

Babylon's power broken

Again, the fate of a city and its people is graphically expressed with the literary device of a call to escape from it while there is still time (v. 6; compare 48:6). Such will be the panic that there will be no time for organized retreat. It will be 'every man for himself'. The moment for God's requital of her sins has come.

He had used Babylon as his instrument for judgment—as the 'cup' he intended her victims to drink (25:15–16). Now, however, the prediction that she, in her turn, would drink the cup of judgment

(25:26) is fulfilled. Even if there had been those who, out of sympathy, would have sought to help her, there would be no 'balm' to be found to cure such a mortal condition (vv. 8–9), just as Israel had been told that there was no 'balm in Gilead' for such a sickness as hers (8:22). Sticking plasters are hopelessly superficial remedies for deep wounds. So even those who once were encouraged to pray for the welfare of the city (29:7) are now called upon to leave and return home, there to proclaim the great things that God has done for them (vv. 9–10).

God's agents of judgment

Again, invading armies are summoned to arms and to battle against Babylon (v. 11). The reference to the Medes is a little strange. They were a people who inhabited the north-west region of Iran. They may have seemed at one time the power most likely to challenge Babylon but, in fact, Cyrus the Persian conquered them in 550BC. Cyrus' mother was a Mede and the two peoples are often associated together in the later Old Testament literature (Daniel 5:28). So perhaps their name indicates here the combined forces of the two peoples, for it was Cyrus who marched victoriously into Babylon in 539BC. The reference to 'many waters' in Babylon (v. 13, RSV) is to the River Euphrates and the many canals that served the city and were the conduits of her wealth (see 50:38). Now, for all her wealth, her end has come. God swears 'by himself' that he will bring about her defeat (v. 14)—literally, 'by his own life' or 'his own soul'. There could be no stronger declarative oath.

A PRAYER

O God, keep me from ever forsaking you. But if ever I prove faithless, make me know that you never abandon those whom you have called to be your own. Amen

BABYLON MEETS HER MATCH

The Creator, Redeemer God

Verses 15–19 are almost exactly a repeat of 10:12–16 (see comment on pp. 62–63). Magnificently they portray in powerful poetry the greatness of God displayed in his marvellous works of creation. Before such a God, how ridiculous are the meaningless idols that people make by their own efforts and then call gods! In form, structure and content this passage closely resembles the oracles of Isaiah 40—55, the work of an exilic prophet who, even in the time of exile and Babylon's unchallengeable might, states his belief in the sole reality and power of Israel's God and the ultimate triumph of his purposes (see Isaiah 40:12–20).

The placing of these verses here therefore underlines one of the main emphases we have found in this whole section of the 'oracles against the nations'. It is to stress the unique being and might of Israel's God, against whom no human power, however apparently invincible, can hope to stand.

But verse 19 shows that he who creates on so vast a scale is nevertheless also the God who knows about and cares for his people, who chooses them in his grace and who plans to redeem them. Indeed, it is just because of his mighty power that he *can* also act as Redeemer, for no power in heaven or on earth is strong enough to oppose his plans for his own.

God's instrument for judgment

In verses 20–23 God addresses an unnamed power by whom he works his purposes on earth. Because verse 24 and, indeed, the whole context of these two chapters tells of the coming fall of Babylon, some have supposed that Cyrus is the one being addressed, for Babylon fell to him, although not by the great battle so vividly described here. Others have wondered whether it is an ironic address to the Babylonians. God has used them for just these purposes of exacting military defeat on those he judges. Now, however, he intends to turn the same kind of power against Babylon itself, as verse 24 makes clear. Perhaps his agent is best left anonymous in these verses.

God can use whomever he chooses for whatever purpose he has in mind. If, in due course, that instrument oversteps its God-given role and limits, then it too can be cast away (Isaiah 10:5–12). God is not dependent on any human being, even if he uses them in his grace.

Babylon's time runs out

Babylon has no chance, for it is none other than the living God who is their adversary, whatever human agent he employs to bring it about ('I am against you… says the Lord', v. 25). The picture of a great nation as a 'mountain', in this case one powerful and high enough to dominate the whole earth, is striking. It recalls the faith of Israel, expressed in the liturgy of the pre-exilic temple, that God dwells on his 'mountain' in Zion (Psalm 48:1–3) and reigns there high above all other powers (Psalm 99:1–2). The mountain which is Babylon will be brought down and even burnt, so that not even stone useful for building elsewhere can be salvaged from it (vv. 25–26).

Again advancing armies are summoned against her. The regions named in verse 27 were among those whom the Medes had subjugated and who are now thought of as her allies in the campaign against Babylon. The names also serve, however, to suggest the vast hordes amassing and the wide territories subject to Yahweh's control. The Hebrew calls on all the participating soldiers to be 'sanctified' (v. 27), which has more significance than the 'prepare' of NRSV. Soldiers participating in the 'holy wars' of Yahweh against the nations needed to be 'sanctified' (Numbers 31:19–24; 1 Samuel 21:4; 2 Samuel 11:11). This campaign is, therefore, God's own war against the Babyl-onians. That is why the earth itself convulses as he marches to war (v. 29; Judges 5:4–5).

FOR MEDITATION

Paul was used by God for very different purposes from those of Babylon. Yet he also was aware of the possibility of even the most dedicated servant of God rendering himself or herself unfit for service, dreading that he might himself 'be disqualified' (1 Corinthians 9:27). No one can live on past achievements— or past commitment.

BABYLON YIELDS UP HER CAPTORS

God champions the captives

Verses 34–37 are spoken in the first person, just like some of the psalms of individual lament and Jeremiah's own laments. As in the psalms, the speaker is voicing the feelings and longings of the whole community, just as Jeremiah suffered to a considerable extent his people's agonies as their representative.

The picture of defeat and exile here is of being swallowed by a great monster—perhaps a picture that inspired the story of Jonah, seen as a type of Israel exiled but delivered by God and given a second chance to fulfil its God-given mission. These words come nearer to a spirit of hatred and revenge than many of the other oracles against the nations where the judgment of God is meted out because of sins committed against *him*. Yet we have to remember that such a spirit occasionally surfaced even in Jeremiah's complaints (for example, 12:3)!

As so often with the psalms of lament and with Jeremiah's own laments, the sufferer receives an answering oracle from God. The word used in verse 36, rendered in NRSV as 'I am going to defend your cause', is law-court terminology. It stands for a legal dispute and here it means that God is going to take up his people's case and be their powerful advocate. Jeremiah had said that he would plead his case before God (12:1) and this received a powerful answer in 50:34 where it is said that the Israelites' redeemer is strong and 'will surely plead their cause'.

God will subdue Babylon, drying up the sea and the waters, the symbol of her power and wealth (50:38; 51:13), so that her capacity to maintain the injustice of her tyranny will be ended. In another instance of 'reversal of judgment', the threat that once applied to sinful Judah (9:11) is now held out to Babylon herself (v. 37).

The predator becomes the prey

Deliberate bathos is used in the mixed metaphors of verses 38–40. They open with Babylon pictured as a pack of lions, threatening in their stalking of their prey and growling in satisfaction over it as they devour it. The passage ends with the picture of the Babylonians as lambs being led away helpless to sacrificial slaughter. Talk of their being sated with their prey leads once more to the picture of God making his victims drunk, a disgusting and helpless state from which they shall never wake (see 25:27).

The monster destroyed

The picture of the 'sea' coming up upon Babylon (v. 42) is partly ironic. She whose 'waters' had made her strong and rich will be overwhelmed by flood waters. But behind it is a deeper, mythological motif. In the Babylonian creation epic, *Enuma Elish*, creation is achieved by the god Marduk (Bel) as he slays the dragon monster Tiamat, the goddess of the chaos waters which cover the whole world. He tears up her body and from the pieces forms the firmament that keeps those waters at bay, thus enabling dry land to appear. Each year, a ritual took place at which this great feat was celebrated by the triumphant cry, 'Marduk is king!' Hints of this, but applied to God, appear in the Old Testament, in Genesis 1, where God creates the firmament to keep the waters at bay and so forms the dry land, in the flood story and in some Psalms (for example, Psalm 74:12–17).

This underlines again the main emphases of these oracles against the nations. God is at war not just with this particular nation or that, but with all the forces of darkness and evil, and these, wherever and whenever they occur, will receive his judgment. And, further, it underlines his cosmic power. Perhaps that is why the name 'Sheshach' appears in verse 41 as a code for Babylon (compare 51:1). Babylon is a 'type' of evil and God's real war is with their god, Bel (v. 44). Yahweh, not Marduk, is the sole creator, redeemer God.

FOR PRAISE

The God who pleads Israel's cause, acting as their advocate (v. 36), has shown himself in Jesus Christ even more powerfully to be the 'advocate' of those who cannot save themselves. 'He is able for all time to save those who approach God through him, since he always lives to make intercession for them' (Hebrews 7:25).

BABYLON'S FATE SEALED

Trust in God's promises

The exiles are again called upon to escape from Babylon as the inevitable end approaches (v. 45). God's wrath is being vented on his enemies but he still cares for his own ('my people') and watches over them. Yet violent scenes of war are never pleasant and the terror and panic as final defeat looms produce ugly scenes. Rumours abound, conflicting accounts come in from all sides, the story changing from one day to the next, let alone one year to the next as verse 46 suggests. Order and familiar structures break down, anarchy is rife and old loyalties are fractured. It is in such a situation that God's people are exhorted, 'Do not be faint-hearted or fearful.' It is hard not to be distracted by all the evil around. But at such times, the prophet urges, the great need is to keep one's eyes on God and believe in the working out of his purpose through all the apparent chaos.

Babylon pays for her cruelty

Once more it is stressed that God's judgment is being directed against Babylon's images (v. 47). In the ancient Near East there was a strong belief in the close connection between a nation's god(s) and the earthly rulers who held power in the name of that god, and who were believed to exercise their power as the god's representative. Nebuchadrezzar, like all the Babylonian kings, claimed to rule in Bel's (Marduk's) name and attributed his victories to the supreme power of his god. It is this false pretension that God is determined to shatter, to demonstrate in action that he alone is the one, sovereign God and all power is given by him.

Further, God is a God of justice. He must establish right rule on the earth. The cries of his people and, indeed, of all the slain of the earth (v. 49) come to him and must be avenged, as Job prayed (Job 16:18). As we have seen, God acts as their 'redeemer' (see comments on 50:34, p. 232). Their oppressor's fate is once more graphically described in verses 52–58.

Return from exile promised

Verses 50–51 link closely to verse 46 where the exiles, in the midst of all the tumult, were bidden not to be faint-hearted. Their very natural feelings are expressed in verse 51, a verse whose sentiment sounds throughout the book of Lamentations and in Psalm 137. All that they had trusted in had been shattered. Others had occupied the land that God had promised them, and even the temple, the place where they believed God dwelt (Psalm 48:3; 132:14), had been destroyed. Yet it is in that very place, 'in a distant land' (v. 50), that they are bidden to remember God. There is no place where he is not present. The exile taught them that God was not bound to one holy place or one set of institutions. He is in fact always present, often where he is least expected. They are also bidden to 'let Jerusalem come into your mind'. In other words, they are to keep a firm grasp of the hope that God would fulfil his promises that the city would one day be reinhabited and rebuilt.

A last act of prophetic symbolism

This long section of oracles against Babylon ends with a dramatic act of prophetic symbolism (vv. 59–64). The occasion is set in the fourth year of Zedekiah's reign, namely 594/3BC. It is similar in nature to the act with the loincloth (13:1–11), except that this is done through an emissary. No visit of Zedekiah to Babylon is recorded, but some think it may be associated with the events recorded in chapter 27 when Jeremiah warned him not to rebel against Babylon. Possibly Zedekiah went at that time, either at Nebuchadrezzar's behest, or on his own volition, to assure the Babylonians of his loyalty. The actual occasion does not matter. The act seals Babylon's fate. The emissary, Seraiah, was Baruch's brother (36:4). Carroll (p. 856) makes the interesting point that both brothers were involved in writing the prophet's words. The scroll that was burned, however, was rewritten. The stone sank, lost for all time. God redeemed his people after the 'fires' of exile. Babylon was never to recover.

A PRAYER

Lord, may I be sure of your presence with me today, even when and where I least expect you. Keep me trusting in all your loving purposes even when I cannot discern your way. Amen

The CAPTURE *of* JERUSALEM

The reason for its fall

The final chapter of the book of Jeremiah serves as a historical appendix to the whole, just as the first section of the book of Isaiah (Isaiah 1—39) ends with a similar, though longer appendix in chapters 36—39. Jeremiah 52 corresponds mainly to 2 Kings 24:18—25:30, although there are some differences, the main one being that no mention is made of the appointment of Gedaliah as governor after 586BC and his assassination by Ishmael (2 Kings 25:22–26). That is probably because it has been so extensively dealt with in 40:7—43:7. Another difference is the detailing of the numbers of those deported (52:28–30). Probably both accounts have a common source which was passed around in various forms. There are a number of small differences between them which it would be pedantic and wearying to detail. It is not really every little fact that is important but the theological vision behind the account and the reason for its inclusion at the end of the book.

That reason is not altogether easy to divine, however. At least in Isaiah 36—39 the prophet plays a significant role in the events narrated. Here, Jeremiah is nowhere mentioned. Further, the account goes back behind later historical happenings already dealt with in the book. This may be because the final editors saw the fall of Jerusalem, the destruction of the temple and the exile to Babylon as *the* pivotal events on which all the preaching of the prophet centred. All the early part of his ministry was spent in warning his contemporaries that this was what would happen because of their sin. There was no way they could avoid it, by military action or political alliance. Repentance was beyond them, so corrupt had their hearts become. Only the other side of this catastrophic judgment would the way be open for God himself to renew his people, bring them home and open a new future to them. This is a truth that may be hinted at in the different fates that befell Zedekiah and Jehoiachin (see below). This chapter is thus the validation of the prophet's message. It shows that, in contrast to the false prophets of shallow optimism, he was indeed a true spokesman for God.

The reason given for it all in verses 1–3 is thoroughly Deutero-nomic. Zedekiah did wrong, and so did the people God 'expelled from his presence'. The Deuteronomists believed that we always involve others in the consequences of our sins (Deuteronomy 5:9), the truth of which they exemplify in this very chapter. Zedekiah was caught up in the web of Jehoiakim's sins (v. 2) just as, they had insisted, Jehoiachin had been caught up in the consequences of the sins of Manasseh (2 Kings 23:24–26). That does not rid each of responsibility (Deuteronomy 24:16), but it does mean that we are each responsible not only for ourselves alone.

The fate of Jerusalem and Zedekiah

The harrowing nature of the events described speak for themselves. Barbarity in war was widespread—David's methods with defeated enemies were far from gentle (see 2 Samuel 8:2). It was a prolonged siege, some of the horrors of which are recounted in Lamentations (4:9–10). It is strange that the first breach in the wall was made by Zedekiah and his family and associates trying to get out (v. 7). Knowing what his fate for resistance would be, he hoped to escape it, but, since it was really God who was judging his people, there could be no escape. His destiny, life imprisonment in blindness, perhaps has for the editors a symbolic edge to it. To refuse to respond to the light that God gives by his word, and to seek to break free from the restraints of his way, is to shut ourselves up in darkness and the con-demned cell of self-centredness.

Destruction and deportation

In graphic but sober prose the unthinkable is narrated. The temple, Yahweh's very dwelling place in their midst (Psalm 46:4–5), is destroyed (v. 13). It took someone with the faith and insight of the prophet to see that God was not bound to any location. Even in Babylon they could both seek him and find him (29:12–13).

A PRAYER

Lord, help me so to live that I may encourage and enrich others by my faith and love. May no words or actions of mine, consciously or unconsciously, harm and diminish another. Amen

The END *of the* OLD—
& PROMISE *for the* NEW

The desecration of the temple

Verses 17–19 describe the looting of the temple of all its rich orna-mentations and the various costly items used in the sacrificial wor-ship of Yahweh. Their institution by Solomon at the time of the building of the temple is described in 1 Kings 7:15–37. Their removal has already been predicted in 27:19–22, but there a note of ultimate hope is sounded at the end, that one day they would be returned—a symbol of the renewal by God of his people's relationship with him. This note of the renewal of the community as a people characterized by their worship of God is also sounded in Ezra 1:7–11, where it is reported that the Persian Cyrus, in the first year of his reign (538BC) gave Sheshbazzar permission to bring the temple items back with him on his return to Judah. So the description of the terrible destruction of the temple and the looting of its contents is not without a note of hope. It was the end of the older order, but there is just a hint of the promise of the new.

The price of rebellion

Conquerors then, as now, tended to show small mercy to those who had resisted them, especially, as in this case, where the siege had cost them so much in time, money and manpower. A number of leading members of the community were taken away to Babylon by the general in charge of the besieging army. There they were beaten and killed (vv. 24–27). No doubt this was intended as an object lesson to any who might have thought of further resistance.

The deportation

Verses 28–30 are the only place where the numbers of those taken away around the time of the fall of Jerusalem in 586BC is given. Numbers for the 597BC deportation with Jehoiachin are detailed in 2 Kings 24:16. The mention of Nebuchadrezzar's 'seventh' year of reign in verse 28 suggests a deportation in 598, which may have been of some Judeans before the assault on Jerusalem in 597. Verse 29 refers to the deportation at the time of the fall of the city in 586, while verse 30 suggests another one, later still. The details are unknown to us and are, anyway, not the important thing for the editors. Throughout the book, as we have seen, it is said that it was those who went to Babylon who formed the true 'remnant', the line of those whom God would renew and with whom he would start again—for all that they are described in this chapter rather contemptuously as 'the poorest of the people' (52:15). This was suggested in chapter 24 with the vision of the baskets of good and bad figs. It is stated again in the letter to the Babylonian exiles in 29:16–20. And, as we have seen, chapters 40 to 44 show that neither those who stayed in Judah nor those who went to Egypt proved themselves a faithful remnant, obedient to God's word spoken through the prophet. Again, as with the despoiling of the temple, all seems at its blackest. Yet there are hints and signs of hope.

Signs of hope in the darkness

The real name of the Babylonian king called here Evil-merodach (v. 31) was Amel-merodach ('son of Marduk'). He succeeded his father Nebuchadrezzar to the throne in 562BC. Possibly as part of a general amnesty at his accession, he freed Jehoiachin from close custody and granted him special favours. Even if there were a general amnesty, however, the way this is described, especially with its suggestion that Jehoiachin's 'seat' was higher than that of any other king (a hint strengthened by the fact that the Hebrew word used for 'seat' also means 'throne'), suggests that the Davidic monarchy is not finished. One of Jehoiachin's sons, Shealtiel, was, as it happens, father of Zerubbabel, the first governor of Judah after the exile. From the human point of view the disaster seems total. But the book ends with the hint that human helplessness can be God's opportunity.

A PRAYER

Lord, you can make even 'the poorest of the people' objects of your grace and channels of your purposes. So, take my life, and when I despair, teach me that you are still at work. Amen

NOTES

NOTES

NOTES

NOTES

NOTES

NOTES

NOTES

NOTES

JEREMIAH

THE PEOPLE'S BIBLE COMMENTARY

VOUCHER SCHEME

The People's Bible Commentary (PBC) provides a range of readable, accessible commentaries that will grow into a library covering the whole Bible.

To help you build your PBC library, we have a voucher scheme that works as follows: a voucher is printed on this page of each People's Bible Commentary volume (as above). These vouchers count towards free copies of other books in the series.

For every four purchases of PBC volumes you are entitled to a further volume FREE.

Please find the coupon for the PBC voucher scheme overleaf.

All you need do:

- Cut out the vouchers from the PBCs you have purchased and attach them to the coupon.

- Complete your name and address details, and indicate your choice of free book from the list on the coupon.

- Take the coupon to your local Christian bookshop who will exchange it for your free PBC book; or send the coupon straight to BRF who will send you your free book direct. Please allow 28 days for delivery.

Please note that PBC volumes provided under the voucher scheme are subject to availability. If your first choice is not available, you may be sent your second choice of book.

THE PEOPLE'S
BIBLE COMMENTARY

VOUCHER SCHEME COUPON

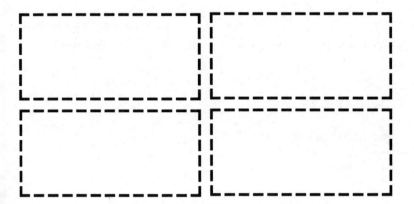

Customer and bookseller should both complete the form overleaf.

TO BE COMPLETED BY THE CUSTOMER

My choice of free PBC volume is:
(Please indicate a first and second choice;
all volumes are supplied subject to
availability.)

❑ 1 & 2 Samuel
❑ 1 & 2 Kings
❑ Chronicles to Nehemiah
❑ Psalms 1—72
❑ Psalms 73—150
❑ Proverbs
❑ Nahum to Malachi
❑ Matthew
❑ Mark
❑ Luke
❑ John
❑ Romans
❑ 1 Corinthians
❑ 2 Corinthians
❑ Galatians and Thessalonians
❑ Ephesians to Colossians
   and Philemon
❑ Timothy, Titus and Hebrews
❑ James to Jude
❑ Revelation

Name: . . . .
Address: . . . .
. . . .
Postcode: . . . .

TO BE COMPLETED BY THE BOOKSELLER

(Please complete the following.
Coupons redeemed will be credited to
your account for the value of the
book(s) supplied as indicated above.
Please note that only coupons correctly
completed with original vouchers will
be accepted for credit.)

Name: . . . .
Address: . . . .
. . . .
Postcode: . . . .
Account Number: . . . .

Completed coupons should be
sent to: BRF, PBC Voucher
Scheme, First Floor, Elsfield Hall,
15–17 Elsfield Way, Oxford
OX2 8FG.

Tel 01865 319700; Fax 01865
319701; e-mail enquiries@brf.org.uk
Registered Charity No. 233280

**THIS OFFER IS AVAILABLE IN THE UK
ONLY**
**PLEASE NOTE: ALL VOUCHERS ATTACHED
TO THE COUPON MUST BE ORIGINAL
COPIES.**